Palgrave Studies in Professional and Organizational Discourse

Titles include:

Cecilia E. Ford
WOMEN SPEAKING UP
Getting and Using Turns in Workplace Meetings

Rick Iedema (*editor*)
THE DISCOURSE OF HOSPITAL COMMUNICATION
Tracing Complexities in Contemporary Health Care Organizations

Louise Mullany
GENDERED DISCOURSE IN THE PROFESSIONAL WORKPLACE

Keith Richards
LANGUAGE AND PROFESSIONAL IDENTITY

H. E. Sales
PROFESSIONAL COMMUNICATION IN ENGINEERING

Forthcoming titles include:

Edward Johnson and Mark Gamer
OPERATIONAL COMMUNICATION

Palgrave Studies in Professional and Organizational Discourse
Series Standing Order ISBN 0-230-50648-8
(*outside North America only*)

You can receive future titles in this series as they are published by placing a standing order. Please contact your bookseller or, in case of difficulty, write to us at the address below with your name and address, the title of the series and the ISBN quoted above.

Customer Services Department, Macmillan Distribution Ltd, Houndmills, Basingstoke, Hampshire RG21 6XS, England

Also by Cecilia E. Ford

GRAMMAR IN INTERACTION: Adverbial Clauses in American English Conversations

THE LANGUAGE OF TURN AND SEQUENCE (*co-edited with Barbara A. Fox and Sandra A. Thompson*)

SOUND PATTERNS IN INTERACTION (*co-edited with Elizabeth Couper-Kuhlen*)

Please see Cecilia E. Ford's website for audio files related to these titles and the current one:

http://mendota.english.wisc.edu/~ceford/

Women Speaking Up

Getting and Using Turns in Workplace Meetings

Cecilia E. Ford
*Professor of English, Language and Linguistics,
University of Wisconsin-Madison*

palgrave
macmillan

© Cecilia E. Ford 2008

First published 2008 by
PALGRAVE MACMILLAN
Houndmills, Basingstoke, Hampshire RG21 6XS and
175 Fifth Avenue, New York, N.Y. 10010
Companies and representatives throughout the world

PALGRAVE MACMILLAN is the global academic imprint of the Palgrave Macmillan division of St. Martin's Press, LLC and of Palgrave Macmillan Ltd. Macmillan® is a registered trademark in the United States, United Kingdom and other countries. Palgrave is a registered trademark in the European Union and other countries.

ISBN-13: 978–1–4039–8722–8   hardback
ISBN-10: 1–4039–8722–X   hardback

This book is printed on paper suitable for recycling and made from fully managed and sustained forest sources. Logging, pulping and manufacturing processes are expected to conform to the environmental regulations of the country of origin.

A catalogue record for this book is available from the British Library.

Library of Congress Cataloging-in-Publication Data

Ford, Cecilia E.
    Women speaking up : getting and using turns in workplace meetings/
    Cecilia E. Ford.
        p. cm. — (Palgrave studies in professional and organizational
        discourse)
    Includes bibliographical references and index.
    ISBN 1–4039–8722–X (alk. paper)
    1. Communication in organizations—Sex differences. 2. Business meetings.
    3. Women in the professions. I. Title.

HD30.3.F66 2008
658.4′56082—dc22   2007052976

10   9   8   7   6   5   4   3   2   1
17 16 15 14 13 12 11 10 09 08

Printed and bound in Great Britain by
CPI Antony Rowe, Chippenham and Eastbourne

In the memory of
Virginia Hart
1914–2007

Activist for women in the workplace
and generous friend

Contents

Acknowledgments

This is a study of women speaking up. It is a conversation analytic study. It is feminist research, and it has been nurtured by colleagues in the broad field of applied linguistics. As I pursued this project, I presented early perspectives and findings to audiences at conferences representing all those areas. Some members of my audiences insisted that I could not use Conversation Analysis (CA) to study women as a "taken-for-granted" social group. While I am grateful for the reflection that those encounters supported, there were also many encouraging voices at those conferences and in other parts of my life and work, and that made all the difference.

Jo Handelsman and Molly Carnes asked me what conversation analysis might have to say about women's struggles with speaking up in the workplace, especially in the fields of science and engineering. Celia Kitzinger and Mary Bucholtz encouraged me when I was first conceiving of a response to Jo and Molly and the members of the Women in Science and Engineering Leadership Institute at the University of Wisconsin-Madison (WISELI). I am indebted to Celia for helping provide the project with a more affirmative beginning, and to Mary Bucholtz and Deborah Cameron for suggesting Jill Lake at Palgrave Macmillan, an editor who powerfully represented language studies at the press. Alice Freed contributed to this book in important ways. Most recently Alice gave of her time at a very pressured moment, offering important input to Chapter 1, where I speak to gender and language scholars.

Emanuel Schegloff fielded my questions and frustrations with CA's power and restrictions, and as always, he gave generous and challenging responses. I thank Charles Goodwin, Mary Ehrlich, Harrie Mazeland, Misao Okada, and, again, Alice Freed, for feedback on my ongoing analyses of questioning actions. I thank Judith Baxter for advice on my book proposal and for helping me situate this research in relation to other kinds of feminist discourse analysis.

Amanda Harrington and Annie Taff, two brave young feminists, inspired me as I completed this project. Annie was also invaluable in getting library resources to me, sometimes overnight, and Amanda translated fuzzy video stills into line drawings, to help illustrate examples while working toward anonymity of participants. Karen Johnson

Mathews and Michelle Quinn are my friends and my creative collaborators. They helped me see this project from beginning to end. My dear friend Junko Mori has been there for discussions of our passions for CA and many other things. I am especially grateful to Barbara Fox, Felicia Roberts, and Joanna Thornborrow for advising me on the entire manuscript at different stages. I hope to have done some justice to their careful advice.

Many other friends, colleagues, and family members have supported this project: Dale Bauer, Grace Bloodgood, Patti Brennan, Mie Femø Nielsen, Joseph Ford, William Hanks, Virginia Hart, John Hellermann, Marjorie Henshaw, Susan Knoedel, A.J.Krill, Doug Maynard, Hanh Nguyen, Michelle Quinn, Deborah Tannen, Sandy Thompson, Irene Tobis, Vicky Vogl, and Elizabeth Weathersbee. Special thanks to Sandy Stark: neighbor, friend, and wordsmith, and to Jennifer Sheridan, WISELI's brilliant research director. A very warm thanks to Jill Lake at Palgrave Macmillan. I know that Jill's wonders will continue as she engages even more fully in the world beyond publishing. Thanks as well to Priyanka Pathak, Melanie Blair, and to the incredible staff of Macmillan India Ltd.

I am profoundly grateful to the women and men in all the workplaces I visited for this project. Without their openness in allowing me to videotape their meetings, this work would not exist. I also gratefully acknowledge the U.S. National Science Foundation (NSF) for supporting the advancement of women in science and engineering. This book is based upon research supported by the NSF under Grant No. 0123666; however, any opinions, findings, and conclusions or recommendations expressed in this material are my own and do not necessarily reflect the views of the N S F.

Finally, thank you to Donna Dallos, my loving companion. Donna tolerates my use of our small home as a "workplace," and more importantly, she helps me rediscover what matters most in life, day to day.

Transcription Symbols

Symbol	Interpretation
?:	Uncertainty in identifying speaker
(.)	A short, untimed pause
(0.3)	A timed pause
(with)	Possible hearing of a word
( )	Indecipherable
hh	Audible out-breath
.hh	Audible in-breath
wi(h)th	Breathiness or laughter in production of a word
thi-	Hyphen indicates a sound cut off
[	Onset of overlapping talk
<u>she</u>	Prominent stress, involving pitch, loudness and/or sound lengthening
SHE	Louder than surrounding talk
°she°	quieter than surrounding talk
@she@	Creaky voice (laryngealization)
she:	Sound lengthening
>a word<	Rapid pace relative to surrounding talk
↑	Arrow up indicates notably high pitch
↓	Arrow down indicates notably low pitch
.	Low falling intonation contour
?	High rising intonation contour
,	Intermediate intonation contours: level, slight rise, slight fall
=	Latching, rush into next turn or segment or Equals signs are also to represent that a turn is continuing, with overlapping talk transcribed on a line that separates one part of a turn by another, an artifact of transcription in vertical lines
((raises hand)) *((looks toward John, on her right))*	Gestures and other non-vocal actions are italicized and enclosed in double parentheses

// [...] *//*	Double slashes and bracketed dots indicate that some portion of talk is not included for reasons of space or focus
// [**discussion of bone density**] //	Content of missing talk may be described

1
Introduction: A Feminist Project

We calculate the charges. We establish the conditions
under which we're going to approve it. Send that on. The
girls type that up.
    Engineer, public utilities workplace meeting, 2005

In a matter-of-fact way, the engineer in this quote encapsulates the gendered division of labor in the professional workplaces I visited for this
project. In North America, as in most of the world, women continue to
be underrepresented at the higher ranks of traditionally male professions
while they are simultaneously overrepresented in support staff positions
in the same workplaces. They are likely to be the "girls" that "type."
Given this asymmetrical representation, even when women and men
work side by side, women experience different work climates than do
men. Gender bias is evidenced in the demographics, economics, and
hierarchical positions of women in professional places of work, and
differences in the status of women and men are also revealed in research
on evaluative responses of *both* men and women toward women (Valian,
1998; Ridgeway & Correll, 2004). Popular self-help books and workshops
urging women to improve their styles notwithstanding, the biases
against women's advancement are far more fundamental than changes
in dress and talk can possibly remedy. In a contribution to a 1999 panel
discussion on language and gender in the workplace, linguist Sally
McConnell-Ginet emphasized the importance of attending to evaluative
bias. She insisted that

> the major issue is not differences in women's and men's competency—
> including their communicative competency. The big problem is people's
> attitudes towards women and men, their sharply differentiated

1

expectations that lead, as psychologist Virginia Valian puts it, to persisting under-evaluation of women's work and over-evaluation of men's.

(2000:127)

The current study rejects the idea that women need to be fixed, as is regularly expressed in popular media and sometimes unwittingly supported by research centered on gender difference. Instead, it concentrates on what women are already doing as valuable participants in workplaces where their presence at higher ranks is relatively new. By documenting women's discursive agency, the findings presented here counter negative attitudes and evaluations of women in settings and positions traditionally associated with men. Using conversation analytic methods, I analyze ways women claim and use turns at talk in a collection of workplace meetings, with attention to both vocal and non-vocal practices.

This is applied research in that it takes up the expressed needs of practitioners rather than the priorities of an area of scholarship, even though conversation analysis, sociolinguistics, functional linguistics, and gender and language studies are fields from which I draw and to which the research findings contribute. This is also a feminist study in that I initiated it in response to women's concerns about speaking up in workplace meetings, and in that my analyses center on the talk of women in the data. As I describe below, I started out with an interest in finding cases of what women experience as "having our ideas ignored," but, after visiting and videotaping the first few workplace meetings for the study, I shifted my attention to documenting women's evident competency in meeting interaction.[1]

As the method I rely upon is conversation analysis (CA), another goal of this study is to contribute to new findings to the corpus of CA-based accounts of meeting interaction (Cuff & Sharrock, 1987; Boden, 1994; Koole & ten Thije, 1994; Bilmes, 1995; Kangasharju, 1996; Wasson, 2000; Huisman, 2001; Barske, 2006; Mazeland & Berenst, in press; Femø Nielson, in press, in prep a, b, c, d). Though my CA lens is focused directly on the talk of women, the practices documented here are functional for and available to persons regardless of sex; these skills are not sex-specific. Thus, the analytic chapters of this book present new CA-based findings on turn-taking in meetings more generally, with meetings understood as scheduled, multiparty, task-oriented institutional interactions.

This introductory chapter outlines the origins of the research and my reasons for moving from a question which focused on women as victims to one regarding women as agents. It then positions the study with reference to trends in feminist language study. The two final sections consider the study as a form of applied linguistics and as an adaptation of CA.

Framing and reframing the research question: from passive to active

The research for this book was prompted by an accumulation of concerns shared with me over the years by women who were my university colleagues and my friends in communities beyond, culminating in an invitation by two women in science for me to join them in a grant aimed at the advancement of women in science and engineering. A prime complaint of women in these fields was that their ideas were ignored, and these colleagues looked to an expert on language in social interaction to help them understand the reported phenomenon. Like other women in the professions, they spoke from direct experience, but they were also well versed on the dismal statistics on women's advancement in the professions and the results of social-psychological experiments on the operation of gender bias.

One of the first books they recommended to me was Virginia Valian's, *Why so slow?* (1998). Valian synthesizes studies and statistics related to women's slow advancement and, in particular, the lower evaluation of women versus men. Study after study has found that, when other variables are controlled (education, expertise, etc.), women are responded to more negatively than men as measured by facial expression, gaze behavior, individual evaluations, and decision reached in task-based groups. As Valian summarizes the research, women "are attended to less, even when they say the same things in the same way as men do" (1998:131).[2] She notes that such findings coincide "with the experience of professional women, who frequently get the impression that they receive less attention than men and that their suggestions are more likely to be ignored than the same suggestions coming from men" (131). Given the consistency of broad statistical studies and of experimental findings, there was reason for me and my concerned colleagues to predict that the analysis of videotaped meetings in professional workplaces would yield insights into the interactional patterns that underlie women's experience of having their ideas ignored.

Thus, at the very initial stage of this project, my guiding question was:

How is the much-reported experience of *women having their ideas ignored* manifested through interactional practices in workplace meetings?

I italicize "women having their ideas ignored" because the proposition it entails ('women's ideas are ignored') became a problem for me as I visited, videotaped, and began to view and analyze meeting interaction. What I was most struck by was the clear evidence of women's competence.

Holding loosely to what originally prompts analytic inquiry is part of a CA approach; indeed, one ideal way into analysis is to engage in what Harvey Sacks called "unmotivated" inquiry (Sacks, 1984:27). Even if we begin with particular questions, in the iterative process of analysis, CA asks us to continually work at setting aside our dearest social understandings and motivations, to the degree that we are able. By striving to do this, we increase our chances of noticing new interactional practices, ones which might be different from what we originally predicted would be important. Elsewhere Sacks (1992 [1966 lecture]) notes in passing that it is easy to "simply fall into the most characteristic error of social science, which is only to interpret the answers to questions and not the questions" (1992:255). Even as I set out with my question of how women's ideas are ignored, I remained open to where the data would lead me. I was prepared for other phenomena to emerge related to women's concern with having ideas taken up. I treated my interest in "women's ideas" and how they are "ignored" as a provisional starting point, one that I would reevaluate as I acquired and analyzed data.

As I started observing, recording, and analyzing meetings, I was impressed with women's evident skill at getting and using turns, and I began to doubt the wisdom and usefulness of searching for instances of women's ideas being ignored. Certainly, arriving at accounts of interactional practices involved in such cases could validate women's experiences, but the undervaluing of women's work and the pervasiveness of women's victimization across cultures and classes is already well attested. How would further detailing of such patterns benefit women? Beyond providing a different kind of empirical validation for women's reported experience, perhaps detailed accounts of how women's contributions are ignored could be incorporated into educational programs aimed at changing workplace climate. Perhaps such findings could be used as supporting evidence when approaching institutional leadership to convince them that inequitable processes are operating in the quotidian but consequential moments of our daily work lives.

A challenge for feminist research on language is that it can become a circular and self-fulfilling process whereby taken-for-granted schemas are embedded in our research questions, leading to findings that reinforce the original schemas themselves. Clearly, the CA method is not immune to the biases of the analysts' taken-for-granted ways of seeing, interpreting, categorizing, coding, highlighting and ultimately sharing findings (Goodwin, 1994), especially in studies like mine which begin with applied interests and priorities.

In reflecting on the question, "How are women's ideas ignored?," I began to realize that letting it guide the project would likely reinforce rather than challenge stereotypes about gender and interaction. First, the question highlights gender as the salient variable, apart from rank, age, race, sexual orientation, or ability/disability, for example. Second, the question treats ideas rather than individuals as points of reference. Both these problems do not align well with my motivations for this research. My interest is neither in exploring sex differences nor in dissecting and defining what constitutes an idea. Rather, my interest is in contributing to our understanding of women's pathways to participation.

But the most problematic aspect of the initial research question was how it positioned women. Although the underlying proposition, "women's ideas are ignored," grants women ownership of ideas ("women's ideas" as the subject noun phrase), it formulates their ideas as objects *acted upon* in a negative and disempowering manner. Following my original guiding question would serve to reinscribe the stereotype of female passivity and powerlessness, directing my attention to women as passive recipients rather than as agents. It is true that the women in the data I collected inhabited male-dominated work worlds and held institutional ranks in which women are underrepresented; they work in settings where men occupy the highest ranks and women are most frequently employed to do clerical work. Yet the women I was videotaping were clearly actors in the meetings. They exercised agency and power.

After reflecting on these issues in relation to the initial data I collected, and after consulting further with my research partners, I decided against formulating women as victims, which is what I would be doing by searching for instances from which I could elaborate and detail patterns of their ill-treatment. I changed my question to one that would guide analytic attention toward ways women actively participate in workplace meetings. Thus, rather than use the meeting corpus as a source for cases of women's ideas being ignored, I used it to explore the question:

How do women get and use turns in workplace meetings in settings where women have been traditionally, and are currently, underrepresented?

This question guided me in documenting ways that successful women claim and frame turns in workplace meetings. Though the question does not address women's experience of having their ideas ignored, it does respond to concerns for speaking up and being heard. This shift in attention allowed me to use CA methods to support reflection on practices women already command.

As noted above, the practices documented in this book serve not only as evidence of women's skills at speaking up in meetings, but they also represent turn-taking and turn-building practices available to and used by meeting participants regardless of sex. In that respect, these research findings should be understood as representing resources for gaining and using turns that are generically useful rather than sex-specific.[3] Nevertheless, because I concentrate on women's turns in the data, my findings are related to and form a contribution to feminist studies of discourse. In the next section, I offer a perspective on that field in relation to the current study.

The backdrop: feminist studies of discourse

For this study interactional practices are understood as functional responses to interactional needs, needs that emerge in the flow of meetings and needs that are addressed by participants in meetings regardless of their sex. But this is a feminist enterprise, attending to women's demonstrated competencies. This section acknowledges and briefly outlines the important intellectual landscape which this project inhabits. I position the current study as one expression of feminist research on language use.[4]

As is true of feminist research in general, gender and language research has been driven by diverse frameworks of interpretation, sharing an "emancipatory purpose" and working for women's interests (Dietz, 2003:399). While not all gender and language research is explicitly feminist, there is a strong feminist outlook in the field. This can be seen in Eckert & McConnell-Ginet's (2003) comprehensive theme-based text encompassing current and enduring issues in language and gender studies. It is also represented in Mary Bucholtz's 2004 reissue of Lakoff's pioneering 1975 book, *Language and Woman's Place*. This newer volume not only presents Lakoff's germinal text but complements it with a set of commentaries by Lakoff, Bucholtz, and 25 other leading scholars with feminist and emancipatory commitments. The contents of these books, along with contributions to *The Handbook of Language and Gender* (Holmes & Meyerhoff, 2003), illustrate how current language and gender scholarship complicates and elaborates earlier feminist studies by including much greater attention to diversity in communities of practice and in forms of gender, within and across class, race, nationality, and sexualities.

As expressed in groundbreaking work by Lakoff (1975) and Zimmerman & West (1975), research on language and gender in the 1970s concentrated on revealing connections between language patterns and women's subordination. While study of patterns of gender, dominance, and discourse continued into the 1980s and beyond, another interpretive framework emerged as some scholars drew attention to similarities between cross-cultural miscommunication and troubles with communication between women and men from the same cultural background. Building on John Gumperz's (1982) framework for studying cross-cultural variation in discourse strategies, Maltz & Borker (1982) proposed that the origins of male-female styles of interaction lay in culture-specific practices resulting from childhood sex segregation. Drawing from developmental research which had pointed to significant differences in the organization of play groups (e.g., Lever, 1976; Goodwin, 1980), Maltz and Borker made a case for male-female interactional style differences as originating in early sex peer styles of producing and interpreting talk. While Maltz and Borker's essay gave rise to a more general dual culture understanding of adult female-male interaction, they also suggested that "at least some aspects of behavior are most strongly gender-differentiated during childhood and that adult patterns of friendly interaction [. . .] involve learning to overcome at least partially some of the gender-specific cultural patterns typical of childhood" (1982:215).

The cross-cultural miscommunication metaphor applied to adult female-male interaction formed the basis for Deborah Tannen's best-selling book, *You Just Don't Understand* (1990). Tannen, a respected linguist and accessible writer, won popular acclaim with this widely read explanation of cross-gender miscommunication. However, her book was also criticized by feminist scholars for its failure to explicitly challenge gender hierarchies. The titles of these critiques point to the fact that the cross-cultural miscommunication metaphor for cross-sex interaction allows for the placement of crucial issues of power and dominance to the side, and thus abandoning the emancipatory priorities of feminism: "Selling the apolitical" (Troemel-Ploetz, 1991) and "When 'difference' is 'dominance': A critique of the 'anti-power' cultural approach to sex differences" (Uchida, 1992). The consequences of the cultural difference approach to gender and interaction was also critically addressed by Alice Freed (1992), Mary Crawford (1995), and Deborah Cameron (1995, 2005, 2007).

Current research in the field of gender and language has developed a productive skepticism regarding the dichotomous conception of gender that was characteristic of much early research, in which, at the extreme, speakers were divided into generic women on one side and generic men on the other. The community of practice framework (Eckert & McConnell-Ginet, 1992) has encouraged the study of groups defined by engagement in recurrently shared tasks. This supports documentation of differences and similarities in language practices in relation to activities, and it leads to more complex and expanded understandings of language variation than those arrived at by primary reference to the social category of gender alone.

Poststructuralism in literary and philosophical scholarship has also meant questioning the adequacy of single and stable identities, and it has provided an impetus for gender and language researchers to reassess their research assumptions. Soon after the publication of Judith Butler's book *Gender Trouble* (1990), research in the mid-1990s began to explore gender as performance.[5] Hall (1995) and Barrett (1999), for example, document how single individuals manage multiple identities through their sociolinguistic repertoires. Multiple identities may be tied to different communities of practice, including intersecting and conflicting membership in those communities (Eckert and McConnell-Ginet, 1992). Such varied and interwoven gender performances complicate claims regarding straightforward connections between gender and language.

This line of gender and language research has also included critiques of the implied playfulness in choice among identities often associated with poststructuralist interpretations of Austin's original insights on language and performativity. The existence of diverse repertoires of identity performance does not in itself lead to freedom from hegemonic gender categories. For example, studies by Barrett, Hall, and others also reveal the misogyny, racism, and the contradictory ways that linguistic performances can reinforce dominant schemes of social categorization. Thus, while feminist language studies have embraced a view of identities as plural and of the language/gender relationship as dynamic and shifting, the dynamics of gender performances bring with them new tensions and complications, especially with respect to the enduring and dynamic power of dominant models of gender (e.g., McElhinny, 1995; Kiesling, 1997; Bergvall, 1996; Cameron, 1997; Baxter, 2002, 2003; Bucholtz, 1999, 2002; Mendoza-Denton, 2004; Morgan, 2004 among others).

Scholarship on "gendered discourses" represents another expression of poststructuralism in feminist language study (e.g., Sunderland, 2004). This research expands the study of language use by exploring "ways of seeing the world" in order to reveal the workings of power. Ideologies are reflected in language use, in multiple forms of representation, and in taken for granted systems of knowledge. Poststructuralist feminist discourse studies investigate systems of knowledge, involving gender as a symbolic and embodied system, intersecting with other categories such as race, ethnicity, class, sexuality, and communities of practice (e.g., Baxter, 2002, 2003, 2006 a & b; Mills, 2003, among others).

Feminist research on language and interaction has also, and from the outset, drawn on CA to document the social construction of women and men, gender differences, and the perpetuation of women's subordination (e.g., Zimmerman & West, 1975; Fishman, 1977, 1980; West & Garcia, 1988). More recently, and simultaneous with the poststructural turn in gender and language studies, researchers are newly tapping CA as a theory and methodology for understanding gender, discourse, and social categorization in action. For example, combining poststructuralism and CA, Ehrlich (2006) examines gender and courtroom ideologies and practices. Citing Butler's notion of a rigid regulatory frame, Ehrlich makes a compelling case for the limits of agency in gender repertoires. She attends to ways that certain question-answer sequences can be structured to support feminist perspectives on rape, but she also demonstrates that other courtroom discourse practices enforce normative and oppressive conceptions of a woman's responsibility for encouraging sexual advances leading to rape.

Contemporary feminist CA is also represented in Speer's *Gender Talk* (2005), and in chapters from Fenstermaker & West's collection, *Doing Gender, Doing Difference* (2002). Celia Kitzinger, in particular, has challenged the limits previously observed with respect to combining feminist research and fundamental CA principles (Kitzinger, 2000, 2007). In collaborative and single-authored studies since the late 1990s, Kitzinger has demonstrated the power of CA to document how social categories, such as gender and sexual orientation, are constructed in and through specific interactional practices. These studies not only attend to the use of reference terms (e.g., self or other identification in terms of sex), but move beyond attention to explicit naming and referential practices to reveal ways that social categorization and hierarchies of social value are displayed in the structuring of talk more generally (Kitzinger, 2005; Land & Kitzinger, 2005).

To provide a source of comparison with the way that I use CA in the current study, let me briefly review one recent feminist CA study. In "Is 'woman' always relevantly gendered?" (2007), Kitzinger demonstrates that even where self- or other-identification through gender categories is evident in the talk of interactants, the action of gender reference is not an end in itself; that is, it may be employed to do more than the action of social categorization. The case Kitzinger analyzes involves a helpline call-taker's reference to the category "woman" as shared by herself and the caller. The call-taker also uses the pronoun *we* in combination with the gender categorization, and in so doing, she draws on both the category term ("woman") and the inclusive use of the pronoun to accomplish the support and empowerment tasks which are the stated aims of the helpline service. Thus, while a sex category is invoked, it is not invoked for its own sake but rather in the service of empowerment through solidarity building. Kitzinger's analysis demonstrates that the "gendering of 'woman'" through explicit reference "is subordinate to, and in the service of" a larger interactional task (2007). Further, she argues that when an analyst locates sex categorization in interaction, this is not equivalent to demonstrating that "doing gender" is the function of that categorization.

Recent applications of CA, such as Kitzinger's 2007 study, employ close analysis of interaction to provide insights not only on gender categorization *per se*, but also on other interactional work done through use of such categories.[6] Notably, my study of women's turns in workplace meetings represents a different application of CA. Rather than using CA to reveal practices through which sex/gender categories are locally constructed (i.e., how the interactants construct themselves, others, or the talk itself), I take woman and man as given categories. I use CA to analyze how female participants gain speaking turns. Beginning with these gender categories requires further explication in relation to core theoretical stances associated with CA, and I return to this later in the chapter.

In addition to pioneering and recent feminist CA, another line of research bears on the current study. Linguistic anthropologists (e.g., Keenan, 1974; Ochs, 1992; Gal, 1991, among others) have examined relations between language and culture from a cross-cultural and cross-linguistic perspective. Much feminist research recognizes and investigates the relative value placed on women's and men's work, and linguistic anthropological studies share this theme. Countering common views that women's ways of speaking bear a causal relation to women's relative lack of power, linguistic anthropologists have argued that women's positions in societal hierarchies are better understood in terms of the relative value of women's work more generally, rather than as a direct result of speech patterns associated with women. This perspective is relevant to the current study as it informed my choice to focus on women's practices for getting and using turns at talk in workplace meetings.

A prime example of anthropological linguistic research calling into question the generality of findings from gender studies of white middle class individuals in North America or Europe is Keenan's 1974 report from fieldwork in Madagascar. Keenan found that Malagasy women's speech styles were distinct from those reported for women in North America. The women she observed were adept at expressing themselves directly, in manners considered "coarse" by standards in the Malagasy community she studied. In contrast, men in her data used styles of speech which had been reported as common among women in the North American context, i.e., mitigated and indirect styles of expression.[7]

Based on previous interpretations of women's supposedly indirect styles as underlying their lack of power, one might predict that women in the Malagasy-speaking community which Keenan studied would wield substantial public and political power as a result of their direct ways of speaking. Indeed, these women did wield power in certain realms of their lives, notably in the home and in market bartering interactions. Yet in the overall division of public and private life in the community, the values placed on speech skills associated with men and women were similar to those represented in studies in the U.S. Specifically, Keenan found that indirect speech (the speech traditionally expected of Malagasy men), rather than direct speech (the speech traditionally expected of Malagasy women), was prized in public oratory, where men dominated. Thus, at the time of Keenan's study, women were excluded from places of public discourse and public power in the community. Had a speech training industry comparable to the assertiveness training that emerged in the U.S. in the 1970s (see Cameron, 1995; Crawford, 1995) been developed for these Malagasy women, it would have been geared to help them learn to modulate and soften their speech in order to get ahead in male domains. The connection between the work that women do and the value placed on talk associated with that work is a theme that Ochs further develops in a 1992 essay, "Indexing Gender."[8] I return to Ochs' insights on the more nuanced ways we need to understand connections between talk, work, and power after I review a recent and related study of women and men in New Zealand workplaces.

A 2004 article by Janet Holmes & Meredith Marra, "Relational practice in the workplace: Women's talk or gendered discourse?," merits special attention with respect to associations between forms of work women typically and stereotypically do, and the evaluation of speech associated with such work. Holmes and Marra draw the concept of "relational practice" (RP) from Joyce Fletcher's book *Disappearing Acts: Gender, Power, and Relational Practice at Work* (1999). In that book, Fletcher introduced RPs as invisible but crucial supportive discourse practices women perform in the workplace. Holmes and Marra (2004) elaborate and critique Fletcher's interpretation of RPs as women's domain. Taking Fletcher's notion of RP beyond interview data and into the realm of attested workplace talk itself, Holmes and Marra study inter-actional practices represented in the Wellington Language in the Workplace database (http://www.victoria.ac.nz/lals/lwp/). In their study, they look at RPs as involving discourse moves that enact and display speakers' concerns for "'face needs' of others," that serve to "advance the primary objectives of the workplace," and that are "regarded as dispen-sable, irrelevant, or peripheral" (2004:378).[9] They illustrate interactional exchanges that do this work and are also treated as dispensable, propos-ing two broad categories of RP: actions which "create team" ("small talk," "positive humor," and "off-record approval") (2004:381–6); and actions aimed at "damage control" ("covert facilitation" and "mitigating humor") (2004:386–90). Of particular relevance to my study, Holmes and Marra demonstrate that RPs in their data, while treated as less significant and less worthy of recognition in the workplace due to their association in general with women's work, are used by both men and women in their corpus:

> In more than half of our [illustrative] examples, the RP was being undertaken by a man, while the manager or the person wielding most authority in the situation, was a woman. Clearly RP is not undertaken only by women.
>
> (2004:390)

Holmes and Marra do not propose that women and men use RP in the same frequencies; indeed, they note that frequency counts are not appropriate for the analysis of the non-discrete categories of talk they consider as representing RP. They stress that, though RPs are identifi-able, they are diffuse practices, verbal or non-verbal, which are by design "invisible, off-record, behind-the-scenes support work which is typically regarded as irrelevant and dispensable" (390). However, these authors do suggest that precisely because facilitative practices are stereo-typically associated with women in society more broadly, this discursive work is predictably undervalued in the workplace.

Holmes and Marra not only offer a critique and a discourse-analytic elaboration of Fletcher's claims about women's invisible discourse labor, but in their reflections on the patterns in their data, they underscore that RPs, as they operationalize them, are not exclusive to women, though they are stereotypically associated with women. Like other recent research on language and gender, their study underscores that relationships between language use and sex of speaker (or recipient or referent) are far from straightforward. More specifically, their study adds empirical support for understanding connections between language and gender as characterized by a web of culture- and community-specific associations.

In "Indexing gender," Ochs (1992) presents a cross-linguistic perspective, complicating direct links between speech patterns and gender of speakers. She articulates a model of indirect, but nonetheless pervasive, associations between particular activities (linguistic or otherwise), stances, and the cultural categories of types of persons who normally do such work:

> we can find particular linguistic features directly indexing social acts or social activities, such as the imperative mode indexing the act of ordering in English or respect vocabulary terms in Samoan indexing the activity of oratory. These acts and activities in turn may be associated with speaking like a male or speaking like a female and may display different frequencies of use across the two social categories.
>
> (1992:241)

Linguistic systems and discourse practices are not exclusively indexical of participant gender; that is, language is not, in general, distinctively used by, about, or in addressing persons based on gender. Holmes and Marra's analyses from the New Zealand workplace data support Ochs' proposal that "the relation between particular features of language and gender is typically non-exclusive . . . variable features of language may be used by/with/for both sexes" (1992:340). Thus, while certain discourse practices may be associated, normatively and/or stereotypically, with women, this makes such practices gendered rather than gender-specific.

In summary, since the inception of modern feminist language studies, there has been a move away from cataloguing gender differences in language use based on understandings of gender as fixed and binary. Indeed, early attempts at correlating language form with sex of speaker often led researchers to perpetuate stereotyped views of women and men. Furthermore, and not surprisingly, research findings were contradictory and inconsistent. Despite the change in direction, issues related to dominance and oppression have continued to be central to language and gender research. As a result, the complexity of gender expression, across boundaries of geography, culture, race, and sexuality are receiving much needed attention. It is distressing to observe, however, that while feminist language research has moved away from simplistic, overgeneralized, and stereotypic conceptions of language and gender, the media and such popular movements as the self-help industry have elaborated and celebrated such stereotypes. Thus, while contemporary researchers are revealing multiple ways that women and men display their gender and other social identities through language and other social actions, the media persist in describing women and men as constituting two different groups each with clear and distinct speaking styles (see Cameron, 2005, 2007). Though the current study does not explore expressions of gender, it does address and provide evidence against popular understandings of women being different from and less competent than men in their ways of speaking in traditionally male domains of work.

Self-help guides: fixing women

The web of associations between the undervaluing of women's work and negatively evaluating the appropriateness of associated language practices, as theorized by Ochs (1992), is by no means easily conveyed and understood. In comparison, accounts that reinforce long-standing perceptions and expectations regarding women are much more accessible and appealing to a general audience; such accounts reinforce the status quo and make no demands for major societal change. Popular media attend to what can be reported as direct causal relations between discourse patterns stereotypically associated with women and women's relatively slow advancement in traditionally male domains. This reinforces the belief that women are the agents of their own subjugation because they speak as they do. Books and workshops aimed at fixing women thrive, with outdated research on differences between women's and men's speech styles cited as explaining women's lack of power.

Cameron (1995) notes that popularizations of early research on gender differences in speech selectively draw from and magnify what otherwise might be considered neutral science:

> As these 'problems' enter the repertoire of public discourse about gender, they provide one more pseudo explanation for women's 'underachievement', one more excuse for the raw deal women get, and one more ingenious strategy for not tackling the root causes of women's subordinate status.
>
> (1995:205)

Cameron treats this as a specific form of "verbal hygiene" directed toward women. Books, articles, and workshops, purportedly designed to help women improve their language practices, actually "create anxiety and encourage low self-esteem in order to sell people quack remedies for non-existent or trivial complaints" (1995:205). The self-help industry "contributes to the very devaluation of women that impels so many of them to turn to self-help in the first place" (1995:205).

In such an approach, gender bias is disconnected from its causes and associated instead with real or imagined speech patterns associated with an oppressed group, whether that group is based on gender, class, race, or some other category. Convincing women that they need fixing is an easily available option, one that holds the victim responsible and keeps her and her allies busy with remedies, while treating more fundamental problems as invisible, or even perpetuating them (Cameron, 1995; Crawford, 1995; Kitzinger & Frith, 1999).

Recent years have seen yet another distressing iteration of the theme that women's communication problems are what hold them back. Jean Hollands (2002) reports designing her "Bully Broads" workshops in response to needs expressed by "top-echelon corporate executives." She shares an example of one plea from an executive:

> Listen. I have to send Cecilia to you. I am finally at my wit's end. I can't protect her again. Being founder of this company doesn't give me enough leverage to help her anymore.
>
> (2002:viii)

Apparently, Cecilia's problem, or the problem that others have with her, is her lack of credibility. In the executive's perception, one shared by Hollands, Cecilia lacks effectiveness because of her style. This harkens back to the deficiencies of the unassertive woman of the 1970s, but now the woman's communicative deficiencies have changed; she has gone too far in the assertive direction. Her problem is not lack of ability to speak with confidence and power; rather, she is a high-performing woman who is evaluated as "intimidating" and "self-centered." In Hollands' workshops, such women share that they have worked hard to reach their high positions in the corporate world. But every one of them, according to Hollands, has had some of the following characteristics applied to her by others in her workplace:

> Abrasive, Caustic, Impudent, Pushy, Sharp-Tongued, Abrupt, Clipped, Intimidating, Rude, Tough-minded . . . Tyrannical, Aggravating . . . Loud
>
> (2002:xxiii).

Hollands' book, *Same Game, Different Rules: How to Get Ahead Without Being a Bully Broad, Ice Queen, or "Ms. Understood"* (2002), is lauded in a *New York Times* review quoted on the cover, "Bully Broads . . . offers a new set of rules for getting ahead."[10] These new rules are designed to temper those that women have been sold for the past 30 years on how to speak assertively. Just when women thought they understood and could take responsibility for what was really holding them back, they are reevaluated and found not to have gotten it right yet. Apparently, learning to speak in ways that are more in line with an imagined assertive male corporate norm has not served women well. We are playing the "same game" as are men, but we are in different bodies and subject to different expectations and evaluations. Hollands observes that

> Our male leadership models have exercised their egos and treated us to their tirades over the years, some without punishment. Women can't seem to get away with it as well as men can.
>
> (2002:ix)

She directs women to, "Stop moaning about that, and start equipping yourself with the soft touch" (2002:ix).

Of course, this brings us to the familiar double bind for women. Hard as women try to learn improved ways of communicating, they can't win. Whether striving to become more assertive, conciliatory, compassionate, flexible, direct, or modulated, women are not rewarded with the ultimate outcome of being taken as equal or superior to a man. It is not the way a woman talks that is negatively evaluated; her fundamental obstacle is that she is *a woman*, how ever she and others locally construct that category. Societal assumptions, norms, and stereotypes are such that, in most settings and on most tasks, a woman is not expected to be equal to a man in authority, intelligence, or leadership: characteristics most valued in the professional workplace and qualities most likely to be perceived as simply in the essential nature of a man.

Thus, what falls by the wayside in the never-ending fix-the-woman approach is the fact that a negative response to a woman's talk is based first and foremost on the fact that she is speaking from a woman's body: speaking not "like" a woman but "as" a woman. It is not directly because one may use a speech strategy associated with women or women's work that one is penalized; a woman is penalized because she is *speaking while being a woman*.[11]

Feminist CA research, in one of its manifestations, uncovers interactional practices through which the category "woman," in interplay with other social categories, is talked into being. In the current feminist application of CA, the category of woman is taken as a starting point, and my analyses are directed at practices through which speaking turns are negotiated and taken up. One purpose for applying CA in this manner has been to provide evidence that women do indeed succeed in speaking up, evidence that my female friends and colleagues, along with popular representations of women and language, have made abundantly clear is needed. At the same time, as noted above, my intention has been to contribute to a CA understanding of meeting interaction more generally. I turn now to a discussion of the current study as a form of both CA and applied linguistics. I return to the relationship between this study and the goals of CA in a subsequent section.

CA and/as applied linguistics

As the broad field of applied linguistics (AL) is the intellectual home in which the current study was nourished, this section offers perspectives on how CA articulates with applied linguistics. While most applied linguists value crossing disciplinary lines, we often avoid these adventures because of the inherent risks of interdisciplinarity, with its dangers of having no institutional home or central publication outlets. CA, like many disciplines represented in the field of applied linguistics, is a theory and method whose practitioners make academic homes in diverse departments and disseminate research findings across epistemological borders. Because, as a rule, CA researchers are based in disciplines where CA is not the dominant method of inquiry, the central questions of particular disciplines do not align neatly and unproblematically with the questions that CA research was originally developed to answer. It is also generally the case that CA researchers, regardless of our disciplinary homes, are committed to both drawing from and contributing to "basic" CA findings. Many of us are also committed to making our research accessible to practitioners in the communities we study.

One conception of AL sees it is an academic discipline "trying to do a more sophisticated job of language teaching," with scholars finding that the title, applied linguistics, adds "an aura of respectability that is lacking in the acronym TESL [Teaching English as a Second Language]"; and that the title also acknowledges that the study of language teaching involves "work on languages other than English" (Stockwell, 1990:151). Yet for many who identify as applied linguists and who are active in national and international societies bearing AL in their names, the field offers an interdisciplinary base for language-related research, with linguistics and language teaching enjoying "no special status" in AL (Schumann, 1990:156). Under the umbrella of AL, interdisciplinary researchers are able to explore applications and explanations for language patterns beyond structuralist frameworks which tend to draw rigid distinctions between linguistics and other fields.[12] For this reason, AL departments, publications, and conferences have been sites of multiple manifestations of conversation analytic research, including the study of grammar and interaction, classroom dynamics, workplace interaction, and interaction within the institution of the family.[13] Understanding CA as a form of AL, though not exclusive to AL, underscores the interdisciplinarity of AL and CA.[14]

Indeed, CA has had applied manifestations for many years, largely stemming from its use to study institutional interaction (see Drew & Heritage, 1992). In the foreword to the 2005 collection *Applying Conversation Analysis* (2004), Paul Drew observes that, while CA was originally created to account for ordinary interaction ("mundane conversation"), it has proved itself fully productive for understanding more task-oriented institutional talk. Furthermore, CA can be both applied and "pure." It can respond to and inform specific settings and fields of practices, while simultaneously contributing new insights into structures of social action more generally. Such new understandings of interactional practices account not only for the settings in which they were first identified, but also have an explanatory reach far beyond those sites. CA can thus serve dual functions: as a method for exploring the basic mechanisms through which social action is done, and as a way of responding to highly consequential challenges for practitioners in specific settings.

One example of the dual functions of CA is the work of Douglas Maynard on news delivery (2003). Maynard's interest in what he reveals to be a ubiquitous set of orderly practices in human sociality, involving the delivery of bad and good news, was originally prompted by his work on important moments when clinicians delivered diagnoses of developmental disabilities to parents of the involved children. Building on those initial observations, Maynard went on to study diagnostic news in other settings. His findings are directly relevant to the professionals whose daily practice he was observing and analyzing when he happened upon this rich area of conversation analytic inquiry; he has, for example, been invited to talk to physicians in "grand rounds" at medical schools and meetings. However, the obvious applications of his findings notwithstanding, Maynard's studies of news delivery constitute fundamental contributions to the study of human interaction.

As I have noted, the present conversation analytic study of women's contributions to workplace meetings was prompted by women who identified communication in male-dominated professional settings as a problem. In that respect, this is an applied conversation analytic project, with goals intersecting those of contributors to Keith Richards' and Paul Seedhouse's 2004 volume *Applying Conversation Analysis*. Studies in that collection involve use of institutionally recognized social categories such as autistic child, parent, clinician, therapist, doctor, patient, and the like, but analysts hold such categories lightly and examine them with a questioning stance. They use CA to investigate how roles and relations are made visible and relevant in the unfolding of the interactions themselves.[15]

In a like manner, for the current study, women are the consultants and the primary foci of my analyses, but the category "woman" is only one among many categories that apply to the participants in the meeting data, as the women themselves reported in interviews (see Chapter 3). My concentration is on how members of these committees manage the local, interactionally constituted roles through their work at getting and using turns at talk. My analyses involve close attention to practices through which participants collaboratively achieve meeting interaction. In the process of documenting women's competencies, I have intended to *draw upon* and *contribute to* CA.

Emanuel Schegloff (1990) has suggested a more synthetic perspective on the relationship between CA and AL, one with which I would also affiliate, though in tandem with a view of AL as addressing "real-world" issues (Brumfit, 1995). In Schegloff's contribution to a 1990 review of definitions of AL, he proposed that by concentrating on participants' practices, CA might be understood as the study *of* applied linguistics— language as it is practiced:

> By "practicing" I mean here exercising a knowledge-based skill, as in "practicing medicine," rather than upgrading or maintaining one's skill, as in "practicing the piano." In this sense, "applied linguists" refers to the ordinary users of a language, the ordinary members of a society or culture who, in the first instance, have knowledge of (the) Language and who apply that knowledge to do the things they ordinarily (or extraordinarily) do with it.
>
> (Schegloff, 1990:162)

From this perspective, using CA to account for practices of talk-in-interaction is an essential way to study AL as what humans do.

Adapting and augmenting CA

While my methods and data are outlined in Chapter 2, I use this section to offer a sense of the place of this study relative to goals and principles of CA. There are two ways in which I have adapted CA for the purposes of this project, adaptations that are not unique to this study. One involves augmenting my primary data, the meeting interactions themselves, with informal interviews. From a CA perspective, interviews are conversations, data in themselves, moments of self-presentation and the co-construction of identities in interaction. As such, they may be used as primary data of talk-in-interaction (e.g., Wilkinson & Kitzinger, 2003). But interviews are also used as sources for additional perspective on the activities under scrutiny (e.g., Kitzinger & Frith, 1999). For the current study, open-ended and informal interviews have given me access to metalinguistic perspectives of women from each of the video-taped meetings. The interviews have enriched my understanding of these women's priorities, and of the challenges they experience in communicating. Thus, while this book primarily presents findings from a CA examination of turns within their interactional contexts, I also include perspectives from these interviews.[16]

A second way that I adapt CA relates to the full power of the method to reveal the workings of social categorization in practice. CA emerged as a method that radically redefines the means through which social sciences motivate analytic categories. Rather than arbitrarily applying social categories and identities, CA sees the analyst's task as one of uncovering or discovering such categories, from the ground up, in the hearable and visible orientations of the actors whose sense-making practices are the subjects of study (Schegloff, 1991, 1992, 1997 and elsewhere). In questioning analyst-based social categories or analysts' adoption of vernacular social categories, CA does not claim that such categories are incorrect. Rather, CA mandates that the analyst elucidate the interactional mechanisms through which identity categories are "talked" into being in and through interaction. The CA outlook is one of constant attention to ways that social categories are locally enacted in moments of talk, along with a productive skepticism regarding *a priori* categorizing of participants' identities. By maintaining this attitude, CA researchers are better able to document how identity work is done. Participants in interaction do identity work quite independently from the analytic categories imposed by an analyst or her general field, be it sociology or linguistics or some other discipline, and one of CA's mandates is that the analyst not only discover categories that the participants demonstrably treat as real but document the social processes through which such categories operate and are enacted in interaction.

As noted above, much recent feminist CA follows this line by exploring practices through which categories such as "woman" are made visible, hearable, and documentable in the orientations of the participants themselves (also see contributions to McIlvenny, 2002 and Kitzinger, 2007). For the present study, by selecting women's participation as the starting point for my analyses, I apply CA in a manner distinct from much current feminist CA. As another expression of feminist CA, rather than exploring mechanisms through which "being a woman" and "being treated as a woman" are performed, my use of CA for this project begins with an assumption that the social category woman exists and affects the lives of the women in the selected workplaces. From that starting point, I document how women do indeed contribute in diverse and skillful ways to meeting interaction, even in settings and positions in which women's participation is new.

In light of tensions within CA and between CA and other frameworks, I want to be explicit about my assumptions and claims about participant gender: I do not propose that the women in my data produce the practices I document *as* "women's practices" *per se* nor as ways of "doing being women" (to use a CA formulation). Indeed, I have found no clear patterns by which men and women in my data deploy communicative practices that regularly distinguish female from male addressees or referents.[17] For the purposes of the current study, I take non-CA-based evidence of pervasive evaluative biases militating against the advancement of women in settings and positions traditionally occupied by men as a point of departure. The feminist CA represented in the present study serves to counter such evaluative stances by documenting interactional practices among a sample of women professionals as they participate in workplace meetings. This project complements the work of other feminist CA currently examining the interactional construction of biases themselves.

That CA recommends itself as a powerful tool for examining the discursive construction of gender in no way diminishes the clear utility of CA for documenting other locally constructed social categories fundamental to meeting participation. As Kitzinger (2000) points out, feminists have long drawn from a variety of other methodologies, finding "ways of adapting these powerful methods and using them for our own purposes" (2000:164). Likewise, the fact that I am particularly attending to women's talk is not a convincing reason for rejecting the use of CA for the current study. CA offers by far the most elaborated and insightful method for understanding the local construction of interactional roles and positions in spontaneous talk; it is precisely women's attested skill at getting and using turns in the moment-to-moment flow of interaction that this book documents.

By using CA methods to analyze particular moments in particular meetings, I document the local construction of social roles and positions such as current speaker, recipient, meeting leader, bidder for speakership, collaborative teller, and the like (see Chapter 2 on methods, and the analyses in Chapters 4 through 6). These are the domains women in the data draw upon to build and expand their contributions to meetings in workplaces where they continue to be underrepresented and in that sense "deviant" participants (Hall, 2003). Thus, in the analytic chapters of the book, while making no claims on whether the women in these meetings speak or interact differently from men in these settings or whether they are interacted *with* differently by men and other women, I investigate a variety of local interactional contexts in which women do get turns, and I document their practices for doing so.

Apart from the inclusion of women's reflections on their interactional work lives in interviews and apart from my primary focus on women's getting and using turns, this research has relied upon fundamental methods of CA: I have examined and re-examined moments in the meetings in which women managed, through combinations of vocal and non-vocal practices, to initiate turns, to project longer trajectories of talk, to expand opportunities for themselves or others to join in topics of discussion, and to manage resistance from other participants in order to complete their turns.

Outline of the book

The book is organized in the following manner: data and methodology are introduced in Chapter 2, parts of which will already be familiar to CA scholars. Chapter 3 offers a selection from women's self-reports in the interviews; in so doing, it frames the analytic chapters by giving voice to some of the women's conscious concerns and reflections on participation strategies. The three core analytic chapters that follow present findings from technical, CA-based examination of turn-taking practices in meeting segments where women took turns. Chapter 4 begins with the collaborative work of multiple participants in constituting a group as entering official meeting mode, a process sketched by Boden (1994) but more fully articulated here. Chapter 4 continues with new perspectives on practices of turn allocation, turn transition, and the specific work done through turn beginnings in meetings. A final section of Chapter 4 considers enactments of connection and ways that participants form alliances in the meetings, analyses related to and building upon research by Gene Lerner (1993) and Helena Kangasharju (1996). Chapter 5 demonstrates how questions in these meetings serve not only as vehicles for initially claiming turns, but they may also serve to present challenges to previous speakers and to open opportunities for the questioner or other participants to expand a new theme in further turns. Chapter 6 shifts to a closer analytic lens, concentrating on the development of two turns within a single longer segment of talk. This intensive analysis documents specific practices through which two different women formulate disaffiliative actions and manage to expand turns in the face of resistance from other participants. In the final chapter, I review the findings, report on applications, and reflect on the conception of claiming and building turns as a manifestation of power (Ainsworth-Vaughn, 1998; Thornborrow, 2002:27–8).

2
Data and Analytic Practices

This chapter provides an overview of data collection along with an introduction to principles of transcription and analysis. Because transcription and analysis are inseparable, CA symbols, terms, and concepts are illustrated by excerpts from the current data, and examples are accompanied by notes on the potential interactional significance of paying close attention to the particulars of sound production as well as non-vocal actions.

Collecting meeting data

To gain access to meetings, I tapped into personal and professional networks of women with jobs in science, engineering, medicine, as well as women working in various forms of management and administration. I had two requirements of meetings for this study: that they regularly involve both women and men, and that at least one member of each meeting would be available to help me identify participants and interpret content as I analyzed the data in the months to come. Participation was voluntary, and I taped only meetings in which all members had signed consent forms.

The collection of taped meetings amounts to approximately 23 hours. The number of participants in individual meetings varied from 7 to 19. The meetings, with names changed, are listed in Table 2.1. In parentheses are number of meetings taped and total time for each group. In brackets are identifications used in examples throughout the book.

With respect to the institutional hierarchies of workplaces where I taped, men in these meetings generally held positions equal to or higher than women participants. Exceptions were Zoology Laboratory 2, Microbiology Laboratory, and Church Staff. The two laboratories were directed by women, and the church rector was a woman.

Table 2.1 Videotaped Meetings

Meeting	Identifications for Examples
Non-Profit Board (1.5 hours)	[Board]
Church Staff (3 meetings, 4 hours)	[Church]
Information Technology Group (1 hour)	[InfoGroup]
University Diversity Committee (4 meetings, 8 hours)	[Diversity]
Hospital Medical Specialty Group (1 hour)	[Medical]
Academic Planning Committee (1 hour)	[Planning]
Engineering Team, Water Treatment Plant (1 hour)	[Plant]
Microbiology Laboratory (2 meetings, 3 hours)	[Microbio]
Zoology Laboratory 1 (1 hour)	[Zoology 1]
Zoology Laboratory 2 (2 hours)	[Zoology 2]

I was present at all tapings, checking the camera sound level, occasionally moving the camera to maintain the greatest number of participants within the range of the wide-angle lens. Shifts in participant configurations occurred when someone used a white board or there was a change from mainly presentation mode to more distributed discussion. Rather than standing behind the camera and thereby further animating the presence of the camera, I spent the majority of my time seated a couple of feet from the camera. When a meeting lasted over an hour, it was necessary to change tapes. In most cases I captured a sound bridge between the video segments with a handheld digital audio recorder.

As all participants had advance notice and all had previously agreed to be videotaped, there was never a problem when meeting participants arrived to see my camera set up on one side of the room. At the beginning of each taping, I collected signed consent forms and reminded the participants that I would turn the camera off at any time they wished, and that I would erase portions of the recording after the taping at their request; this information was also printed on the consent form.

I had prepared for the possibility of sensitive issues emerging in meetings, and there were times when my access to all or part of the meeting was affected by such concerns. In one case, I was scheduled to videotape a meeting but subsequent to gaining consent from the participants, my contact person asked me not to come. This individual recognized that the group was becoming contentious and felt the risk was too great that a video camera and the presence of a researcher would heighten anxieties. In another case, I recorded only the first half of a two-hour meeting, as the agenda for the second hour involved "brainstorming" on confidential issues. There were also moments in meetings in which the issue of being recorded was explicitly referenced by participants. In two tapes there are gaps because one or more of the participants requested that the recorder be turned off temporarily. In one instance this involved a discussion of specific corporate clients, and in another case a meeting participant emailed me after the meeting, requesting that I erase a segment because of sensitivity of the topic. I do not believe that the missing segments result in a problem with the representation of turn initiation and building practices, which are the focus of my analyses.

Analytic practices

My analytic process began as I positioned the camera in a meeting room and then found myself compelled to change its position or the direction of its "gaze" as a meeting developed (Duranti, 1997: Ch. 5 and Appendix). The need for this kind of adaptation underscores that configurations of participation are emergent and dynamic even in relatively formal, institutional interactions. For example, the existence of a predetermined meeting leader did not determine how turn allocation was controlled from moment to moment, nor did it determine toward whom most talking and gaze orientation would be directed. The existence of a planned agenda did not determine who would speak up during another person's report to the group.

Focal segments

After recording and digitizing each videotape, the next step was to review the tape in full. As I did this, I noted segments in which one or more of the women spoke. As these observations accumulated a collection of focal segments took form. This represented the beginning of my documentation of practices for securing turns at talk, including practices for opening up longer agendas of action that led to further participation. I transcribed the focal segments in detail, and as I analyzed the segments, I continued to elaborate the transcription, including more notations on gaze, gesture, and other visible but non-vocal behaviors. From my analyses of focal segments, there emerged a number of recurrent practices for turn initiation and turn-building. In the process of working with each new meeting I taped, I regularly came across phenomena I had not noticed in previous meetings. This prompted me to review previous tapes looking for similar cases which I may have overlooked.[1]

Thus, focal segments became objects of repeated CA inquiry along the lines of what is presented by ten Have (1999:101–28) and Pomerantz & Fehr (1997). In addition to documenting ways that participants gained turns at talk, I made observations about the actions done in the turns. For example, I might note, "Stephie seems to be disagreeing with John and Charles." I would then ask, "What, in the actions of the participants, makes me think this is disagreement?" Another pass through the segment, often including attention to more of the previous interactional context, might provide me with grounding for my initial observation, or it might lead me to rethink my initial interpretation.[2] Beyond the focal segments themselves, I also looked closely at the opening of each meeting in order to account for the initial constitution of a group as in meeting mode, a shift in the local structuring of participation.

Concepts, terms, and transcription symbols

CA is a theory and a set of methods aimed at accounting for the collaborative production of "talk as social organization" (M. H. Goodwin, 1990:1–17). Among CA's methods is the close transcription of talk. Transcription supports detailed analysis of the construction of social interaction, but video and audio recordings always serve as the primary data, and analysts are continually adding detail to existing transcripts. Fine-grained transcription as a component of analysis reflects CA's view of interaction as ordered and orderly, predictable and accountable; accumulated findings on the sources of interactional order support an assumption that no level of detail can be assumed to be trivial for participants in interaction and thus for analysts. In other words, analysts attend to detail because participants in interaction produce and respond to detail. We try to notice and notate the features of vocal and non-vocal action which participants use to create this order and this improvisation. The transcription symbols, originally developed by Gail Jefferson, note features of sound production and the timing of vocal actions, and the symbol system has been augmented over the years as new features of interaction have been noted. In this section, I offer an introduction to some conventions, methods, and concepts central to the analyses I present in Chapters 4 through 6.

Working with transcripts and videotapes

As transcription and analysis go hand in hand (Ochs, 1979), in principle CA treats all hearable sound production features as potentially consequential for understanding interaction. However, a transcriber's filtering of sounds, based on her hearing and her analytic preconceptions, make all transcription a provisional, fallible, and iterative process. Access to previous, simultaneous, and subsequent talk and gestures is a crucial source for analytic understanding of the way the participants organize their interaction and what significance they may be making of it. For example, when the gaze of a participant or several participants shifts, such movements may be responsive to less audible or previously unnoticed (by the analyst) actions.

Working with the present meeting data involved viewing the video recordings, with the transcripts serving as aids to analysis rather than as the primary data. A key to the transcription symbols used in my examples is found on pp. x–xi. In order to underscore how such details captured in transcriptions may have potential significance, let me illustrate some fundamentals of the order in ordinary talk, drawing attention to how transcription supports the analysis of that order.

Turn-taking and turn construction

One fundamental task to be managed in interaction is turn-taking, including speaker selection and the interpretation of what it takes to complete a turn. Next speakers may be unilaterally selected by a current speaker or they may self-select, beginning to speak without being explicitly chosen. In the meeting data, it is also common for speakers to perform separate, non-vocal bids to speak and then wait to be recognized by the chair or by another participant currently holding the floor (some specific practices for turn transition are discussed in Chapter 3). Videotaped data allows for detailed analyses of the coordination of both vocal and non-vocal actions. In order to capture and reflect upon the ways that speakers coordinate vocal and non-vocal actions as they managed turn transfer, I regularly include non-vocal actions in my transcriptions for this study. For example, at line 3 in excerpt (1), Hank uses a hand gesture to make a bid to speak. Transcribed between double parentheses, in bold and italicized font, is a short description of Hank's gesture, and at line 4, double parentheses frame a note on Amanda's non-vocal response:

(1) [Planning] Non-vocal actions and speaker selection

1   Amanda: Uh- in the interim this is still the committee that is
2   responsible for- (ethnic) studies credit.
3   Hank: .hh ***((raises hand with index finger pointed up))***
4   Amanda: ***((gaze and vertical head movement toward Hank))***
5   Hank: Gloria just brought up a relevant question.

It is no coincidence that Hank prefaces his gestural bid to be called upon with an audible in-breath, transcribed as ".hh" (line 3). Obviously participants are breathing all the time, but audible in-breaths are not the norm; they are salient occurrences and can indicate that a person is about to speak. In (1), the in-breath and the hand raise (line 3) draw Amanda's gaze and her non-vocal response (line 4). The non-lexical and non-vocal actions in lines 3–4 constitute a short sequence of bidding by Hank and acknowledgement by Amanda. In addition to parenthetical notations of non-vocal actions, I also include simple line tracings of video stills for some examples.

Transcripts also include indications of prosodic stress. Example (2) illustrates the potential significance of and interaction between a speaker's stress and a non-vocal action by a recipient:

(2) [Medical] Non-vocal action and prosody

```
1   Ned: You can measure the right hand, you can measure the right arm, you can
2        measure the head, or you decapitate [ folks. (0.7) And that's what[. . .]
3   Gwen:                                    [((moves head forward, gazes toward Ned))
```

Ned's loudness and higher pitch on the second syllable of "decapitate" (line 2), represented by underlining, could be a way of marking that information as potentially of interest, both to him and for the recipients. Just after Ned produces this word, Gwen moves her head forward and turns her gaze toward him. The left brackets in lines 2 and 3 mark the point where Gwen's movements are simultaneous with Ned's talk. These movements may be directly responsive to Ned's production of the word "decapitate".[3]

Example (3) contains cut off sounds, segments of speech delivered at rapid pace, along with several restarts and repairs. Repairs involve notable halts in the progress of a turn unit, with resumption regularly involving repetition or revision (Schegloff, Jefferson & Sacks, 1977). Though such processes and features of articulation are commonly thought of as speech problems and errors, CA research has shown their orderly nature and the interactional work they may do (e.g., Goodwin, 1979; Schegloff, 1987)

(3) [Diversity] Other features of sound production

```
1   Mary: >Oh no no no(if I)< eh- (.) and this may be stating- (.)stating
2         obvious, bu:t uh the two years would (.)enable you >not only
3         >>then<< to set up< a la:b, but to find (.) possible dual- dual
4         career positions:
```

The inward pointing less than and greater than signs indicate that what comes between them is produced more quickly than surrounding talk, with the double signs around ">>then<<" marking even greater speed. The hyphens, as in line 1, "eh-" and "stating-", represent a sound cut short. This represents a hearable stop in the progress of a sound (or a word, phrase, or sentence; see Jasperson, 2002). In line 1, Mary cuts off her completion of "stating-" and then says that same word again, moving past its ending and into the completion of that predictable unit of turn construction, that is, a unit of grammar, prosody, and action which is currently in production rather than possibly complete.[4] She also executes the cut off and redoing of a word at the end of line 1, and she produces multiple pauses at points where there is clearly more projected in her turn (lines 1, 2, and 3). These production features in Mary's turn are worth investigating. One might interpret them as enactments of care in speech production (see Chapter 6 for an analysis of Mary's turn-building process). My purposes here is to note that both the lexical content of Mary's turn and the details of her turn's delivery invite a closer analysis of how she is formulating her action.

As with all CA investigation, attention to the details of vocal and non-vocal actions relate to the basic analytic question (and the question that participants are constantly responding to): "Why that now?" Why would one select this form of delivery in this location and for these recipients (Schegloff, 2007:1–4)? Transcription symbols do not answer that question, but they serve as heuristics to support further inquiry.

Projection

Turns at talk and the interactive courses of multiparty activities are recognizably reproduced in interactional encounters. Repeated engagement in interactional tasks results in repertoires for participation in the sequences of action that make up our social lives (Schegloff, 2007). Our skills at interacting rely on an ability to flexibly, but precisely, anticipate these courses of unfolding action in each new encounter. That is, in order to participate, we must be able to recognize a trajectory of action as it is still in the process of unfolding. For example, to respond in a timely way to any current speaker's turn, we need to have a good sense of what action she is producing and what range of predictable forms (e.g., grammatical and prosodic patterns) the action normally takes. Each increment of an unfolding turn offers further cues as to where the turn is going and what it will take to complete it, with turn completion serving as a primary juncture for next speakers to begin their talk.

CA refers to the recognizable and expectable nature of emergent talk and action as *projectability*. Bits of talk project potential trajectories, the talk and action that may follow.

Careful study of recorded interaction reveals the workings of projection, and the current meeting data is no exception. As in more ordinary, casual interaction (Sacks *et al.*, 1974), participants in these meetings do not generally wait for pauses to develop before processing and responding to what other persons are saying, nor do they treat silence between turns as open time to be freely used for composing responses before speaking. For example, in (4), Jan asks Florence to introduce Lynn to the rest of the group, and Florence produces her response at the completion of Jan's turn, without any gap:

(4) [Diversity] Precise timing of next speaker turn beginning

Jan: Uhm, So I guess our first introduction is Lynn:= Florence would you like
    to, do the honors?
Flor: Sure,

While Jan is producing her turn, Florence and others are interpreting the action Jan is producing. As they do so, they are able to anticipate what it will take for Jan's turn to reach possible completion; that is, the participants project a trajectory, a grammatical and prosodic shape, for talk yet to come in Jan's turn. It is projection that allows Florence to produce a response to Jan without waiting for a pause; Florence has already projected the possible completion point of Jan's turn, and she is prepared to begin precisely as Jan's turn reaches its end.

Pauses, hesitations, and preference

In CA transcripts, pauses are timed and transcribed in tenths of a second. The ability to project possible completion points before their arrival supports specific interactional significance for pauses and hesitations. One potential significance of a pause after the completion of a turn is that the next speaker may disagree; thus, when a next speaker may be about to disagree, that disagreeing turn is regularly (though not universally) preceded by pausing. For example, a pause in place of Florence's "Sure," in (4), above, might have been interpreted as a problem: Jan and others could interpret such a pause as projecting upcoming hesitation and refusal by Florence (Pomerantz, 1984; Sacks, 1987; Schegloff, 2007). As speakers treat pauses in certain contexts as projecting disagreement, they may extend and modify their actions in pursuit of response or agreement. Even when a disagreeing turn begins to be delivered, it may be prefaced with hesitation markers ("uhm," "uh") or other forms which, in such a position, project potential disagreement (e.g., "well"). The projection of disagreement, before the disagreement is fully delivered, allows further opportunities for the previous speaker to speak again in order to pursue agreement.

Disaffiliation is a general term used to encompass a broad range of actions that, in their local interactional contexts, are understood as disagreeing, disaligning, or otherwise taking issue with a prior action or stance, and thereby, creating potential interactional trouble between two or more participants. Disaffiliative action is done in special ways, including the pattern mentioned above of the emergence of pauses before disaffiliative responses. In other words, it is in part through the relationship between the present turn's action and previous actions that disaffiliation may be evident, but it is also through hesitations, delays, and the addition of accounts and explanations that a speaker displays that what she is doing is indeed problematic, i.e., not the normative, agreeing, or aligning way of acting in that sort of context. Actions positioned and/or packaged such that they do disagreement or disaffiliation are termed *dispreferred* (Schegloff, 2007). Using forms associated with dispreferred or "delicate" actions (e.g., delays, hesitations, mitigations, restarts) can thus, in itself, display dispreference, a stance toward the action as problematic or not aligned with the normative expectations. Indeed, if a speaker delivers an action with delay and hesitation, for example, it may be interpreted as a dispreferred action, even if the lexico-grammatical content alone seems to be delivering agreement and affiliation in other ways. In this book, I will use disaffiliative, disagreeing, and disaligning interchangeably, though some researchers distinguish them (e.g., Keisanen, 2006).

Given the status of pauses and hesitations as forms of action (projecting and formulating dispreferred responses, for example), it becomes all the more crucial that interactants recognize action sequences, of grammar, of sound production patterns, and of non-vocal behavior as simultaneous and interrelated sources for projecting possible points of turn completion. Such recognition supports participants' ability to target specific points for launching their turns. Observation of interaction has made it abundantly clear that humans are remarkably precise in how they place turn initiation relative to current or previous speakers' projectable points of possible completion. Only if we recognize the vital projection skills humans command, their practical knowledge of the recurrent shapes of actions and their possible end points, can we account for the split-second timing evident in interaction.

Projection of completion points is not only useful for avoiding pauses and overlaps as a means of doing affiliation. Projection also supports variations in the operation of the turn-taking system; it supports the interactional significance placed on the deployment of overlaps and pauses. Gaps and overlaps are used and interpreted in relation to the possibility of precise, on-time, start ups. For example, recognizing the emerging shape of a turn allows a recipient to initiate a response precisely *before* a projectable end point is reached. The interpretation of an overlap depends on the specific action being done in an unfolding turn. Overlapped turn beginnings may be done as a way of joining in with encouragement and agreement, or they may act as interruptions and reinforce strong disagreement.

Example (5), below, includes an illustration of non-interruptive overlap. Stephie articulates the word "<u>co(h)</u>lleg(h)e" with a breathiness, transcribed by the parenthetical "h"s and interpretable here as laughter. John produces laughter in overlap with the end of Stephie's participial phrase "being on- the other side of the <u>co(h)</u>lleg(h)e". Note that this phrase projects more to come in this context, as Stephie has not produced a previous independent (or "main") clause which this dependent clause could be seen as extending:[5]

(5) [Diversity] Overlapping as joining in with laughter

```
1   Steph: Being on- the other side of the co(h)lleg(h)e[.
2   John:                                              [huh eh heh
```

The grammatical dependence of Stephie's participial phrase in line 1 projects continued talk before completion of a main clause. John's overlap here, though not coming at a point of turn completion, is not interruptive. His laughter is precisely placed so as to display his affiliation with Stephie's stance: he literally joins in with Stephie's display of a humorous stance toward her location in the college.[6] As will be discussed in Chapter 6, Stephie's interweaving of laughter with her production of this phrase is specifically designed to do work relative to particular recipients, one of whom is John. CA uses the term *recipient design* to refer to the particular ways talk is crafted with reference to particular participants; this is a form of indexicality that can both reflect and posit local relations between speakers. In (5), Stephie's laughter-infused production of the word *college* invites and enacts solidarity between herself and John.

Just as an overlap can have different sorts of interactional significance, so a pause after the possible completion of a question can project disagreement or it can indicate a problem of understanding. In (6), below, Jill's pause in line 1 is part of a projectably incomplete turn because Jill has not yet specified the subgroup of "alendronate users" whose percentage she is requesting. Jill then comes to the possible end of her question at line 2. However, another pause emerges just after Jill has stopped speaking (line 3), and just where Ned could have initiated a response:

(6) [Medical] Pause interpreted as an understanding problem

```
1   Jill: Ned, uhm what- what's the- percent of alendronate users,(0.4)
2         have you seen that ar- you would call sort of failures.
3               (0.4)
4   Jill: Bone marrow density failu°res.°
```

Through what Jill adds at line 4, she displays her interpretation of the pause as indicating that Ned has a problem in understanding what she means by "failures." At line 4, she repairs and recompletes her turn, adding more specifics through the modification, "Bone marrow density failures."

Examples (4) through (6), and others in these meetings and in numerous CA studies, illustrate how projectable shapes of turns and sequences of turns support a norm of split-second timing in turn-taking, and how projection supports the deployment and interpretation of overlaps and pauses. In this system, both overlaps and emerging pauses after the possible completion of turns carry a range of locally determined meanings.

Contingency and relevance

Though interaction is fully orderly and relies on predictability (as in projection), it is far from predetermined. To propose that interaction is *contingent* is to counter implications that the operation orderly practices of talking implies predetermined patterns and clear distinctions between appropriate and inappropriate discourse practices. When we look at sequences of action—questions and answers, tellings and their uptake (or lack of uptake)—we can identify normative trajectories that such interactional sequences *may* take, as participants and analysts we recognize that the course of a projected trajectory is *only* a normative course; it is open to revision in the process of its production. For that reason, we explicitly state that a given point represents a *possible* completion, as I have done above. Actual completion is a matter of negotiation from moment to moment. In the case of turn-taking, then, while projection is based on recurrent and expectable turn trajectories, built through grammar, prosody, and patterns of vocal and non-vocal action, participants may nevertheless begin vocal and non-vocal actions before possible completion points. Conversely, they may allow pauses to emerge after previous speakers have come to points of possible turn completion, a situation which regularly leads to the same speaker adding to her (previously possibly complete) turn. The last two examples in the previous section are cases in point. In (5) John initiates his laughter at a point where Stephie has projected more talk to come, and in (6) Ned is silent at a point when Jill's turn is possibly complete. Possible completion followed by a pause may be interpreted as a problem. This is a contingency that Jill responds to by speaking again, adding more specification in pursuit of uptake from Ned.

Further aspects of the contingent production of a single turn are explored by Charles Goodwin in his 1979 analysis of a speaker's shaping of a single sentence. Goodwin demonstrates that what we traditionally take as progressive parts of a single speaker's turn can be intricately responsive to simultaneous actions of recipients.[7] Thus, even the projectable trajectory of an unfolding grammatical unit (a sentence in Goodwin's example) is subject to contingencies, features of the emerging interaction that are not predetermined. While sound production notations are relatively uniform in use among CA researchers, the representation of non-vocal action is not standardized; Goodwin is exceptional in his longstanding representation of gaze and body movements in his illustrative examples (Goodwin, 1979).

Example (6), above, also illustrates how the CA notion of *relevance* is useful as a corrective to treating interactional structures as predetermined rather than contingent. A response from Ned is projectable based on Jill's possible completion of her questioning turn (at line 2). In such a context, we say that Jill's action makes a response from Ned relevant next. However, Ned does not speak at that juncture. In CA terms, Jill's action has created a condition under which a response from Ned is anticipated; a response is *conditionally relevant*. Thus, the silence at line 3 is not just any silence; it is a silence in place of a response by Ned. How Jill and others interpret that silence is constrained by the relevance of a response. Using the terms *relevant* and *relevance* underscores that while the next action is not predetermined, the slot itself—that moment at the possible completion of Jill's turn—involves a frame of reference largely shaped by Jill's just completed action. The concept of relevance supports analytic attention to contingency and the local construction of context. Thus, while interaction is highly ordered and predictable, and there are consequential relevancies created by each next action, talk is also highly contingent.

Connecting contingency to the predictable shapes of preferred and dispreferred turns, Schegloff notes that

> Which of alternative contingent next actions a speaker will do [. . .] is not in principle predictable. Still, although whether an invitation will be accepted or declined, for example, is in principle indeterminate, much can be said about how either will be done if it is chosen—for example, whether it will be done promptly or delayed, explicitly or indirectly, baldly or with an account, etc. [. . .] There are various places at which another can initiate talk and action, various practices for doing so, and (in multiparty interaction) alternative participants who can do so. But who, when and where are always contingent.
>
> (1993:21–2)

Contingency also operates in another component of the turn-taking process. In the classic CA account for turn-taking in interaction, Sacks *et al.* (1974) provide a framework for understanding turn-taking, including the necessity that participants be able to allocate turns in a spontaneous manner. Sacks *et al.* also point to the fact that turn-taking requires a flexible notion of a turn unit, which they call a *turn-constructional unit* (TCU).[8] With respect to the study of meetings, Sacks *et al.* sketched principles for distinguishing "ordinary conversation," the most basic form of interaction, and other forms of *talk-in-interaction*—a broad term for ordinary conversation and other interactional activities. Institutional talk involves special adaptations and transformations of ordinary practices. For example, ritual interaction, parliamentary procedures and the like, have *specialized speech exchange systems* (Sacks *et al.*, 1974).

Even though meetings involve adaptations of the turn-taking system, meetings are not exempt from patterns of preferred and dispreferred action formulation, or from the operation of contingency and relevance. In their introduction to the collection *Talk at Work* (1992), Paul Drew and John Heritage list and elaborate features that distinguish institutional interaction from ordinary talk. These include, among other features, the sorts of restricted "goal orientations" found, for example, in the agendas of meetings. In her book, *The Business of Talk* (1994), Dierdre Boden notes some practices through which ordinary talk among individuals gathering before a scheduled meeting is transformed into official meeting structure (also see Cuff and Sharrock, 1987).

Such practices are evident in the present data as well. There are clear shifts in the allocation of speakership as meetings are officially opened. Meeting leaders act as representatives of the shared agenda, and they are, to varying degrees, the persons through whom speakership is coordinated. However, contingency, shifting relevancies, and ongoing projection of turns and courses of action characterize the events I recorded. In none of the meetings is talk rigidly controlled, nor are agendas rigidly followed. Interactants jointly achieve a shared sense of what they are doing together. They constantly update, revise, and sometimes resist orientations to what they take as the interactional task at hand; how members of the group are structuring their activity; and when and how they may be called on or when and how they may select themselves to contribute.

Position and composition of turns

A sequence is an ordered course of action. Sequences are, as Schegloff describes them, "general patterns or structures *which [participants] use* (and which we can describe) to co-produce and track an orderly stretch of talk and other conduct in which some course of action gets initiated, worked through, and brought to closure" (2007:5). The significance of a turn, for participants and for the analyst, is determined by both its *position* and its *composition*. The term composition refers to turn design, the selection of vocal and non-vocal forms that build a turn. Recognition of what action is being done in any moment, then, depends not only on the shape or composition of a piece of talk (including sounds, words, phrases, sentences; prosody, and gesture) but on where it is used, its position, in a recognizable sequence. The intersection of position and composition provides for the interpretation of a piece of talk as doing a particular action.

In example (7), we can see how position and composition contribute to interpretation of potentially cryptic aspects of a turn's formulation. Because Laura, an important member of the Non-Profit Board, has not yet arrived Jaimie offers to call her if someone has her phone number:

(7) [Board] Position and composition in the interpretation of Jim's talk (lines 7 and 10)

```
5   Jaimie: =if someone has- Laura's- number, I will, if you have the board
6           directory, I'll give her a quick call.
```

7⇒ Jim: [Ahh
8 Jaimie: ['Cause I talked to Monty yesterday. And said I'll see you tomorrow
9   at the meeting, and (0.8) he said ↑Oh: yeah.
10⇒ Jim: Uh it is uh: doo doo doo doo >three two five< zero six nine five.

Jaimie's turn at lines 5–6 combines a request for information and an offer. At the possible completion of her turn, it is relevant for "someone" to provide her with Laura's number. At line 7, Jim produces the token "Ahh" as he flips through his board directory. Jim vocalizes in a position where a specific range of responses are relevant, actions responsive to Jaimie's offer and request. Combined with Jim's visible engagement in looking through the directory, a turn composed of "Ahh" is interpretable as drawing attention to his search and simultaneously projecting and delaying further talk in which he will produce the requested information. That Jim's turn is in overlap with Jaimie's continuation has to do with mechanisms we discussed earlier; that is, possible completion not always being actual completion.

After Jaimie's elaboration (lines 8–9), Jim begins to form a clause with, "it is" which has a pronoun that, in this position in the sequence, links to "Laura's number" in line 5, the information Jaimie is requesting. But simultaneous with this turn beginning, Jim is running his fingers over a page. In this position, the syllables he produces, "doo doo doo doo" are interpretable as a kind of turn-holding practice involving "sound effects" for his continuing search. After these searching sounds, Jim reads Laura's number. Both line 7 and line 10 illustrate contributions whose composition might ground a different interpretation in another position. For example, Jim's "Ahh" after a bite of food, might be heard as an expression of satisfaction. Likewise, after a question about the time, a clause starting with "it is" simultaneous with a gaze at a watch might project the delivery of an hour and minute reading for the completion of the turn. A similar contrasting position and interpretation could be imagined for the syllables, "doo doo doo." Participants thus build and interpret what a turn or other action is doing by reference to an intersection of its composition and its position in an unfolding sequence.

Having discussed fundamental CA practices and concepts that I draw from in the analytic chapters of this book, let me provide an orientation to the collection of interviews and the continuing dialogue I carried out during my analytic process.

A continuing dialogue: interviews, informal consultations, and feedback from formal presentations

In an essay on the challenges of feminist fieldwork on gender and language, Sara Trechter (2004) reflects on the challenges of describing the language of persons in settings that might not be familiar to the researcher.[9] The priorities of the researcher, including her feminist commitments, may not be aligned with the ideologies of the persons whose language she is documenting. As do many qualitative researchers, Trechter encourages respect for the perspectives of participants:

> Much like a conversation—an apt linguistic metaphor for feminist fieldwork—no single participant knew or had ultimate control over the end product, nor will participants interpret that product in the same way. And like a good conversation, aspects of this dialogic research process may be repeated in new contexts.
>
> (2004:274)

The issues Trechter raises bring to mind Linda Alcoff's essay, "The problem of speaking for others" (1994) and Kitzinger and Wilkinson's essay "Validating women's experience? Dilemmas in feminist research" (1997). There is an unavoidable and ultimately beneficial tension in feminist research between the priorities and commitments of the researcher and those of the researched. While I did not find the settings of the meetings I taped remarkably unfamiliar, I regularly reflected on how I might be reading more or less into particular exchanges than would the participants themselves, consciously or unconsciously.

In an effort to keep the project responsive to women's explicit questions I continually compared my developing analyses with the experiences and priorities of the women in the meetings I visited and videotaped. I continued my dialogue with the women whose concerns prompted this project in the first place by offering formal and informal presentations of my findings on the data. Additionally, for each meeting group, I maintained contact with one or two participants who had agreed to take part in informal dialogue with me via phone calls and email exchanges. In these exchanges, I checked my understanding of terminology and of how participants viewed their workplace climates, roles, and relationships. I learned about concerns and tensions they felt in those particular meetings as well as in their work lives more generally.

Along with sharing my ongoing observations and inviting feedback in presentations, I conducted open-ended interviews with 14 women, at least one from each of the videotaped meetings.[10] The interviews included questions about the women's ranks relative to others in the taped meetings, how they described their identities, and their reflections on experiences interacting in their workplaces. I also invited each woman to share advice they would give others concerned about speaking up in such settings.

In the conversation analytic chapters (4–6) and in the final chapter of this book, I bring in reflections from the interviews. However, before moving to the technical analyses and findings on turn-taking, turn extension, and participation, I use Chapter 3 to draw from the interviews and offer an initial sense of these women's reflections on their worklife and experiences in interacting.

3
Reflections on Participation

One way I invited women's perspectives on participation in meetings was through open-ended interviews. These conversations lasted from 20 minutes to two hours, and they were rich with information and insights. While Chapters 4 through 6 introduce technical detail on participation patterns in the meetings, the present chapter provides a brief backdrop of reflections from individual women who took part in the videotaped meetings. This is a sampling from these women's reflections on their styles of interacting and on their experiences participating in institutional settings.

The women I interviewed have much in common: most specifically, all are among a minority of women in their ranks in their workplaces and in their professions more generally. However, these women were far from uniform in how they perceived themselves as participants, how they compared themselves to others, and how they saw themselves treated or positioned (Baxter, 2003; Davies & Harré, 1990) by peers and superiors in their institutions. In addition, though they all reported conscious strategies for planning before meetings and for getting turns in the flow of meetings, they varied in their assessments of the success of their strategies: some were quite happy with their participation, while others reported problems and continued frustration.

Multiple senses of difference

Though my analyses (Chapters 4–6) focus on women's turns in meetings, it is noteworthy that in response to open-ended prompts regarding their experiences interacting in their workplaces, the women I interviewed did not report that being a woman was the fundamental obstacle to their full participation. All the interviewees knew of my interest in women's participation in meetings, but none of them pointed to gender as the sole source of challenge for them in workplace communication. Several of the interview prompts related to interactional style and personal history of interacting. Among the 14 women I interviewed, it was most common that they articulated a number of factors affecting how they positioned themselves and were positioned by others in meetings and other institutional interactions in their lives. They described intersecting sources for their experiences and their styles of interacting, including intelligence, race, institutional rank, and particulars of their personalities and preferences (e.g., being social, being shy, being cautious, hating to waste time).

Reference to multiple identities resonates with CA's caution regarding analysts' imposition of social categories as uniquely relevant to accounts of interactional practices (e.g., Schegloff, 1997). The performance of multiple identities is also a key element in poststructuralist research on gender, with current trends in feminist research questioning monolithic views of social categories. Individuals fit into, draw upon, and are treated by others with reference to multiple possible identities and social positions; the women I interviewed were no exception. That the women I interviewed cite various intersecting positions from which they speak and toward which others orient in speaking to them added support to my commitment to avoid any claim that the turn-taking practices documented in this book, though focused on women's talk, should be viewed as exclusive to persons identifying as women.

In the following sections, I use excerpts from the interviews to illustrate a range of social categories or identities which, in addition to gender, were cited by interviewees as significant for their interactions and their interactional styles.

Socialization, brilliance, and social class

Pam, a white middle class, accomplished scientist and high-level administrator, cited her early experiences with interrupted schooling and evident brilliance as relevant to the formation of her interactional style.

> *You know I haven't ever thought this through quite like this, except when you asked about how I interact, I felt that I should go back to the fact that I have been bold and outgoing and loud and unafraid to speak up for as long as I remember . . . . I wasn't socialized very well before I went into kindergarten, and I was there for just half mornings a half year because of some ill health [. . .] I could already read and, when I went to kindergarten because my mother had home-schooled me while I was, while I had to stay home when I was ill.*

Pam was also exceptionally confident in her intelligence:

> *I have wanted to be a [scientist] since I was ten. And I was very, very good in math the whole way through. [I] skipped a couple of grades, and so forth. [I had] very high math aptitude and achievement. And when we had teachers who I thought were stupider than I was, I was pretty obnoxious. So, at some point I actually got separated from the rest of the class. [. . .] I would interrupt, and I started learning that you should not interrupt, but I really had not been socialized very well. So I was kind of a loud-mouth and assertive.*

The combination of her illness, her intelligence, and her unusual display of confidence (which she attributes to lack of socialization) led to Pam's being separated from other students on several occasions during her elementary and secondary education. She credits this separation for saving her interest in math, since she knew "that teacher was not competent enough." The down side was that being separated from other students affected how well socialized she was to norms of interacting.

As a young woman, Pam's sense of otherness increased when she attended a highly competitive and prestigious private university. The students in her classes, mostly men, were better prepared in subject matter and better "socialized" into schooling, as Pam put it. Though she acknowledged being one of very few women in her classes, she explained her feelings of difference as stemming from the educational advantages of her peers in the university:

> *I had not gone to New York/Bronx High School of Science, that sort of thing. I was in with people who were, who had better study habits, and were basically better prepared. So, being the only or one of the few women in math and science classes was, um, . . .*

Interestingly, Pam abandons her reference to being one of relatively few women. When she restarts, she focuses exclusively on educational background rather than gender as creating the conditions leading her to pull back from participation at that point in her academic career:

> [continuation] *I was not ever afraid to speak-up, but at some point part way in to the semester, when I realized they were getting it immediately and I wasn't getting it immediately, I did stop speaking up. I mean I stopped asking questions in class when I realized that I was probably the only one who didn't understand something. And the reason I wouldn't understand it was because I was in fairly advanced classes. For example in*

calculus, I took the two-year, ah, hoity-toity calculus instead of the regular calculus. And it was taught, the two years were taught by luminary mathematicians. And everybody in the class had a very good background in math. I did not have a good background in math, and I did not have a good background in physics. So my high school background was not as good as the other people's. And that did make me start to shrink from asking questions in class.

Although Pam stressed that her path to success was difficult, she did not speak of her status as a woman in a male-dominated profession as the fundamental obstacle. Pam's experience of competition and intellectual challenge stood out as affecting her attitude toward participation in institutional settings. She also pointed to social class and educational background as affecting her ability to succeed at one of the best universities in the US. Nevertheless, and despite emotional upheavals and continuing serious health issues, Pam became an acclaimed scientist, university administrator, and advocate for diversity in higher education.

Gender, race, and institutional rank

Other women I interviewed pointed to race and institutional hierarchies as intersecting with gender to affect their workplace interactions. Gloria, a middle class, African-American with a doctorate in the humanities, was serving as a university dean at the time I interviewed her. She reported that when she spoke in meetings she felt she received less attention and uptake than others:

I've noticed it's white, male faculty who have the most power and privilege at these meetings. And then it kind of goes down from there. Being a black female staff member, I have often felt as if my voice is not going to be as important or my opinion is not going to be as valued as someone else's.

Gloria identifies as black and female, but she also identifies as a "staff member." In most North American universities, faculty members have greater prestige than staff members. While Gloria's self identification as a "black female staff member" indexes the contrasting category, "white male faculty member," it also contrasts with "white female faculty member." Gloria thus invokes rank in the institutional hierarchy as a source of biased treatment in meetings.

Gloria's experience is one of intersecting identities and multiple biases. Thus, even though her position at the time of my interview was relatively high, since she was an administrator at a respected university, for Gloria, a combination of gender, race, and rank posed challenges to her full participation.

Institutional rank and personality

Florence, a white middle class woman with a Ph.D. in economics, directs an interdisciplinary research center housed in a college of science; this is an administrative position comparable to Gloria's. Like Gloria, Florence reported dealing with bias based on her position in the university hierarchy, but she also saw her personality as contributing to her experiences in meetings. Florence generally preferred "to be quiet." She noted, however, that as she had gained expertise and the recognition that accompanied it, her communicative style had begun to change. She also noted that she was using different strategies for speaking up:

> *Florence: The more I participate in meetings, the more I get that feeling of success.*
> *Cecilia: Are you aware of things that work?*
> *Florence: It's just um, I think it's just taking [a turn].*
> *Cecilia: Just jumping in?*
> *Florence: Yeah. Not trying to be polite, not waiting my turn. If what I think I have to say is important enough then I finally just do it. And I'm getting more comfortable with doing that.*

Nevertheless, Florence viewed her rank as continuing to contribute to her relatively restrained participation in meetings, a restraint that she sees as partly self-imposed but also a result of her treatment by others in higher ranks:

> *Although I will say with over time I've become more bold, in meetings, I still defer to faculty. You know, I'm not going to interrupt anybody. They interrupt me, and I let them. Is what I have to say so important that I'm going to be more aggressive? I have to make that decision a lot during meetings.*

Florence is an experienced researcher and the director or an influential center. However, she finds herself questioning the importance of what she has to say, and she views her status as an administrator rather than a faculty member as a factor in the undervaluing of her participation.

Gwen, a white, middle-class physician, holds a high rank in several institutions where she teaches and practices medicine. She reported numerous ways that she and other women of her rank and accomplishment are poorly treated because they are women. Gwen was quick to point to race as a factor that further advantages or disadvantages women in medicine, and she is extremely active in advocating for diversity. But she also pointed to her personality and interactional style as problematic. In particular, she saw herself as perhaps speaking up too much, but doing so nevertheless:

> *I'm kind of loud, obnoxious, and interrupting. You have to [interrupt] or you never get heard.*

Gwen compared herself negatively to a woman with whom she regularly collaborated. She admired and longed to share her colleague's poise:

> *You know I watch Jan, and she's so serious and quiet and paced, and she's so effective. And I'm more kind of loud and I don't know, how would you describe it? I mean humorous I guess, loud and energetic.*

Gwen is recognized as an out-spoken advocate for women and racial minorities in the institutions where she works, and while this gains her great respect and trust from some, it is a source of tension between her and her male superiors.

Being an out lesbian

Sexual orientation figured in at least one woman's experience of interaction in her workplace. Lonnie, a white, middle class systems analyst on an engineering team, deals with regular gender bias, but as an out lesbian, she felt she had an advantage as compared with heterosexual women in her workplace:

> *I think it really helps sometimes. I saw [my advantage] where a heterosexual woman—you know, because there are all these guys—was always hesitant. And I'm just like, "Ah, I'm not risking anything." I don't know. It was just easier.*

Lonnie also identifies as a weight lifter, and she spends lunch hours lifting with her male colleagues. She saw that as enhancing her solidarity with her male co-workers.

Personality and expertise

Lonnie's report of feeling less stress than heterosexual women in her workplace prompted me to ask about her co-worker Sally. Sally, a white, middle-class, middle manager, was the only other woman present in the meeting I taped at Lonnie's workplace. In reflecting on her perceptions of how Sally is treated, Lonnie cited Sally's personality and expertise as counterbalancing the obstacles she would otherwise face as a heterosexual woman in a male-dominated workplace:

> *It's not a problem for Sally, but Sally is—she has a very strong personality. And she's also somebody who's very knowledgeable. So I think in a technical environment they respect somebody who's knowledgeable. But there are people she supervises who are called "girls"* and treated in a little different fashion.*
>
> *"girls" = clerical staff

Strategic silence and learning to listen

While status characteristics were viewed as sources of bias, and speaking up was reported as a challenge by some, other women reported consciously, and in some cases strategically, limiting their vocal participation. Thus, whereas Florence saw her quietness as a personal preference, Lonnie reported intentionally refraining from speaking so that she would be taken more seriously when she did speak:

> *I usually try not to say very much because people stop listening. I think I'm more effective if I say something then, because people usually listen.*

Carol, white, middle class scientist working in a government position, characterized herself as an enthusiastic participant but one who could be a better listener. And Mindy, white and middle class, employed in a university science department, had developed a strategy of being quiet to avoid conflict both in her childhood family and later in her department at the university. Remarkably to her, this choice resulted in her moving into a chair position, as she had not made enemies in an otherwise polarized workplace. Like others who viewed being quiet as a choice, Mindy reported

> *[my silence became] a powerful tool, because then when I say something everybody looks over and thinks, "Wow, she spoke!"*

In another institutional context, Moira, a white Episcopal priest, from a middle class background, also reported a strategic use of silence. Moira was very aware of her power in church staff meetings, and in those settings she purposely did not take advantage of her special rights to speak:

> *The priest is the boss and when she needs to say something it's not hard to get the floor. I try to share it. I don't like to own it, because then I never hear anybody else's perspectives.*

Moira also reported limiting her speech in larger church governance meetings, where she was not "the boss." Like Lonnie and Mindy, Moira saw her relative silence in these events as adding power to her contributions when she did choose to speak up:

> *If I'm not facilitating the meeting, I knit. Always. I am Madame Defarge in this diocese. And I have gotten the reputation now: "Moira may not say much, but she listens, and when she does say something, you'd better listen." And I would much rather have that kind of reputation than somebody who's always shooting off her mouth, that people kind of tune out.*

Moira saw her default practice of knitting throughout meetings as creating a background against which others interpreted even small movements on her part:

> *If I look up from my knitting, people know I have something to say.*

In yet another variety of self-evaluation of communicative style, Lynn, a white, middle class information scientist, viewed herself as not only speaking up too much, but also as needing to learn better listening skills:

> *[Getting a turn] is not a problem, I'll bet you can guess, for me. I'd probably be guilty of brushing past something I thought was irrelevant or a time waster, or that's not appropriate. The skill I would have to focus on would be being a good listener. Being efficient but being a good listener.*

Stephie, is a white, middle class engineer. Like Moira, Stephie works to hold back from speaking, but like Lynn, being silent and listening does not come easily to her:

> *I get really impatient with people when I think they're talking about things that I think are really off point, and I just can't believe you're wasting our time with this or being manipulative. But sometimes I really do work to hold off, to not be verbal in a meeting unless I think that it's essential. I mean I work very hard not to get the floor, because I think I dominate meetings. I'm very articulate, and I can very easily take control of a meeting. And I know that I don't always have the only or the best answer for something.*

What these excerpts illustrate, then, is that these women consider multiple aspects of identity as affecting their experiences communicating in the traditionally male professional settings and in the specific positions they hold. Thus, while all the interviewees were among the few women in their ranks in their workplaces, they varied in how they reflected upon the combinations of social categories and personal characteristics that intersected to affect their experiences and their conscious practices in meetings. Among these women are some who view themselves as quiet, and others who see themselves as outspoken to a fault. These differences result in contrasting concerns regarding participation—from needing to push oneself to speak up, to holding back and trying to listen to others.

Conscious strategies: preparing in advance and speaking up in the flow

In addition to reflecting on the multiple factors that affect their experiences of meeting participation, these women reported conscious strategies related to what CA terms projection. Their reports on strategies came up in response to the prompts, "How do you get the floor to speak?", and "What has helped you to be an effective participant in meetings?" A general practice that all the women mentioned in one form or another was cultivating connections and alliances with co-workers, outside of meetings and also within the flow of meetings. The women also shared strategies for preparing before meetings and particular ways of getting a turn in the real-time unfolding of meetings, both kinds of work related to the CA notion of projection (see Chapter 2, p. 30). In this final section of the current chapter, I report on ways that my interviewees consciously reflected on and strategized about projection and participation.

Projecting meeting agendas

Projecting ahead begins before the actual meeting, especially when a meeting agenda is circulated well in advance. Almost all the women I interviewed emphasized the value of not only having an agenda for a meeting, but also having that agenda well ahead of time:

> It's about knowing what the agenda is in advance, knowing what the goal of the group is.

A shared agenda allows participants to plan for points they may want to make and to evaluate their commitment to specific outcomes, whether they are very attached to achieving particular ends, or whether they are willing to let things go. When an agenda listed issues of particular consequence to them, some women employed pre-meeting strategies to insure that their concerns would receive adequate attention. A pre-circulated agenda also allowed for preparatory interactions. Some women had specific ways of preparing in advance of meetings, these included networking among their co-workers before an important meeting:

> *Sometimes if I know a meeting is coming up, I send out a preparatory email. Say there's going to be a sensitive issue and I know there's going to be a lot of talking, I'll email, "I know this meeting is coming up and I just want to set a little background." It usually works pretty well because people usually talk about it in the meeting. I got what I needed out there.*

Several women stressed the value they placed on meetings actually following a pre-set agenda. Here are two illustrative excerpts:

> *[An effective meeting] is one where we had an agenda and all the bullet points were addressed or we said who was going to do the follow up and by when.*

> *When I chair a meeting I'm pretty hard core about what's going to get accomplished, because time is precious.*

Getting in: projecting within the flow of interaction

While meeting agendas project action at a broad level and in advance of an actual meeting, interviewees were also conscious of the local work required within the contingent and shifting flow of a meeting. In addition to preparing for a meeting beforehand, then, some women (for example, Lonnie and Florence, but not Pam, Stephie, or Lynn) reported difficulty initiating turns in the rough and tumble of ongoing meetings. As they told me about their strategies for getting the floor, they also noted that those very strategies were less than effective. At one end was concern that they would accidentally interrupt; at the other end was the possibility of missing an opportunity to speak up. Here are two reflections on projecting in real time:

> *I have to kind of prepare myself [. . .] like find my opening. And if I feel like my topic is slipping, then I sometimes just let it go.*

> *What I do is I look for pauses. Sometimes I'm not very skillful at it and sometimes I find that I may interrupt somebody. I don't mean to, but there aren't often a lot of pauses.*

Looking for openings and waiting for pauses were considered problematic strategies, ones that do not work very well. This is interesting in relation to the fact that none of the meetings I taped followed formal rules of order. In light of this, CA findings on turn projection and turn transition in casual conversation are particularly relevant. They help to explain why waiting for pauses would not be the most successful practice for getting the floor.

Recall that in the classic model of turn-taking (Sacks *et al.*, 1974), smooth turn transition results from fine-tuned monitoring of turn trajectories. This monitoring allows participants to project upcoming points of possible completion before the actual completion is reached. As discussed in Chapter 2, close monitoring of projectable completion points supports split-second timing in the launching of next turns, and it also provides for meanings to be made through pauses and overlaps. In multiparty interactions, such as the meetings I collected, it becomes even more of a challenge speak up, since two or more persons may begin their turns after the same projectable point of possible completion in a current speaker's talk. Under such circumstances, consciously waiting for a pause before one launches a turn could be problematic indeed. If one waits for pause, this strategy will regularly result in either overlap or the opportunity "slipping" away.

Summary and looking ahead

This chapter has presented selections from my interviews with participants in the videotaped meetings, including their reported strategies for getting turns in meetings. The interviews provided me with a sampling of women's experiences, of their articulation of challenges, and of their ideologies of meeting interaction. One theme which emerged was that the women's experiences were varied rather than uniform, with each woman reporting identities and influences beyond gender. The interviews reveal that gender is one among a number of intersecting influences on each woman's evaluation of her participation and her experiences in what they identify as a male-dominated institution. Each woman experienced herself as different or other in some sense, but difference took a variety of forms. They pointed to aspects of their identity such as race, gender, sexuality, personality, and they also cited what they understood as their essential speaking styles.

The interviews also provide a sense of these women's conscious strategies for participation, including communicating ahead of a meeting and working to place their participation in the contingent flow of meetings in progress. Though participants' intended contributions may be planned well before a meeting begins, some women struggle, moment by moment, to calibrate their real-time participation in the unfolding, collaborative, and contingent structure of the real-time meetings. Others work to refrain from taking the floor in order to be more effective when they do speak up. A commonality is that all the women valued having allies among their co-workers in meetings.

This chapter has offered a glimpse of these women's perceptions, experiences, concerns, and conscious strategies with respect to participation in meetings. We now move to a technical analysis of recurrent practices through which women in the collection of videotaped meetings gained and constructed turns. Chapter 4 begins with a look at how the move to official meeting organization is orchestrated, and it then concentrates on contexts and practices for gaining speakership, practices for turn initiation, and a consideration of the enactment of connections and alliances between participants.

4
Meeting Organization: Openings, Turn Transitions, and Participant Alliances

This first of three core analytic chapters considers practices of getting and using turns in the meeting collection. These are practices through which women come to speak, but, as I have emphasized, they are not exclusively women's practices. Indeed, in a section on epistemic downgrades at turn beginnings, I offer a case of a man doing a similar practice; I insert this case because hedging action may call up stereotypes of women's language, and in my data this practice is not exclusive to women. In focusing on women's pathways to speaking, the illustrative examples serve not only to contribute general findings regarding turn-taking in meetings, they also stand as evidence of women's control of such practices.

This chapter provides an overview of meeting order as a "local, *in situ* production" (Cuff & Sharrock, 1987) including how meetings are opened, how turns are allocated within meetings, and the significance of turn beginnings. The first point of analysis is the collaborative achievement of meeting opening. We move then to contexts and practices for turn transfer, with attention to both vocal and non-vocal actions. A section on turn beginnings examines the special work of such junctures for projecting actions to come, both within and across turns. The chapter ends with an exploration of cases where women are parties to connections and alliances with other participants; the value of cultivating alliances was stressed by interviewees in response to the prompt, "What advice do you have for people who want to be effective in meetings?"

Achieving a shift to meeting order

Meeting interaction begins, naturally, with meeting openings. These shifts in the structuring of participation establish a single person as leader or chair, with others moving in and out of speaking turns, some short and some quite expanded. How is the shift to official meeting order accomplished? In these meetings, people arrived with expectations about who would lead the meeting and what specific roles others might take, in light of the norms for the group and the particular day's agenda. However, having knowledge of regular roles and responsibilities did not create real-time meeting structure.

At each taping, I had already set up my camera before people entered the room. Very brief mention was sometimes made of the presence of the camera and of me, but for the most part, as people entered, they exchanged greetings and began conversations. As more participants arrived, separate exchanges emerged (Egbert, 1997), with the prospective meeting leaders also involving themselves in informal conversation. While the leaders were not necessarily acting *as* leaders in those initial moments, it was common that they were approached by individuals with specific requests or inquiries regarding a meeting's agenda.

One non-vocal action engaged in by leaders and others was to look toward the door and the clock. Leaders often combined such glances with other moves toward consolidating attention (see Atkinson & Drew, 1979; Boden, 1994). The moves toward a shift to meeting order were normally initiated by a single person, one who thereby began to propose and enact a leadership role. Arrival at meeting order was evident when the participants were divided into interactional roles, with one person as leader and other participants forming a party addressed by the leader. This served as a default frame of reference for turn allocation and turn transition.

Drawing from Erving Goffman, Dierdre Boden described components of meeting openings as "bracketing out" and "bracketing in" to construct "the local meeting membership . . . the interaction order and the organizational tasks at hand" (1994:90). Movement to meeting order in the present data involved a number of components and actions similar to those initially sketched by Boden (1994:90–9). For example, leaders in the present data regularly used discourse markers such as *okay* and *alright*, produced in markedly louder volume than their previous talk. In this way, they drew attention to themselves and began to close down non-meeting talk and initiate moves toward meeting order. While leaders regularly used explicit directives to open meetings, any turn by a potential leader that treated the rest of the group as a single party could serve to initiate the shift to meeting order. Meeting initiating actions consisted of recognizable preparatory issues.[1] Thus, regular vehicles for shifting into meeting order included questions about background readings, shared handouts or other materials; meeting preparatory issues might also concern the number of people in attendance and those missing. Examples (1) through (4) illustrate the openings of meetings.

In line with my interest in demonstrating women's competence, I use cases involving women as leaders.

In (1), Amanda, the committee chair, explicitly initiates the meeting through her directive at line 10, "Let's go ahead and get started"; however, we can see that her earlier action at line 1 has already initiated movement to open the meeting. In fact, the shift in the organization of participation is achieved across several turns, coming before and after her explicit directive:

(1) [Planning] Moving to meeting order

```
1  Amanda: I wish we did have more people, for the conversation about
2       the (    ).
3  ?:     [oh yeah.
4  Amanda: [Our brainstorming output.
5       (.)
6  Frank: Yeah.
7       (.)
8  Amanda: Power rests in too few hands. Otherw(h)ise. huh huh=
9  ?:     =uhm
10 Amanda: But let's go ahead and get started, [ and talk through some=
11 Frank:                                       [mm hm
12 Amanda: =of the things topic, maybe we'll- some uh (    ) will
13      arrive.
14      (0.3)
15 Amanda: Was the agenda (0.4) uh went out on (0.7) email. Do people
16      have copies of it?
```

By sharing her concerns about attendance (lines 1–8), Amanda proposes an understanding of the people already present as constituting the meeting's attendance for the day. When she checks to see if everyone has a copy of the agenda (lines 15–16), she guides them to jointly attend to the official tasks at hand. Thus, she uses a combination of interactional practices for calling a meeting to order.

At the beginning of example (2), Gwen, the co-chair of her committee, is interacting with Clive, while Stephie is chatting with Vivian. The two columns at the start of the example (lines 2–9) represent the separate exchanges; only parts of each are audible enough to be transcribed. Other groups are in similar small configurations of interaction. Thus, although the members of this meeting arrive with the knowledge that Gwen will be the leader, the shift to an official meeting participation structure requires local and collaborative work.

Gwen uses *alright* two times (lines 7 and 10). In the first instance, it proposes a close to the sequence she's engaged in with Clive, and, at line 10, her *alright* serves in a manner akin to what Boden calls a "standard topic transition marker." In Boden's data, as in mine, such markers can function to preface "an assessment of attendance and/or a proposal to 'get started'" (96). Gwen's *alright* at line 10 is not produced as a separate unit but as continuous with what follows: her estimation of whether there is a quorum. She produces this assessment of attendance with rising intonation, but she does not pause to allow for spoken response. Instead she moves immediately into her declaratively formatted but rather explicit call to order, "we'd better get going":[2]

(2) [Diversity] Multiple practices to move to meeting order

Gwen & Clive ⇐	⇒ Stephie & Vivian
1 Gwen: We appreciate it a lot.	
	2 Steph: I am not- We're not- um
3 Clive: Well we're honored.	
	4 Steph: I somehow value it more than
5 Gwen: uh huh huh	5 drug companies.
6 Gwen: You don't have to say that.	

7⇒Gwen: **Alri̠:ght.**
8   Steph: Maybe (   ) isn't as
9   fascinating as [(   )
10⇒Gwen: [>**Alright**< well
11   **I thi̠nk we have a quorum? so we better [get going,**
12 Steph: [(   ) eh heh heh
13⇒Gwen: [**U:m, (.) there are agendas for the meeting here, (.) if people**=
14 Steph: [(   )
15 Gwen: =**didn't get them maybe (.) pass them around they're right there at the**
16   **end of the table? If anybody needs an agenda, =and then I also have um**
17 Dan: No that's- that's Flo's copy. *((addressing Ellie))*
18 Ellie: Does anybody need an agenda?
19 Gwen: **Does any- anybody need an agenda.**
20   (.)
21 **Gwen: And also I have extra copies of the minutes from last time (.)**
22   **if anybody needs them,**
23   (0.7)

24 Gwen: U:m.
25 Dan: Parking (   )
26 Gwen: PARKING. YES.

As in cases of moves to order in other meetings, Gwen's explicit move in lines 10–11 does not constitute a stark or absolute opening boundary for the meeting. Other talk overlaps with her meeting initiating moves. On the transcript, we can see Stephie's talk overlapping with Gwen's at 12 and 14, and on the video, it is clear that Stephie's gaze and torso are turned toward Vivian, her primary interactant. Within several seconds, however, all the other groupings cease to be audible or visible, and Gwen, in collaboration with others, is constructed as leader of the meeting.

While Gwen's turn at lines 10–11 is interpretable as addressing the whole group (note, for example, the use of *we* and *let's*), she has been gazing down at the papers in front of her. The fact that Gwen is not looking up may allow for the smaller interactional clusters to continue a bit longer. At the end of line 11, Gwen gazes up and scans the group. This leads to a quieting of other voices, along with visible adjustments in the facing directions of participants, as they shift to positions displaying shared attention toward Gwen. In what follows, both Dan and Ellie are collaborating in the meeting preparatory actions Gwen has initiated: their turns address issues of getting materials circulated and committee members' parking passes officially endorsed. Example (2), then, is another instance of multiple practices achieving the shift to meeting order, resulting in the constitution of the group as organized around shared activity.

Another resource for initiating meeting order involves introductions of new committee members or visitors. Again, with such actions, a leader treats the meeting participants as a single party, a group addressee. By enacting a division of participants into a leader-plus-others formation, introductions, like questions about shared materials, serve as identifiable moves toward meeting structure. In example (3), Jan, a microbiology laboratory director, uses introductions as a component action for shifting to meeting order:

(3) [Microbio] New participant introduction as a vehicle for move to meeting order

1 Jan: *((looks to Don, a lab member who is joking around as the group waits for*
2   *the meeting to begin))* You're in a funny mood today, aren't you.

3   Don: WHAT:?

4   (0.8)

5   Don: I didn't say anyth-

6⇒Jan: *((moving her gaze away from Don and toward the center of the meeting table))*

7⇒   **S::o has everybody met Wineth?**

At line 2, Jan is addressing one individual, and at 6, she returns her gaze toward the center of the group, prefaces her turn with *so,* and introduces a visitor.

While all the meetings involved a shift to official meeting order, in the meeting of the non-profit board the shift was delayed because, unexpectedly, neither of the co-chairs was in attendance. After about ten minutes of waiting, one of the members, Fred, addressed a question to the group, "So who's running this meeting anyway." Jaimie then volunteers to call one of the missing co-chairs. She leaves the room to make the call, and she returns with notes on the agenda in hand. Through her actions, Jaimie begins to take the role of leader:

(4a) [Board] A problem with opening the meeting

1   (3.4)

2⇒ Fred: **So who's running this meeting any[way.**

3   Jaimie: [Well I was gonna say=

4   Paula: [eh heh

5   Jaimie: **=if someone has- Laura's- number, I will, if you have the board**

6   **directory, I'll give her a quick call.**

7   Jim: [Ahh

8   Jaimie:['Cause I talked to Monty yesterday. And said I'll see you tomorrow

9   at the meeting, and (0.8) he said ↑Oh: yeah.

10 Jim: Uh it is uh: doo doo doo doo >three two five< zero six nine five.=Wait

11   that's- that's his too. Wait no ₒthat's the one I use.ₒ

12   (1.5)

13 Lyn: **'Cause I didn't even get the agenda.**

14 Fred: Well we had a meeting to set one up.

15 Lyn: Yeah.(.)

16 Fred: and Laura

17 Lyn: has it. eh huh

18 Jaimie: **Yeah. She'll have it, but- if she isn't coming, maybe I can get it**

19   **via the phone.** *((Jaimie raises phone to ear & steps out into the hallway))*

20   (3.0)

The others continue with casual rather than task-oriented interaction(s) characteristic of pre-meetings. After two minutes, Jaimie returns to the room:

(4b) Jaimie is co-constructed as leader

1 Jamie: *((still in hallway but now audible in the meeting room))* Okay. Take care.
2 Lyn: <u>Nice</u> pen, though. ⇐CONTINUING A SEQUENCE OF CASUAL TALK
3   (1.0)
4 Fred: She wants it back.
5 Lyn: eh heh heh heh
6 Jaimie: *((moving into the room and toward her seat))* (   ) **for the meeting**.
7 Lyn: What's that?
8 Jaimie: .hhh She [=LAURA] (.) got. (.) caught up um with some stuff with her
9   daughter, and just- thought the meeting was next week.
10   (.)
11 Paula: ehhh and she j(h)ust got back from Chicago?
12⇒Jamie: **SO::, I have the agenda.[and the question is-**
13 Jim: [It's on the back (   )
14 Jaimie: **[whether we have a quorum until Mel gets here.**
15 Jim: [And (   )
16 Jaimie: **I think when Mel gets here we'll have a quorum.**
17 Jim: You know I said they do get [(   )
18 Lil: [How many-=
19⇒Jamie: **=Seven. Seven's a quorum. Then let's start.**

When Jaimie returns reporting she has the agenda (line 12) and then addresses the question of a quorum (lines 12–19), she performs meeting opening actions typically done by leaders. At line 19, she adds the directive, "let's start." As in other meetings, then, movement to meeting order involves multiple practices, though in this instance, leadership is at first treated as a problem.

That a group is engaged in official meeting order does not mean attention is uniformly focused on a single task. However, even when side conversations occur, the meeting order is still treated as relevant. When participants have exchanges apart from the shared group focus, they employ practices that contextualize that talk as subsidiary; that is, participants enact these exchanges as spatially, temporally, and socially bracketed. They move into closer proximity (e.g., leaning a head closer to the head of another), and they speak more quietly. These modulations enact a display of recognition of and deference to the primary attention of the group. Thus, while potentially disruptive, side exchanges still reinforce the operation of official talk and the default norm of joint attention.

We have seen how movement to official meeting order is orchestrated through identifiable practices. Through these practices, participation is shifted from casual and simultaneous talk in small formations to joint attention on shared activities. The shift also achieves the transformation of participant roles into leader and others, with the leader now serving, in principle and—for the most part—in practice, as the moderator of speakership.

Speaker selection and turn transitions

In analyzing turns initiated by women, I attended to broad domains of function within and across meetings—in particular, the projection of possible turn completion, the selection of speakers, and the organization of turn transitions. A fundamental way to understand the variety of practices through which women come to speak is by noting the various sorts of sequential contexts constructed as meetings develop. As in interaction more generally, particular moments within the social organization of meetings provide diverse and fleeting opportunities for speaking up. Also in line with what we know from fundamental CA work on turn-taking and the contingent nature of collaboratively constructed activities, practices for turn allocation and turn transition vary with shifting activities and the specific sequential opportunities for participation that activities and their subparts afford.

Choices of when to take a turn, of how to speak, and of how to orient one's body (while speaking or listening) display understandings of relevant configurations of participants and of the unfolding activity itself. Momentary choices to be more visible or audible are further constitutive of the activity at hand, and they may also propose and enact changing positions and relationships within a group. How one speaks demonstrates one's understanding of the talk so far, and it projects specific kinds of actions as relevant next.[3] Speech, gaze, gesture, and body orientation all contribute to this process of coordinating actions, as participants respond to one another and continuously co-create a shared activity.

Let us first examine practices of turn allocation, including non-verbal practices for displaying heightened interest and readiness to speak; we will then examine the special work of turn beginnings. After meeting order is established, the leader guides transitions between the items on the agenda. Other participants look toward the leader, literally and figuratively, as the primary arbiter of turns. Participants may be called on by the leader or another participant. They may make vocal or non-vocal bids for the floor. And it is also possible for participants to speak up without first requesting a turn, vocally or non-vocally. Thus, though meeting leaders regularly select other speakers, unilaterally or in response to bids, leaders are not uniformly in control of turn allocation.

Unilateral selection of next speakers by meeting leaders

Speaker selection, particularly at the beginnings of meetings or of new agenda items, is often done by the leader unilaterally, that is, with no previous bid from the designated next speaker. In examples (5) and (6), meeting leaders engage in unilateral next-speaker selection. In (5) and (6), the leaders not only allocate turns to other speakers, but they also project specific kinds of action for those turns. In (5) Amanda asks Bea to give a background report, and in (6), Jan asks Florence to introduce a new committee member:

(5) [Planning] Leader selects participant to report

Amanda: **Bea, do you want to give us some background, on**
        that [course,
Bea: [U:m:: This is ah:: request we received from S-A-S.

(6) [Diversity] Leader selects participant to do introduction

Jan: Uhm, So I guess our first introduction is Lynn: =**Florence would you like**
      to, do the honors?
Flor: Sure, (.) This is Lynn Rhine. (.) Lynn is a dissertator in the history of
      technology. Uhm, she will be working as our P.A.,* next year,

                                 *P.A. = project assistant

This specification of next-speaker action may project longer turns, turns made up of multiple grammatical and prosodic points of possible completion (Houtkoop & Mazeland, 1985; Schegloff, 1996; Selting, 2000 among others).

Displaying interest in speaking: making bids

When participants other than the leader or current speaker initiate bids for turns, it is often the case that their readiness to speak is initially displayed through non-vocal actions; this regularly involves hand raising, but non-vocal displays of incipient speakership go beyond hand raising.

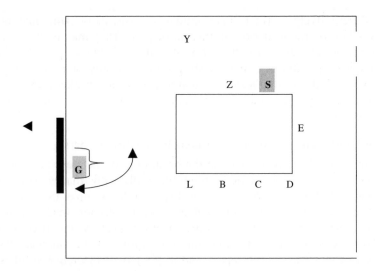

Figure 4.1 Gareth's gaze relative to seated participants

Figure 4.2 Gareth's position relative to Sally

In (7), Gareth, standing at the front of the group, has been shifting his position between facing the group and facing a blackboard. This results in his turning his back to the group on repeated occasions. At the start of the extract, he has shifted toward his right while using hand gestures to guide attention toward features of a diagram. For most of his long turn, Gareth has been moving his gaze only far enough back toward the group to include participants to his right as he faces the group (LBCD & E).

When Gareth is facing the group, Sally, the head of accounting for the group, is seated to his left and across the table. In this location she has not been central to Gareth's field of vision during much of his talk in the segment leading up to example (7). At line 4, Gareth comes to a point of possible completion and begins to scan the group more widely, now including Sally in his gaze. After a short pause, he adds a turn-constructional unit to ask whether his long turn has made "sense" (line 7).

(7) [Plant] Bidding for a turn with a hand raise

```
1  Gare: But ultimately keep in mind your involvement in this, and how would
2        you like to use the system, (0.4) What would you like to- (.) to:- What
3        would you like to s̲e̲e̲, with the thought that we're gonna try to make it
4        as e̲a̲:s̲y̲ for you to use as we can.
5            (0.3)
```

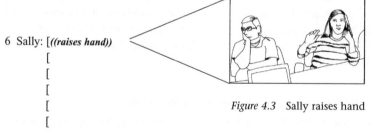

```
6  Sally: [((raises hand))
         [
         [
         [
         [
```

Figure 4.3 Sally raises hand

```
7  Gare: [ >That make sense?< Yes. >Questions.<
8  Sall: The- the one key I don't see here is o̲n̲b̲a̲s̲e̲.*
```

                                *Onbase = database software

The pause at line 5, Gareth's gaze toward the whole group, and his question all converge to treat his previous span of talk as possibly complete and to make it relevant for another person to speak. Just as Gareth begins the question, "That make sense?" (line 7), Sally raises her hand (line 6). When Gareth produces, "Yes. >Questions.<" (also, line 7) he is specifically responding to Sally's non-vocal bid, which emerged as he produced the first unit of his turn. Sally then takes a turn and presents a problem she has with the model Gareth has introduced: a database program (Onbase) is missing. The coordination of gaze, gesture, and speaker selection between Gareth and Sally in (7) is typical of speaker selection practices in the meeting collection: as a speaker comes to a point of possible completion, another participant makes a bid for a turn.

Bids may be wholly non-vocal; they may be prefaced by an audible in-breath; and they may also be accompanied by use of the leader's (or current primary speaker's) name. Similar to Sally in example (7), Jill, in (8), is among a group of recipients of a report by Ned, and the meeting is interactionally structured around Ned's long and continuing hold on the floor. In such a context, waiting for an "opening" might work—more specifically, waiting for a recognizable topic transition, marked by tokens such as "Okay," by pauses, and by the presenter's orientation to materials for the presentation (here, the laptop and screen). In this kind of activity, there is less pressure for quick next turn beginning, as one person holds the floor and is projecting more to come in a long, multiunit turn.

Ned is acting as leader and presenter in this meeting of a medical specialty group. He has been looking toward his laptop as he manages slides for his long and continuing presentation. Jill's bid to speak is responsive to indications that Ned has reached a point of possible topic transition in his report. After producing a summary in lines 1–2 ("and so . . ."), he has allowed a pause to develop. At line 6 he produces a closing relevant *okay*, and at line 7, along with his quieter production of *okay*, he moves his gaze up toward the group. In coordination with Ned's vocal and non-vocal actions, Jill raises her hand, and Ned selects Jill with his second and louder *okay*.[4]

(8) [Medical] Bidding for a turn with a hand raise

1 Ned: And so if you've g<u>o</u>t somebody, who's >just< d<u>e</u>vastated by osteoporosis,
2   and those people ↑exist, (.) I think >that< th<u>is</u> is s<u>o</u>mething to consider.
3   (0.8)
4 Ned: ((sniff))
5   (2.3)
6 Ned: °okay° ((Ned turns toward screen while touching laptop keyboard))
7   ((Jill moves her hand first out (1) then up (2), following Ned's head movement as he
        turns to face the group))
8 Ned: Okay. ((Ned reverses direction of head movement, displaying responsiveness to Jill))
9   ((Ned gestures toward Jill, places hands in lap and leans back in his chair))
10⇒ Jill: Ned, uhm what- what's the- percent of alendronate users, (0.4)

(1) hand out   **(2) hand up and open**

Figure 4.4   Jill pursues and gains Ned's attention with a sweeping hand raise

11   have you seen that ar- you would call sort of <u>fail</u>ures.
12   (0.4)
13 Jill: Bone marrow d<u>e</u>nsity failu°res.°

Just after Ned's first *okay* and just as he begins to look up, Jill initiates her gestural bid for a turn (line 7). With his next *okay* (line 8) and his simultaneous gaze toward Jill at line 9, Ned responds to Jill's bid to speak.

In response to a participant's bid for a turn, the current speaker, here most commonly the leader, may nod and/or gesture toward the bidder. The leader's calling upon a bidder may also involve a verbal token such as *yes* or *okay*. In (8), Ned uses both gesture and an *okay* to respond to Jill's hand raise. In example (9), Cindy raises her hand, and Jan gazes toward Cindy and uses her name:[5]

(9) [Diversity] Gaze and name to call upon bidder

1   (1.2) *((Cindy raises hand))*
2 Jan: [°Cindy°
       [*((J leans forward to gaze toward C))*
3 Cind: Um, I think (0.6) the question I was going to have is related to
4   Stephie's, so this is so Stephie's question has partly may answer
5   this but um (1.2) I'm wondering about [. . .]

In the examples so far, turn transfer is coordinated through leaders, either unilaterally (as in 5 and 6), or as a response to a participant's bid to speak (as in 7–9). By turning (literally and figuratively) toward the leader to coordinate their entry into a turn, participants renew the interactional structure of the meeting: that is, along with myriad other orientations by participants, by addressing their bids to speak to the leader, they participate in co-constructing the meeting order. Likewise, of course, the leader renews her or his role on a moment-to-moment basis by selecting speakers, whether unilaterally or responsively.

In these meetings, speaker selection is also done by non-leaders, particularly when a participant has been in the local role of primary speaker; that is, when a non-leader is producing an extended turn. We have already seen two earlier cases where a leader invites another participant to take what may be an extended turn: a report of background by Bea in (5), above, and an introduction by Flor in (6), above. Speakers of extended turns may thus act as temporary coordinators of speakership. In such cases, in addition to orienting to the leader in bids for the floor, participants may also coordinate their turn initiations with the current primary speaker.

In example (10), John has been producing an extended turn, but Jan is chairing the meeting. From the beginning of John's talk, Mary has held up her hand in a bid to speak. Though Mary's raised hand has likely already been available in John's visual field during the duration of his turn, it is not until line 11 that John's facing direction clearly reaches Mary. At line 13, John, rather than Jan (the meeting chair), selects Mary to speak. He points toward Mary and simultaneously apologizes, presumably for having held the floor while another wanted to speak:[6]

(10) [Diversity] John, rather than Jan (the chair) responds to bid for speakership

1 John: And also being a former recruiter, I found that, your chances of
2   hiring somebody,
3 ?: m hm.
4   (0.4)
5 John: are m:uch better, if you establish, (0.5)a interactional
6   relationshi[p.
7 Steph: [Right,
8 John: early o:n, and meet with 'em, year in, year out,
9 ?: mhm
10   (.)
11 John: couple of times a yea:r, *((gazes toward Mary, whose hand is raised))*
12   (0.4)
13⇒ John: °**Sorry.** ° *((quick pointing gesture toward Mary))*

14 Mary: >Oh no no no(if I)< eh- (.) and this may be sta̲ting- (.)stating
15   the o̲bvious, bu:t uh the two ye̲ars would (.)ena̲ble you >not only
16   >>then<< to set up< a la̲:b, but to find (.) possible dual- dual
17   career positions:.

Just prior to example (11), below, Amanda, the meeting chair, has
asked Bea for a report. (see [5] above); and what follows, in (11),
provides another illustration of turn transition coordinated without
orientation to the chair. In reporting on the background for the
proposal under consideration, Bea produces an extended turn (lines
1–8), acting as primary speaker. In lines 7–8, she suggests that the meeting members look over the proposal, implicitly opening the floor,
though not necessarily returning control to Amanda. At that point,
most meeting members are flipping through the pages of the proposal,
but during the pause at line 9, Gloria looks up and proceeds to ask
a question. By responding, Bea treats this question as directed toward
her:

(11) [Planning] Non-chair selecting next speaker

1 Bea:[U:m:: This is a request we received from S-A-S. for a service learning
2   course. (.) Ummm, at the present time there's something in here, uh,
3   where he talks about L and S students cannot get credit for this course,
4   although they can arrange to sign up, like he says-for some sort of-
5   independent study with- someone in their own department or something,
6   it's um, (0.7) uhhh, (1.3) It's a service learning course that they would
7   uh- background information and some of it's here, so we can just take a look
8   at it.
9   (1.2)
10⇒Glor: **So this course currently exists, but it's a- [it's a null course.**
11 Bea: [It's a null course.

Example (11) is intended as an illustration of how it is possible for a
turn transition to take place without the chair's direct involvement.
In the environment of a non-leader producing an extended turn, a
request for clarification is directed to the current speaker rather than
negotiated through the leader. The example also illustrates two other
potential features of turn transition and construction. Both Gloria
(line 10) and Bea (line 11) speak up without first making a bid, and
Bea produces her turn clause in overlap with Gloria's continued talk, as
a collaborative completion (Lerner, 1991). We touch on these practices
in the next section.

Speaking up without explicit negotiation

While it is regularly the case that women in these meetings make explicit bids to speak, they also regularly initiate contributions without such negotiation. In addition to offering a case of next-speaker coordination through a primary speaker other than the meeting leader, example (11) illustrates two different participants initiating talk without explicit bids or negotiation; Gloria and Bea just start up. Speaking up without negotiation can involve independent actions, as in the case of Gloria's declaratively formatted question at line 10; or it may involve collaborative completion or an extension of the current or previous speakers turn structure, akin to what Bea does at line 11.

In example (11), Bea's choral completion of Gloria's turn is neatly fitted to the local sequential context. Bea's position as next speaker is conditioned by at least two factors of the developing interaction: Bea is the recipient of a question, and she is also acting as the primary speaker in the local interaction. At line 10, Gloria delivers what Labov and Fanshel (1977) term a B-event statement (also see Heritage & Roth, 1995). Gloria's turn does questioning by producing a *so*-prefaced declarative whose content is in the domain of knowledge that Bea controls. Gloria first formulates a complete clause, and she then begins another with the contrastive connector *but*. However, she briefly cuts off her turn production part way through the next clause, just as she produces the indefinite article *a*. Both Bea and Gloria chorally recycle "It's a" and complete it with "null course" (Lerner, 2002). While Gloria's production of the clause serves to complete her questioning action, Bea's production of the same clause functions as a response to Gloria's question. Bea has interpreted Gloria's hesitation and the questioning potential of the turn so far as enough to prompt an answer. By initiating her talk before a point of completion in Gloria's turn and by positioning her turn beginning precisely as Gloria restarts her clause, Bea is able to display both her understanding of Gloria's turn as a question and, at the same time, provide an answer to that question.

Even in contexts where there is no clearly interactional conditioning that might make their talk specifically relevant, it is regularly the case that participants begin to talk without first producing visible or audible bids to speak. One way this is done is by producing an extension of a previous speaker's turn. We see such a case in example (12). Ned has been responding to a question and comment from Jill. At line 5, Beth, who is also an expert on the osteoporosis medication under discussion, begins her turn with *and*, introducing her action as an addition to what Ned has been saying:

(12) [Medical] Beth extends Ned's response to Jill

1 Ned: and if you have a good calcium inta:ke, (.) you can be pretty sure that
2   bisphosphonate therapy's gonna work.
3 Jill: °mmhm.°
4   (0.6)
5⇒Beth: and that's true among our older:- patients too:,that it's rare that
6   I'll see a true decrease, as interpreted by the Ned on the Dexa*, .hh if
7   somebody is no:t-(.)>you know< still pretty darn immobile. and smoking
8   like a chimney.

*Dexa = bone density measurement device

In adding to Ned's turn, Beth positions herself as a co-expert with Ned in responding to Jill's question.

Example (13) offers a further case, in addition to Gloria's turn (example [11]), in which a woman speaks up without negotiation. In this case, as with Gloria's turn initiation, the turn is a fully separate action, not a coordinated completion or an extension of previous talk. In (13), Amy is coming to the close of a practice run-through of a presentation. She ends by showing a slide crediting co-present members of her team for helping with the material she has reported. Brian, the leader of the laboratory group, responds to Amy's final slide and her turn at line 1 with an expression of surprise and appreciation, "Oh look we're all there" (line 3). At this juncture, Amy has not projected any further talk by herself nor has she explicitly invited comments or questions. Carol is one among seven participants who could open the postpresentation questioning and commenting activity:

(13) [Zool 2] Carol speaks up without negotiation, producing a new action

1 Amy: Anyway so I [thank you all of you guys for (.) all of your help.
2 ?:   [(We keep all that)
3 Brian: Oh look we're all there.
4 Eva: eh heh
5⇒Carol: **Back it up a couple of slides.**

As we will discuss later, another participant, Eva, raises her hand before Carol begins her turn. Carol does not raise her hand but rather starts up without a preceding bid for a speakership, and Amy responds by following Carol's directive to back up her slides. An exchange between Carol, Amy, and Brian ensues.

Examples (11) through (13) illustrate ways that next speakers start up directly without any negotiation: one may collaborate in the completion of a previous turn and overlap with its production; one may also add to another's talk; or one may simply start a new turn without extending the previous turn structure.

Non-vocal coordination

One striking feature of turn transitions in these task-centered multi-party interactions was the fine-tuned, non-vocal work of incipient speakers as they indicated interests in taking the floor. At the point where a participant begins a vocal contribution, she may have already engaged in considerable non-vocal coordination, which is interpretable as displaying heightened interest and/or a readiness to make a vocal contribution. Schegloff (1996) and Linton and Lerner (2004) have used the term "pre-beginnings" for certain actions which project the possibility that a non-speaking participant is moving toward vocal turn initiation, and Streeck and Hartge (1992) have documented gestures coordinated with transition places. In the present meeting data, recipients coordinate bodies and gaze behaviors with precise points in current speakers' turns, though not exclusively at places of possible transition. Through these temporally specific displays, a recipient can indicate not only her readiness to speak but also the specific content of a currently unfolding turn to which her projected talk will be responsive.

Let's look at one segment in which a participant coordinates non-vocal actions with the ongoing turn of a primary speaker, and through this coordination offers pre-turn projection of her interest in speaking and of the specific content to which she will respond. In (14), Gwen is seated on the same side of the table as Ned, and for that reason she is not in his field of vision. Ned has been discussing methods for evaluating the effects of a certain treatment for osteoporosis. In response to Ned's description of one method of testing bone density, Gwen moves her head and upper body forward and gazes toward him. In this way, she makes herself visible to Ned and in a manner tightly coordinated with Ned's developing talk. Thus, before she launches her vocal action, and simultaneous with specific points in Ned's ongoing talk, Gwen makes herself visibly responsive. By the time she speaks, at line 11, Gwen has already displayed heightened interest in specific parts of Ned's previous talk:

(14) [Medical] Fine-tuned non-vocal actions that indicate heightened interest and readiness to speak

```
1  Ned: You can measure the right hand, you can measure the right arm, you can
2        measure the head, or you decapitate* [folks. (0.7) And that's what=
3  Gwen:                                      [((moves head forward, gazes toward Ned))
4  Ned: =they did. So they did densitometric decapitation in this and
5        and in the female study. (0.7) I find that kind of worrisome,
6        in that the [cranium is a big reservoir of cortical bone,=
7  Gwen:            [((moves head forward, gazes toward Ned))
8  Ned: =and there's still this issue that we'll come to about, are we robbing
9        Peter to pay Paul,=are we taking cortical bone to put it into the
10       tribecular component, and it (.)just smells bad.
11⇒ Gwen: [Does it ↑scientifically make ↑sense to decapitate?
12  Gwen: [((moves right hand up and out as she starts speaking))
```

> *Decapitation = a method that excludes the head from post-mortem bone density measurement.

Gwen's non-vocal actions are simultaneous with Ned's talk, but she does not begin her spoken turn until a predictable location relative to Ned's turn design, at a point of grammatical and prosodic completion. With non-vocal moves, Gwen has displayed heightened attentiveness at lines 3 and 7. Her first forward-head motion and gaze toward Ned (line 3) is placed precisely after he completes the word "decapitate," and her second movement is placed right after Ned negatively assesses the use of decapitation by stating, "I find that kind of worrisome,".

By the time Gwen leans forward and launches her spoken turn, but before she utters any of what we traditionally consider linguistic material, she has already non-vocally indexed the points in Ned's talk that she will address in her turn. Through her bodily movements, Gwen demonstrates not only *that* she is interested but also *what aspect* of Ned's talk is drawing her attention.

In coordinating non-vocal behavior with specific points in the current speaker's talk, a potential next speaker begins to distinguish herself from the field of recipients. Such displays may involve vertical or horizontal head movements, and they may also involve leaning one's whole trunk forward or in other directions in order to create an unobstructed line of vision between oneself and the current speaker. This is especially useful when one is seated on the same side of a meeting table as the current speaker, with others between you, as was the case with Gwen in (14).

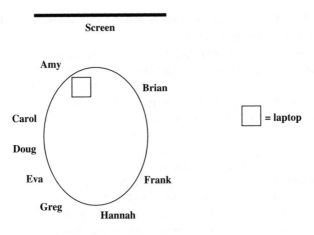

Figure 4.5   Seating of zoology lab participants

With regard to differing practices for coordinating entry to participation, in these meetings, it appears that hand raising *by itself* may not be the most effective practice for gaining immediate access to a turn. To compare hand raising to speaking up directly, let me expand a bit in (13a) on a segment we already looked at in (13), above.

(13a) [Zool 2] Eva's hand raise vs. Carol's speaking up directly

1 Amy: Anyway so I [thank you all of you guys for (.) all of your help.
2 Eva: [*((raises hand))*
3 *((by end of Amy's "help", her gaze includes Eva, whose hand is raised by that time))*
4 Brian: Oh look we're all there. *((Amy gazes back at screen, away from group))*
5 Eva: eh heh
6⇒Carol: Back it up a couple of slides.
7   *((Amy looks at projection screen as she taps her laptop keyboard to move to previous slide))*

Eva raises her hand at line 2, just as Amy is showing her final slide and thanking the group, actions that make completion of her presentation and shift in participation relevant. Although Eva keeps her hand raised even into Carol's turn (at line 6), it is Carol, seated in a position that excludes Eva from her field of vision, who successfully launches a turn. Amy responds to Carol's directive at line 6 by manipulating her slide show (line 7), and Eva lowers her hand to the table. First (vocal) starter, in this case, gets the turn (Sacks *et al.*, 1974).

Figure 4.6   Eva raises hand while Amy, Carol, and others gaze at screen

In (10), above, we saw another case in which getting a turn through hand raising is trumped as another participant speaks up. As noted, Mary had raised her hand almost simultaneously with John's self-selection as speaker. It is only after she has held her hand up throughout John's lengthy turn that Mary gains the floor, with his selection of her through a gesture and an apology.[7]

Cases like (13a) and (10) suggest that hand raising in itself, unaccompanied by other and earlier non-vocal coordination, may be less effective than simply starting up, if getting a turn immediately is the goal.[8] John and Carol both simply started up, leaving Mary and Eva to wait and possibly find that the relevance of their contributions has, as one interviewee put it, "slipped."

Overall, the data show a variety of interrelated and sometimes co-occurring practices for the coordination of turn launches. As in non-institutional interactions, next speakers can be selected by current speakers, though other selections can appear more formal and explicit in these meetings. As a regular alternative, in my data, a participant may make a bid to speak by raising a hand, an action that is probably only done as a joke in ordinary talk. Again, this can open a usually brief sequence involving the bid and the granting of the bid (both may be done non-vocally). In addition to unilateral selection and bidding followed by granting, we also see speakers launching turns without any preceding bids or other action-projecting behaviors. This can take the form of collaborative completions, extensions, and turns opening new sequences of action.

Turn beginnings

The preceding section examined turn transitions, but it also included aspects of turn beginnings. For example, with collaborative completion or extension, the next speaker begins her turn with a structure that clearly continues the previous turn. We also noted earlier in this chapter and in the previous one that the size of a projectable unit in the meeting data ranges from the meeting agenda, through the trajectory of one topic or activity, to the very local grammatical, prosodic, and action trajectories of single turn units. We have seen evidence of close monitoring of turn projection, as participants construct their turns and as others precisely place their turn beginnings at points of possible completion. We now take a closer look at turn beginnings in themselves, since they are prime locations for the projection of what is yet to come.

This section concentrates on ways that initial parts of turns serve as frames for projecting talk that will follow. Given the importance of turn beginnings for displaying connection to previous talk and for projecting what action a speaker is initiating, I highlight some alternative ways of using the salience of initial position in turns.

A turn beginning constitutes a particularly consequential moment for projecting the trajectory of the unfolding turn. Initial position in a turn is a space in which one provides guidance for what will come next, what sort of action one is building, and what sorts of responses may be invited or anticipated (Sacks *et al.*, 1974; Jefferson, 1978; Houtkoop & Mazeland 1985; C. Goodwin, 1996; Ford, 2004).

In the meeting data, it is common for turns to be prefaced with tokens that delay the action of the turn. This is especially true for turns not tied through linguistic structure to previous talk (i.e., not extensions or collaborations), and turns which start up new sequences. In (15), Belinda begins with the token, *um*.

(15) [Microbio] Turn-initial token

Lynn: one housekeeping note, about test tubes? °um°, people are (.)
     kinda forgetting to erase the marker on their test tubes, it means we have to go
     through the whole entire <u>bas</u>ket, so if you could please just take a little
     acetone or ethanol to it, (.) it would save us (.) a <u>ton</u> of time, °thanks.°
     (1.4)

⇒Bel: Um, I wanted to bring up the issue of <u>sto</u>rage, again, so, actually, Mary did
    the: research (0.3) on on this, it tur- turns out storage of important films: in
    (libraries and that kind of thing), an:d (0.6) we have several issues, u:m, one is
    do we use glycerol

This segment is from the beginning of a lab meeting, and both speakers
use the opening moment to make general announcements not officially
on the meeting agenda. Like the non-vocal pre-turn actions already
discussed (e.g., gestures, audible in-breaths), such turn-initial hesitation
tokens may serve to draw a large group's attention to the speaker before
she begins the central action of her turn.

In addition to the use of turn-initial tokens, there are some formats
and actions that appear to be specific to the initial units of turns in
the meetings. A fundamental way of using the first part of a turn is to
project that one will be producing more than a short turn. Projecting
a longer contribution involves using a first turn-constructional unit
to establish one's intention to speak further (Sacks *et al.*, 1974). When
Belinda, in example (15), above, follows her initial token with the
statement, "I wanted to bring up the issue of <u>sto</u>rage," she is projecting further talk, and probably a multiunit turn.

In example (16), Pam uses her first turn-constructional unit—
the complete clause and prosodically bounded unit, "So I've ( ) two
suggestions."—to project that her contribution will have two components. She thus proposes to produce an extended turn, consisting of
multiple points of grammatical and prosodic completion which will not
constitute her ceding the floor. Pam proceeds to introduce the first part
with "one of them is"; and as she completes the first portion, she prefaces the second part with "the <u>oth</u>er thing is." Through these devices,
she guides her recipients through her extended turn, inviting only
limited responses from others until she has finished:

(16) [Diversity] Projecting a two-part turn

    ((Pam raises hand))
    Jan: °Pam,°*((simultaneous with talk, gestures toward Pam))*
⇒Pam: Um, so I've (   ) two suggestions. A- one of them is to really pop that
      point in the introduction, (0.3) telling about ourselves.
    // [Pam makes first point and receives uptake from Gwen and others] //
⇒Pam: The <u>oth</u>er thing is (.) tha- a-addresses what Cindy was was wondering
      about, wh(h)at, what can these people who come to this anticipate will
      come out of it,
    Jan: °um hm°

In (17), Stephie projects an extended turn, launching her turn at a point of possible sequence and topic completion. Her turn initiation is a particularly clear case of the potentially elaborate work one may do to organize the beginning of a turn. She uses an audible in-breath along with a hand raise to gain the attention of the group. With the first clause of her turn, Stephie points back to "tha:t," a reference to the whole previous topic as what she will address, and she also projects a multiunit turn, her "brief comment" (which ultimately extends for several minutes; see Chapter 6).

(17) [Diversity] Projecting an extended turn

Jan: It'll be fun to work ou:t, I think. *((nods as lifts and turns papers over))*

    (0.6)

⇒Steph: [.hh **Can I make a-   (.)brief comment on tha:t, I- uh- uhm:**

        |
        [*((S begins hand raise))*

Like Pam, in (16), Stephie uses her turn initiation to provide guidance for recipients as they orient to her multiunit extended turn.

At a turn's beginning, participants may also do explicit work to pre-frame their projected contribution. Such framing appears to be related to the projection of disaffiliative and delicate actions. For example, in my data I find initial framings occupied with hedges and other epistemic downgrades, as can be seen in these fragments.

(18) [Medical] Pre-framing

  Gwen: **This just caught my eye, and I don't know if this is r̲elevant, but** [---]

(from 10) [Diversity] Pre-framing

  Mary: [---]**this may be st̲ating- (.)st̲ating the o̲bvious, bu:t** uh the two
      ye̲ars would (.)en̲able you >not only >>then<< to set up< a la̲:b, but to
      find (.) possible dual- dual career positions:.

(from 9) [Diversity] Pre-framing

  Cind: Um, **I think (0.6) the question I was going to have is related to
      Stephie's, so this is so Stephie's question has partly may answer this
      but** um (1.2) I'm wondering about [---]

In these hedged beginnings there is usually a cataphoric pronoun, or what Goodwin (1996) has termed a prospective indexical, such as *this* or *it*. The pronoun projects that more is to come and treats the current unit as clearly preliminary to the projected action. The initial pre-framing units in these turns addresses the relevance or the potential redundancy of what one is about to say. In (18) Gwen indicates that what she will say has not involved great thought and planning: it "just caught my eye." In (10), Mary downplays the potential newsworthiness of what she will be saying by suggesting that it may be "stating the obvious." And in (9), Cindy acknowledges that what she will say may no longer be relevant. These hedged beginnings are regularly followed by the contrastive *but* and then the projected action itself.

This pattern of hedging or mitigating may call to mind the notion that women express more insecurity in their speech than do men (e.g., Lakoff, 1975). While I have not undertaken a comparative study of such initiations in women's and men's turns, I can report that hedged pre-framing of turns is not exclusive to women in these meetings. One case in point is Richard's contribution to the church staff meeting, reproduced in (19). This meeting took place at a time when the Boy Scouts of America's declared policy of not allowing openly gay leaders was a news topic and a subject of debate. The question under discussion in (19) is whether St. Barnabas should allow a Cub Scout troop to meet in its facilities. Richard suggests that, like another church in the same city, St. Barnabas might reach a special understanding with the local troop:

(19)

Rich: **Well I'm (tal-) I mean (2.0) for what it's worth** Hope Congregational
     does have a boy scout troop. (.) and they (0.5) have as- an understanding
     with the boy scout, with that individual troop, that they are (0.7) affirming.
     (0.5) that they're open.=
Paula: [>But if their council finds out,<
Rich: [Now if,
Rich: That's right. If the council finds out, they've got a problem,

While there are differences between contexts and formulations if one compares Richard's hedge with those of Gwen and Mary, the fact that a man produces a hedge stands as evidence against any absolutes regarding women's and men's hedging strategies in framing meeting contributions.

Hedged beginnings are not the rule for women or men in these meetings. Indeed, women also initiate turns with strong assertions of disagreement, displaying very minimal deference. For example:

(20) [InfoGrp] Unmitigated disagreement

Gary: this model holds except under certain c[ircumstances, [and some places
Rick: [oh okay,   [well those

are places where it's not invariant,
(0.4)
⇒Steph: **No there's a place where it do[es vary,**
Gary: [where it'll vary,

(21) [InfoGrp] Strong and unmitigated disagreement

Rick: I know you don't [wanna (put it) that way.
⇒Steph: [**TWO YEARS AGO, NO NO, TWO years ago,**
       I tried to say that, that you, that you might have a different weight for
       something that contributed, so, let's say resources, might be weighted (.)
       very very important in terms of success, but not all that important in terms
       of failure, (.) so that t[he weight actually would would vary with the =
Conni: [mm
Steph:=directi- with with the: the actual value,

In both fragments, Stephie disagrees without mitigation, and in (21) she
even places her disagreement in competitive overlap. She begins her turn
at a point where Rick's turn is not complete prosodically or grammatically, and she speaks loudly until Rick's continuing talk is finished, and
she is able to continue in the clear.[9]

There is another recurrent practice for turn design in the women's talk,
and it involves initiating a sequence with a questioning action. In these
cases, a woman opens a shift in participation beyond the questioning
turn itself. I examine this practice in more detail in Chapter 5, but to
complete this section, I provide one example of the phenomenon.

In example (22), Jill produces a question that is recognizable as such
from very near its beginning due to the question word, *what*. The question is, of course, a turn in itself, and it is the first part of a two-part,
question-answer sequence. However, her question initiates a sequence
which is expanded beyond Ned's response (Schegloff, 2007:13, 115–26).
Jill asks Ned what percentage of alendronate users do not have positive
outcomes for the treatment of osteoporosis, and after Ned completes his
response to Jill's question, Jill takes the opportunity to expand with a
further display of her knowledge on the topic of bone treatment with
the medication alendronate.

(22) [Medical] Question plus opportunity for elaboration

⇒ Jill: Ned, uhm what- what's the- percent of alendronate users, (0.4)have you
       seen that ar- you would call sort of failures.
       (0.4)

Jill: Bone marrow density failu°res.°

// [*Ned responds at length-- partially deleted for space reasons*] //

Ned: (ya know) It's just no:t that- It's just no:t, i- In my: practice, I- I see basically none. .hh uhm, *((clears throat))* (.) I think tha:t,(1.0) that eh- (2.1) the literature suggests that failure, (.) would be really high, because of non-adherence.

((Jill nods and points toward Ned))

⇒Jill: And that's what it sounds like. I mean if y- if you: .hh If you >can< loo:k, I mean if you know you have good adherence, (.) it sounds like the likelihood of failure is very, (.) [very low.

[*((Ned nods repeatedly))*

Ned: (Correct).

Jill: °Okay:,°

This section and the previous one have documented recurrent practices for managing transitions from one speaker to the next and features of turn beginnings along with the work that they do. Segments from the meetings have illustrated how the move to meeting order is generally achieved and how turn-taking is organized and managed during the meetings. There is variation in whether or not a participant requests a turn or whether she launches her turn without negotiation. When she launches without deliberation, she may do so with a wholly new unit, or she may formulate her turn as a continuation of an action and/or a grammatical unit begun by a previous speaker. It is notable that incipient speakers coordinate their turn beginnings through non-vocal as well as vocal means, exhibiting possible interest in speaking well before the point when they actually start their turns. One form of non-vocal indication of readiness to speak is, of course, hand raising, but gestures and body positioning employed in the course of a current speaker's talk are also evident as strategies in these meetings.

There is one further configuration of participation that emerged in the meeting data and which deserves illustration. In several instances and through a group of related practices, participants enact connections and alliances. I turn to these cases in the next section.

Connections and alliances

Many of the women I interviewed emphasized the value of alliances with and support from others in meetings and in workplace interaction in general. As one woman put it,

It's important to get allies. I think that's probably the most important thing, because if you're the lone voice then you're probably not going to

> *get the outcome. Let's put it this way, if you really care about the*
> *outcome, then it's important to get allies.*

These women consciously worked to make connections between themselves and others in various ways, and they stressed the importance of alliances with persons whom they considered more powerful in their workplace hierarchies. The emphasis my interviewees placed on these alliances prompted me to look more closely at their interactions with persons they had identified as supportive. I was interested to see if alliances were evident in the interaction. In this section, then, I illustrate some forms of interactional connection and alliance that are enacted in the meetings.

Transitional beginnings crediting previous speakers

As participants begin new turns, they sometimes very explicitly tie their talk to ideas of other speakers. One interviewee had a name for this consciously crafted format for turn initiation. She referred to them as "transitional beginnings"; for her, they always included the name of a person whose idea she was responding to or upon whose previous contribution she wanted to elaborate.

In (23), Stephie and others have been discussing how they might take results of a workplace climate survey and usefully share them with administrators. Tanya ties her turn back across several sequences to an earlier contribution by Stephie:

(23) [Diversity] Tanya credits Stephie in her transitional beginning

Tanya: One idea **building on Stephie's comment about how the results would**
      be used later in the semester, one thing that I'd really like to see, I'm
      betting that there are going be questions he:re (.) where the results are very
      (0.3) unexpected at least to: (.) deans an and administrators, And I- I'm
      kind of envisioning, ya know, with this (coming in here) watching the
      numbers flash up, that part of the presentation could be basically asking (.)
      the deans to predict, how do you think people would answer those
      questions,

The structuring of Tanya's long turn is quite complex, as she folds in background and thereby delays the end of her turn, the idea that "part of the presentation could be basically asking (.) the deans to predict. . . ." In relation to making connections between participants, this example is a case in which a speaker enacts connection by using a "transitional beginning." Tanya explicitly acknowledges that her turn, her idea, is founded on Stephie's previous talk; by doing this, she both credits Stephie and also ties back to previous talk, demonstrating the relevance of her own contribution.

Examples (24) and (25) are taken from a long discussion of how to plan a public gathering that the diversity committee is planning. The goal is to get more of the community involved with the committee's mission. Stephie has been presenting her views on how the gathering might best work. In (24), Cindy uses a transitional beginning connecting to a problem Stephie has just addressed:

(24) [Diversity] Cindy includes Stephie in her transitional beginning

```
Steph:  If we finish with a broadening discussion, I think it will be very difficult
          to ( get the[  )
Gwen:              [ ↑Yeah, that is great. Because then also, it will get them excited
          about the pro[cess.
Steph:                   [yes.
?:      yep.
?:      °right.°
?:      That's good.
Viv:    It's a warm up.
          (1.2)
Jan:    °Cindy,°
⇒Cind:  Um, I think (0.6) the question I was going to have is related to
          Stephie's so this is- so Stephie's question has partly- may answer
          this but um tsk (1.2) I'm wondering about what (.) uh:m the consequences
          would be fo- i- what- sense the participants will have (.) to begin with,
```

A little later, Pam produces the extended two-part turn that we saw as example (16) above. Recall that, in the second part of Pam's projected two-part turn, she links back to Cindy's earlier contribution:

(25) [Diversity] Pam ties back to Cindy's previous contribution

```
Pam: The other thing is (.) tha- a-addresses what Cindy was was wondering about,
          wh(h)at, what can these people who come to this anticipate will come out of it,
```

The strategy of using specific names of previous speakers in transitional beginnings seems to be used in turns that are in agreement with the prior talk, building positively upon the named person's idea. While I have not systematically studied this possibility, I have yet to find a case (in women's or men's turns) where initial parts of a turn involve explicit naming of persons responded to *and* where what follows is a disaffiliative action. It may be that connections are more likely to be made when the action is neutral or positive and that the action of naming in the meetings is associated with affiliation. For example, in (17) from above, when Stephie begins what will turn out to be a delicate and disaffiliative action—calling into question what has been proposed in the previous talk—she makes no mention of John, Charles, or Jan, the persons whose ideas she is taking exception to:

(17 repeated) [Diversity] Tying back without naming a participant

Jan: It'll be fun to work ou:t, I think. *((nods as lifts and turns papers over))*

   (0.6)

Steph: [.hh Can I make a- (.)brief comment on tha:t, I- uh- uhm:

Thus, explicitly naming persons from previous talk may be avoided when one is formulating a disaffiliative action, and it may be preferred in formulating ties of affiliation or agreement (Sacks 1987).

   Another kind of connection involves participants acting as a "party" in multiparty interaction (Mandelbaum, 1987; Lerner, 1993; Kangasharju, 1996). Among the engineers at the Water Plant, Lonnie, Gareth, and Brent work together as peers in software development. The meeting I taped was occupied with a report from these three to others who will be using a new program under development. The project involved taking paper and spreadsheet data that Gareth had produced and managed over many years and synthesizing that data into a digital database for all members of the group to access. The meeting was called to offer an in-progress overview of the program and to invite suggestions from the larger group. Gareth opened the meeting by outlining the components of the program and the purpose of the gathering. He then turned the floor over to Lonnie, and she reported on specific parts of the program for which she had major responsibility and knowledge. As questions arose during Lonnie's report, Gareth jumped in to respond. Indeed, Gareth and Lonnie's contributions were interwoven as they moved in and out of speaking roles. As we will see in examples (26) and (27), Lonnie positions herself as the authority and maintains her role as the primary speaker during the presentation of her report. While Gareth joins in and presents himself as a co-authority with Lonnie, he also defers to her.

   In example (26), Lonnie has been reporting for a few minutes, with her gaze moving between the PowerPoint she is controlling from her laptop, the screen on which the slides are projected, and the group. At line 1, she has glanced at the group and seems to project the possibility of a question (though no visible or audible actions seem to condition this). Jerry raises his hand and launches a turn, which we see is quickly cut off by Gareth:

(26) [Plant] Gareth and Lonnie speaking as a "party" in the meeting

```
1 Lonn: I'm just gonna go- quickly through this, if you have (( directs gaze to group))
2        a quick question to ask me I don't mind ((Gareth directs gaze to group))
3 Jerr: ((raises hand)) Yeah, I [ just go-
4 Gare:                          [We- We're gonna try and get through this whole thing
5        in an hour.=
6 Lonn: =Yeah, so I'm gonna try to go a little fast but I- I'm happy to sit
7        down one on one with anybody after this and go through °the database
8        again,°
```

At line 4, Gareth produces a response to Jerry's turn beginning which effectively cuts off Jerry's turn in progress. By producing this response, before Lonnie has had a chance to respond to Jerry, Gareth acts from a position as co-reporter. He uses the pronoun *we* to refer to himself, Lonnie, and perhaps Brent, co-developers of the software program. At line 6, Lonnie produces an agreement token, *Yeah*. This asserts agreement, but it also confirms what Gareth has said and thereby enacts a position of authority relative to Gareth. That is, in doing a confirmation, Lonnie enacts her position as one with the knowledge and power to confirm (or deny) Gareth's statement. In her agreement token and her continuation, she also enacts her primary speakership. Note as well that Lonnie uses the pronoun *I* rather than *we* in lines 6–8, thereby reinforcing her role as reporter and, to some degree, the main person with knowledge of this part of the program development.

Working as collaborators while also commanding specific separate areas of expertise, Lonnie and Gareth enact and manage shifting positions toward the rest of the group and toward one another as they report on the software development. In (26), both Gareth and Lonnie responded to Jerry's turn beginning by deferring comments in the interest of time. In the next segment, example (27), a bit later in Lonnie's report, Jerry speaks again. This time, Lonnie, rather than Gareth, begins a response before Jerry completes his turn (line 4). By initiating her turn in overlap with Jerry's talk, Lonnie asserts her rights to respond, and she does so before Gareth can intervene.

Lonnie begins her response (lines 4–5), but Jerry overlaps her response to provide some motivation for his question (lines 6–7, "It would really help searching . . ."). After Jerry's elaboration comes to a point of possible completion, Gareth once again joins in as a co-expert with Lonnie. In this instance, the start of Gareth's response to Jerry overlaps precisely with Lonnie's own response (lines 8 and 9). Note that Lonnie disagrees with Gareth as the sequence continues (lines 15–20):

(27) [Plant] Lonnie and Gareth as a "party"

1 Jerr: One of the fields there- that interceptor field is common
2   across a lotta stuff, are you trying to use common names or (do they
3   have [names already)
4 Lonn: [*((tongue click))* ↑um, that's a good question. 'cause um, we-we
5   c[alled it
6 Jerr: [It would really help searching if you knew it was always called the
7   same thing no matter which database you were in.
8⇒ Lonn: [Right, so we'll-
9⇒ Gare: [WE'RE GOING TO STANDARDIZE THIS ONE [BASED ON WHAT=
10⇒Lonn: [Yeah,
11 Gare: =WE GOT IN G-I-S*,=
12 Jerr: =Okay, >eventually it will °be.°<
13 Gare: Yep[, so[this- so::[:,
14   [[[*((G gazes to[ward L))*
15⇒ Lonn: [↑Well: [yuh (no-)
16   *Lonn*:   [*((quick pointing & lateral head movement))*
17 Gare: [No[:?
18   *Gare*:   [*((q[uick lateral head movements))*
19⇒Lonn: [Yeah, no:,=because we- remember, we ran
20   into problems that (.) this one is too general?

*GIS = GEOGRAPHICAL INFORMATION SYSTEM

As it turns out, Lonnie is very skillful in dealing with Gareth's overlapping talk. At line 9, Gareth's talk is louder than Lonnie's, and Lonnie cuts off the progress of her response to Jerry (line 8). But she speaks again as Gareth is still talking, and, as in (26), Lonnie produces a confirmation of what Gareth is saying (line 10). Lonnie asserts her role as expert and primary speaker by producing the token *Yeah* (line 10) and by doing so overlaps with Gareth's turn. Lonnie's *Yeah* has a very slight rising intonation, which makes it sound tentative rather than fully confirming. So in the process of reasserting her authority, through this rise in intonation Lonnie may also be projecting possible disagreement with or at least ambiguous confirmation of Gareth's assertions regarding Lonnie's domain of expertise. And a careful disagreement is what Lonnie indeed produces, both through gesture and talk (lines 15–16, 19–20). Let us look closely at features of Lonnie's disagreement that come off as careful.

There is a coordinated shifting of orientations in the talk, gaze, and gestures of both Gareth and Lonnie between lines 13 and 20. Gareth is initially responding to and addressing Jerry, with "Yep, so this-" (line 13), but as he produces these words, he can hear Lonnie, across the table from him, producing *Well* (line 15), a common pre-disagreement marker which sometimes allows for the avoidance of explicit disagreement altogether (see Chapter 2, section on "pauses, hesitations, and preference"). As Lonnie speaks, Gareth can also see her doing a quick pointing gesture toward him, along with a very rapid lateral head movement (line 16). To the *Well* and the non-vocal actions, Gareth responds with a candidate understanding, "No?" (line 17), and he accompanies this with a lateral head movements of his own. By cutting off his turn in 13, and by producing these responses to Lonnie, Gareth shows his understanding that Lonnie is beginning to disagree, though she downplays her disagreement in a number of artful ways: her pointing hand is held low, and her head shake is very subtle. In terms of the general patterns observed in CA, we can see that Gareth's "No?" produced as it is as a question and a candidate understanding works to transform this exchange into one closer to agreement. In line 19, Lonnie starts with "Yeah," agreeing with Gareth's candidate understanding ("No?"). She then produces a "no," which now is a further confirmation rather than a clear interactional disagreement. Her "Yeah, no:," is interpretable as, "Yeah I confirm your understanding that what you were saying was not correct."

By this time, neither Gareth nor Lonnie is directly addressing the rest of the group. They are clarifying the facts between themselves. Lonnie is skillful in not simply correcting Gareth but doing so in a manner that reminds him of what they discovered together, thereby highlighting their collaboration. As she continues (line 19), she includes Gareth as an agent in the discovery of the problem, and her reminder to him ends with a slightly rising intonation, "remember we ran into problems that this was too general?" This can serve as a prompt for Gareth's confirmation of remembering.[10] Note her use of *we* here, as opposed to *I* in (26) (line 6).

While the interaction between Lonnie and Gareth in (26) and (27) seems to reveal tension, in my interview with Lonnie, she described a very positive working relationship with Gareth. She had no complaints with his style and felt supported by him in her work. She remarked that this was sometimes surprising to her given that she is an out and proud lesbian and that he is outspoken in sharing his Christianity, assuring her he is praying for her. Lonnie stated with no uncertainty that she and Gareth respected each others' areas of expertise and had a consistently warm working relationship. She trusted Gareth as an ally in her workplace.

An alliance between peers was also visible in one of the Zoology labs as well. After Amy's presentation (see [13] above), you may recall that Carol takes the floor and directs Amy to move back a couple of slides in her presentation. Before Carol had spoken up, Eva had already raised her hand in a bid to speak. Carol's strategy of simply speaking up rather than raising her hand gets her the floor, and Eva ultimately lowers her hand. But note that Greg acts as Eva's ally when he witnesses her bid to speak being superseded by Carol's subsequent talk. At line 5, Greg makes his first intervention, followed by Eva's repetition plus laughter, as she keeps her hand up:

(13b) [Zool 2] [Expanded]

1   Amy: for (.) all of your help.

2   *((Eva raises her hand, keeps up till line 12))*

3   Bria: Oh look, we're all there. hh

4   Caro: Take it back a couple of slides.

5⇒ Greg:We have - (-) questions.=

6   Eva: =We have questions. uh[huh huh

7⇒Greg: [y' There- There's a   *Figure 4.7*   Greg points to Eva
                                                      (lines 7–8)
8   question, over her[e. *((E turns toward G))*

9   Caro: [Yeh- because you were [thi- ya know:,

10⇒Greg: [huh huh huh

11 Caro: Beca[use we were just-talking about it wasn't 'n=

12   [*((E lowers her hand))*

13 Caro: =in your conclusions,

      // [*the exchange between Carol and Amy continues for some time*] //

At lines 7–8, Greg reasserts his call for attention to Eva, "There's a question, over here." But rather than picking up on these calls by both Greg and Eva, Carol continues her talk at 9 and 11. Both Eva and Doug gaze toward Greg, with Eva smiling and keeping her hand up. Eva then lowers her hand at line 12. Though unsuccessful in its outcome, Greg's work to support Eva is another illustration of connection and alliance. Interestingly, this segment does involve someone being "ignored," at least by the primary participants (Carol and Amy). Relative to that primary dialogue, Eva's raised hand and Greg's verbal intervention are "sequentially deleted" (Schegloff, 1987:110). That is, although Eva and Doug acknowledge Greg's intervention by gazing toward him (and with a smile in Eva's case), the primary speakers at this juncture, Carol and Amy, continue without reference to Greg's actions.

A final case of an alliance in action is found in the Planning Committee. On first reviewing the tape of this meeting, I noticed that Hank was in a sense speaking for Gloria. Since I was looking for cases of women speaking up, I was not sure what to make of this case. It seemed to recommend itself as primarily a case of a woman remaining silent and not contributing, yet Gloria is credited with the idea, and Gloria does contribute later in the discussion. In my interview with her, and without my drawing attention to this moment in the meeting video, Gloria referred to Hank as an example of a more powerful member of the institutional hierarchy who used his power to her benefit. She spoke of the value she placed on having Hank as an ally. I first present the interaction and then quote Gloria's independent reflections on the importance of alliances and specifically on her relationship with Hank.

The intervention takes place as Amanda is reporting on a request for a two-credit course, which is a problem because most courses earn three credits. Just prior to this moment, but during Amanda's long turn, Gloria leans toward Hank and speaks to him quietly. Their exchange is inaudible on the videotape, but that they are talking is visible (see earlier discussion of how subsidiary interactions are framed and produced as such). Hank then gains a turn in the meeting, and initiates his turn by crediting Gloria for the question he raises. We can see that, by the end of the excerpt, Gloria joins in with Hank, but clearly it was Hank who got the issue on the floor. I reproduce a generous portion of this segment in order to include the point when Gloria herself speaks (arrow 2, at the end of the example):

(28) [Planning] Hank voices Gloria's question

Amand: Uh- in the interim this is still the committee that is responsible
     for- (ethnic) studies credit.
Hank: .hh *((H raises index finger; A does vertical head movement toward H))*
⇒Hank: **Gloria just brought up a relevant question. This is a two credit
     course.**
Amand: *((vertical head movement))*° mm [hm.°

Hank: [We have uhm, in general avoided
        giving ethnic studies (.) credit to two credit courses because a student
        takes AN ethnic studies course [but it's a three credit requirement =
Amand: [mm hm
Hank: =actually, there was a- JAZZ course in music for seven years that
        was h.h a two credit course and it caused enough problems that-
        we: took the ethnic studies away from it.
Amand: mm h[m
Hank: [so as a separa- a SEParate question from the h QUALity of this
        cour- particular course is-should we be giving ethnic studies=
        THEORETICALLY you could take a two credit course and one credit
        course,
Frank: [mm-hm]
Hank: [and me]et the requirement, but there aren't any one credit courses.
        there aren't any two credit courses at the moment. so:
Frank: [so this would be doing more-[not be doing a service to the student.
Hank: [the students would   [go OH NOW I have to take another one-
⇒Gloria: **[cause they want to satisfy ethnic**
        [studies requirement.
            [*((Gloria looks from Frank to Amanda))*

When I asked Gloria what advice she might have for people who want
to have more success in contributing to workplace meetings, she spoke
of the crucial nature of cultivating allies, and she drew on her experience with Hank to illustrate her point:

> *Maybe this is obvious, but [one needs] to have allies that are seen as the*
> *more privileged voices—knowing who those voices are, if the outcome is that*
> *important to you. I can use Hank Carr as an example. Hank Carr is an*
> *example of a white male who does tend to talk a lot at meetings. He's very*
> *articulate and has a lot of good ideas, and he understands that about him-*
> *self. Sometimes he'll even say, "Oh I'm talking too much. I better shut up."*
> *But he's one person that I will, after a meeting or before a meeting, just go*
> *to his office and run some ideas by him. I talk with him so that when we*
> *get to the meeting—because I know he's the talker and he might be heard*
> *more than I would—maybe he can back up some of my ideas or bring my*
> *ideas to the forefront in a way that I wouldn't be able to do, or I might not*
> *feel confident in doing. I do think it's important to establish those kinds of*
> *relationships. I think it's important to know who those people are and use*
> *them. The meetings that happen outside of the meetings are important too.*

It was Gloria's emphasis on the importance of alliances and her specific use of Hank as an example that prompted me to look back at the case where Hank raised Gloria's issue. More generally, Gloria's explicit noting of allies, along with similar explicit reports of connections and connection strategies in my interviews, motivated me to look for interactional evidence that such relational links might be functioning in the meetings.

In principle, getting one's ideas introduced through more powerful institutional voices, here a black female's raised by her white male colleague, would seem to reinforce the status quo of power relations in the institution. On the other hand, Gloria, like other women in these meetings, insisted that getting her most cherished ideas heard and acted upon successfully was more important than having her own voice be the vehicle for raising ideas or getting direct credit for her ideas.

My intention in this section has been to begin to shed light on alliances, an aspect of workplace interaction that women point to as consequential to their work lives. The fact that support through alliances is cited in the interviews suggests that these experiences may be particularly valuable to women seeking a place at the table in institutions where they have been traditionally underrepresented.

Conclusion: openings, transitions, turn beginnings, and participant alliances

In order to understand practices through which participants gain and use turns in these data and with women's turns serving as the sources for illustration, in this first analytic chapter we have looked at the initiation and the interactional unfolding of meetings. An initial section documented how meetings are brought to order, a process resulting in a significant shift in the structuring of participation such that one main activity is shared by members of the group. Subsequent sections explored the variety of ways that participants come into speakership, the kinds of work they do in turn beginnings, and ways in which connections and alliances are enacted. One notable feature in the coordination of turn transitions was non-vocal coordination, both before a point of possible turn transition and at such points. Gestures, gaze direction, and other bodily movements played a significant role in such coordination, with the coordination going well beyond hand raising to include the marking of specific points of heightened interest in a current speaker's turn. We also noted that, while hand raising is effective in many cases, this practice can easily be trumped when another participant simply speaks up; speaking up without formal bids or negotiation of a turn is common in meetings without formal rules of order, as were all the events I videotaped. The chapter concluded with a discussion of alliances and support between participants, an aspect of workplace interaction that women in my interviews considered especially important.

While the chapter was divided into sections on shifting to meeting order, turn allocation and transition, turn beginnings, and enacting alliances, the social practices and interactional processes illustrated in each section are interwoven and simultaneous in the meetings themselves. That is, though I offer various perspectives on domains of turn-taking and meeting organization, these are not discrete or ultimately separable organizations in the flow of the meetings themselves. The collaborative structuring of talk with respect to leaders or primary speakers, speaker selection, non-vocal participation, and the enactment of alliances (or lack thereof) are interwoven and mutually elaborating or contextualizing. For example, turn transitions, turn beginnings, and non-vocal coordination are all in play as participants collaborate to shift into official meeting order. And although turn allocation and speaker selection were treated in a single section, these are domains relevant to the examples in all sections. Clearly, turn allocation is relevant for enacting a leadership position, for initiating contributions, and for constituting alliances, and it is done through a combination of vocal and non-vocal means.

This overview of the range of ways women initiate and build contributions both confirms the fact that the women are competent at initiating turns in the meetings, and it also demonstrates that they do not share a single general pattern or style. Just as we saw in the interviews where the women reported different preferences and perspectives on meeting interaction, this chapter has shown how these women command a variety of ways of gaining entry to participation and ways of maintaining that participation. In the case of turn beginnings, hedged pre-framing of turns was noted, but, as this could be considered a stereotypically women's move, I added a case of a man using a similar strategy in order to emphasize that this is not an exclusively female strategy.

This chapter adds to our understanding of meeting interaction by providing a functional typology of general practices for organizing meeting order and for initiating contributions. Chapters 5 and 6 document two different sets of practices, examining them at different levels of granularity. Chapter 5 elaborates on the use of questioning as a way of opening participation and also as a way of displaying knowledge and presenting challenges. Chapter 6 zooms in on two women's contributions to a single segment of a Diversity Committee meeting, investigating the practices through which both women take issue with the talk of other, higher-ranking participants. We examine how they launch these delicate actions, and how they succeed in extending their turns in the face of competing participation and directions of talk.

5
Questions: Opening Participation, Displaying Expertise, and Challenging

In keeping with the combined goals of documenting women's skill at speaking up in the meetings and also contributing to a CA-based understanding of meeting interactions more generally, this chapter reports on interactional functions accomplished or set in motion through the action of questioning. Questions in themselves would not have stood out were it not for the fact that the action of questioning, in these data, regularly leads to further participation; that is, sequences initiated by questioning actions regularly open at least one further opportunity for the initial questioner to speak again. In addition, questioning turns can serve as knowledge displays and they can present challenges to other participants. Thus special attention to questioning is warranted not by a particular interest in question forms *per se*, but by the fact that, within the larger set of women's turn initiations, questioning serves to shift the local organization of participation and the local sense of who is in control of knowledge. From another perspective, however, the fact that questioning serves to bring women into participation in these meetings is notable in relation to some early research on women, men, and questions. Certain question forms have been associated with relative lack of power and even insecurity. The current findings suggest another perspective on the function of questions.

After a brief review of trends in the interpretation of questions in discourse, gender, and language studies, the remainder of the chapter examines questioning actions in the current data, with special reference to questioning turns which display expertise, present challenges, and open expanded participation.

Related research on questions and questioning in discourse and gender studies

Questions have received considerable attention in discourse studies and specifically in language and gender research. That attention has led to intersecting and contrasting interpretations of the work that questions do and how questioning relates to women's power and self-presentation in discourse. Questions figured in the first contemporary studies of language and gender that emerged from what is now referred to as "second wave" feminism. Robin Lakoff's 1975 book, *Language and Woman's Place*, drew linguists' and feminists' attention to women's (over)use of question forms—particularly tag questions and declaratives delivered with rising intonation. Lakoff viewed women's use of these question forms as fitting into a range of practices through which women showed a "pervasive tendency toward hesitancy, linguistic and otherwise." She suggested that women's tendency to use these question forms enacted their lack of authority and their need for "reassurance" and "acceptance" (Lakoff, 1975:143).

As Lakoff's suggestions were taken up by other scholars, her claims were connected with studies of question functions more generally. Independent of interest in women and language, questions were receiving attention for their multifunctionality (Austin, 1962; Hudson, 1975; Ervin-Tripp, 1976; and Freed 1994). It is not surprising, then, that in an empirical expansion on Lakoff's research, Pamela Fishman (1977, 1978, and 1980) found functions of questions that seemed at odds with Lakoff's findings. While Fishman's quantitative findings supported Lakoff's claim that women used these questions forms more than men, Fishman did not interpret the relative frequency in women's use of tags and declarative questions as a direct reflection and enactment of women's insecurity. She inspected the interactional contexts in order to understand local interactional forces that might explain why these forms were used.

Fishman drew upon the newly developing framework of CA, and specifically Sacks' 1972 work on adjacency pairs, fundamental, two-part interactional sequences through which one speaker's action makes expectable or relevant a response by her addressee. Questions are prime examples of actions that make responses—answers—relevant. Looking closely at the contexts where women used these specific question forms, Fishman noted that they involved sequences of turns in which a male is being unresponsive or only minimally responsive to a topic raised by his female partner. In connection with this pattern, while overall the women in her data had less success than men in having their topics taken up, when women used these question forms to pursue topics, they succeeded in having their topics taken up more frequently. From her analyses, then, Fishman argued that rather than enacting hesitancy or insecurity, women in these couples used questions as vehicles for strengthening the force of their turns as they attempted to get more than silence or minimal responses from their partners. She concluded that these specific question forms were used as upgrades in the pursuit of response. Rather than standing as evidence of women's essential insecurity, using questions was a practice adapted to the emergent contingencies of pursuing uptake from reticent recipients.

Employing another interpretive framework, Deborah Tannen (1990) found asymmetry in women's and men's reported use (or non-use) of a specimen case of questioning: asking for directions from a stranger. Attitudes and experiences with asking or not asking in these situations present insights into connections between power, gender, and questions in practice. In her 1990 book, *You Just Don't Understand: Women and Men in Conversation*, Tannen drew from women's and men's self-reports of their interactional practices and experiences. She noted frequent complaints from women that men refused to ask for directions, whereas women reported being willing to do so. Tannen interpreted these reports from an interactional sociolinguistic perspective (Gumperz, 1982), elaborating a "dual cultures" approach to gender differences in discourse practices (Maltz & Borker, 1982). By this interpretation, gender difference in willingness to ask directions is one manifestation of fundamental differences in the interactional styles of women and men. Such styles are connected to evidence that girls and boys develop distinct styles as they are socialized in and through sex-segregated peer groups.

The dual cultures framework builds upon findings that competition and hierarchy are managed differently by boys and girls, at least those in the groups most commonly studied. Whereas girls, in the groups studied, develop less explicitly hierarchical modes of interacting, boys learn to be openly competitive in constructing and maintaining hierarchies. As a result of these differences in peer interactions earlier in life, men avoid positioning themselves as "one down" in interaction, while women are not as vigilant about such hierarchical distinctions. Given these distinct interactional patterns, it is inferred that women's reported readiness to ask directions is related to their relative lack of concern (as compared with men) about placing themselves, even temporarily and with a stranger, in a lower hierarchical position.

Tannen's interpretation is relevant to the current study as it provides us with another voice in the ongoing research dialogue regarding questions, gender, and power. In Tannen's interpretation, it makes perfect sense that men avoid asking strangers for driving directions. Revealing one's ignorance and vulnerability puts one immediately into a one-down position. By not asking for directions, men are manifesting their deeply socialized habit of maintaining a "one-up" position.[1] Of course, asking directions from a stranger occurs in a different context and constitutes a different action than the questions Fishman studied among women and men in heterosexual relationships. In those cases, women used questions to pursue uptake from an intimate partner rather than to gain specific information from a stranger. Noting variation in data sources and contexts of use brings us again to the importance of analyzing language forms and functions in their interactional contexts.

Coinciding with Tannen's elaborations of the dual cultures perspective but resonating more with Fishman's research, other scholars moved beyond frequency counts to nuanced attention to social interactional functions. Indeed, over the years, gender and language research has produced results that complicate an easy positing of speaker or recipient gender as the main source for explaining language practices. Research has continually underscored the importance of attending to local sequential contexts for forms such as questions, forms which had previously been treated as associated with women's talk (O'Barr & Atkins, 1980; Holmes, 1984; Cameron *et al.*, 1988; Greenwood & Freed, 1992; among others).

To place divergent findings on questions in a broader research perspective, it is instructive to consider James and Drakich's (1993) review and synthesis of difference-based studies of men, women, and quantity of talk. They point to problems in researchers' cultural assumptions and to varying data collection methods and contexts as complicating the interpretation of divergent findings. Among the many studies they review and compare, there is significant variation in the settings and activities from which discourse data were drawn. For example, settings and events might involve casual and non-task oriented interaction or more formal and task-oriented talk. One overall pattern they find is that women appear to take more talk time in less task-oriented and more casual interactions, an observation that resonates with Edelsky's 1981 study of women's varying participation within specific subtypes of talk in faculty meetings. James and Drakich suggest that socio-emotional and facilitative practices are culturally expected of and associated with women (see Fletcher, 2001; Holmes & Marra, 2004). Question forms are common vehicles for doing facilitative work in interaction, which James and Drakich reason may be a factor in the pattern of increased talk by women when they participate in less agenda-driven, task-oriented, and formal interactions. This harkens back to Fishman's call for putting primary emphasis on understanding the interactional contexts in which linguistic forms emerge if one is interested in understanding the complex associations between language and gender.

While the current study is not aimed at discovering differences between women and men, it is aimed at documenting women's attested ways of getting and using the floor; thus the findings I present in this chapter not only provide general insights into the work of questioning in meetings, they also move us further away from a deficit model of women's language practices. We move next to the interactional understanding of questioning for this study.

Questioning in interactional terms

For this study, questioning is not defined by grammatical structure, i.e., by a set of forms associated with doing questioning. Rather questioning is understood as an interactional function. Specifically, a woman was doing questioning as part of the action of her turn *if*

1) she pointed to a lack of information or knowledge, or she expressed a stance of uncertainty with respect to a proposition, *and if*
2) she stopped speaking, opening an interactional slot for response from her recipient(s).

This two-part, interactional definition allows for inclusion of structures that are not formally questions or identifiable as interrogative structures. While questioning can be done through interrogative syntax, it may also be done through a B-event statement. In such a case, the speaker produces a declaratively formatted turn involving knowledge understood to be controlled by a recipient (Labov & Fanshel, 1977; Heritage & Roth, 1995). Questioning action can also be performed through reports of missing information or uncertainty about a claim. In another variation, a speaker may embed a questioning action in a report about having a question. All these types of action invite answers. What the definition excludes are turns which, although formulated with interrogative syntax, do not invite or open a slot for a recipient to respond.

Let us look at two examples in order to clarify what does and does not count as doing questioning for this study. Example (1) includes a case of questioning achieved without interrogative syntax. Note that Bonnie communicates that an issue has "always bothered" her. She is concerned about the use of parathyroid hormone in treating osteoporosis, and her recipient, Ned, is an expert on osteoporosis. Within Bonnie's long turn, she reports never having "gotten a good answer from Beaudry" (Beaudry is a pseudonym for a large pharmaceutical company).

(1) [Medical] Questioning without a question form

Bonnie: Ned, **one of the things that's always bothered me, and I've never gotten a good answer from Beaudry, either,** is that (.) unless you giv:e (.) parathyroid hormone intermittently, it's getting subcue*, so that you get, it's that *((gestures))* it's basically emulsion, you don't have that good anabolic effect, a:nd, you know, that's what might scare us more about the osteosarcoma, I guess that's what the rats have too, but when people have primary (.) hyperparathyroidism, it doesn't just, *((gestures up and down, indicating fluctuation in hormone level))* you know, so it's it's rea:lly a kind of a different drug in a way, and that that concerns me.

Ned: Yeah, I mean, I think, I- I- you're exactly right, Bonnie, this is:, you're comparing apples and oranges, (.) for sure, (0.3) °um:°, and I- ya

⇒ know **I'm not enough of a molecular biologist to explain the pharmacokinetics to you,**

*subcue = subcutaneously

Drawing on Labov and Fanshel's model, we can categorize Bonnie as the _A_ speaker and Ned as the _B_ speaker with regard to osteoporosis and its treatment. Thus, Bonnie is making B-event statements when she refers to aspects of the osteoporosis treatment in question. Furthermore, Bonnie's reference to not having gotten an adequate answer points to a lack of information.

Ned responds to two actions in Bonnie's turn. He first confirms her presentation of the issue:

Yeah, I mean, I think, I- I- you're exactly right, Bonnie,

In performing the action of confirmation, Ned co-constructs himself as expert in the domain (the _B_ recipient of a _B_-event statement). Next, by delivering an account for not being able to answer the technical part of Bonnie's question, Ned displays his understanding of Bonnie's turn as including that questioning action:

I'm not enough of a molecular biologist to explain the pharmacokinetics to you,

Thus, although there is no grammatically formatted interrogative in Bonnie's turn, we see that Ned responds to a questioning action. With respect to the second criterion for doing questioning, Bonnie cedes the floor to her recipient, Ned. Bonnie's turn fits my interactional definition of questioning.

Compare Bonnie's action in example (1) with Stephie's first clause in example (2). Stephie uses *yes/no* interrogative syntax:

(2) [Diversity] Interrogative form without a questioning function

> Jan: It'll be fun to work ou:t, I think.
>
>   (0.6)
>
> ⇒Stephie: .hh **Can I make a- (.)brief comment on tha:t,** I- >yuh<- uhm: (1.6)
>
>   Being on-the other side of the <u>co(h)l</u>leg(h)[e,
>
> John: [huh eh heh
>
>   (0.6)
>
> Jan: ↑We've never had a ↑search committee in our °(department).°

A first note is that Stephie ends her first clause, "Can I make a- (.) brief comment on tha:t," without the rising intonation associated with *yes/no* interrogatives doing questioning. Second, Stephie allows no pause after that first clause; she continues into the beginning of a next grammatical and prosodic unit. In so doing she holds the turn past a point of possible completion, and she only pauses after she has arrived at a place where the grammar of her unit projects further talk for completion, "I- yuh uhm (1.6)".[2] After the pause, she repairs her talk, reformulating the continuation as a dependent phrase, "Being on-the other side of the <u>co(h)l</u>leg(h)[e,." In short, Stephie produces *yes/no* interrogative syntax (although without rising intonation), but she rushes through into another unit of her turn, without opening a slot for recipient response. I do not consider the initial clause of her turn to be doing questioning; instead, Stephie uses this first clause of her turn to project a multiunit turn, and she moves directly into the next unit of that turn.[3]

In the remainder of this chapter, I will use the terms *questioning*, *questioning action*, and *question* interchangeably, but the cases under examination all fit the interactional criteria I have outlined and exemplified in this section.

Opening a sequence through questioning

Adjacency pairs are basic two-part structures in sequence organization, but in many activities a third turn serves to either close or expand the course of action of an adjacency pair (Schegloff, 1968; Sacks, 1972;

Jefferson & Schenkein, 1978; Schegloff, 2007:13, 115–167). This is true for question-answer sequences, which regularly involve a slot in which a questioner does acknowledgement, receipt, or evaluation (Sinclair & Coulthard, 1975). In describing two-party interactions, Sacks (1972) uses the term "party," which can be applied to collections of one or more persons under certain circumstances (Lerner, 1993; Kangasharju, 1996). In meetings, for example, a chair may be addressing the rest of a committee as a single party. When an individual speaks up with a question for the chair, that individual may speak as a single party, with the chair treated as the recipient and the two forming a public dyad in the context of the committee.

It is common in my meeting collection that, when an individual does questioning, it opens a sequence in which multiple subsequent turns elaborate on a theme. This brief section introduces the expansion of adjacency pair into a three-turn sequence, in its most minimal form. The sections that follow further illustrate such expansions, and they also demonstrate other actions done by questioning turns and their expansions.

Expansion after a response can be very minimal, doing no more than acknowledging the response. In example (3) Beth's questioning turn initiates a minimal three-part sequence: at the first arrow she does an understanding check, one kind of repair initiation (Heritage, 1984a:318–20). After Pam responds with disconfirmation plus correction (Ford, 2001, 2002b), Beth produces a non-vocal acknowledgment (arrow 3). Pam is in the midst of a long turn, reporting on a survey of women in physical sciences. She is explaining that her funder requires that the interviews be conducted by female-male pairs; that is, she is required to have a man co-conducting each interview:

(3) [Diversity] Minimal expansion of a questioning sequence; Pam is in the midst of a longer projected turn

```
Pam:    They wanted a man and a woman, both on the telephone, in the
                interview. [(0.8) And=
Vivian:                    [huh. Interesting.
⇒1 Beth:                   [They meaning (.) the Satellite Exploration
                Center?=
⇒2 Pam: =No:, the the chair of the committee, [ had, had, in consultation with=
⇒3 Beth:                                       [((multiple head vertical head nods))
Pam:    =the committee, had concluded that this was the way to do it,
                I was surprised, but that's what our committee decided
                that we should do.
```

At the first point of possible completion in Pam's turn, Beth acknowledges the response through a series of vertical head nods. These non-vocal tokens constitute a minimal third turn expansion of a question-response sequence. To foreshadow the manner in which questioning may involve multiple functions, it is worth noting that Pam not only responds with a disconfirmation and a correction, but she goes on to share her own surprise: "I was surprised, but that's what our committee decided that we should do." In this component of her response, Pam registers that Beth's understanding check might contain an implied challenge and could project disaffiliation.[4] By adding an account to her disconfirmation and correction, Pam acknowledges that Beth's question could also be an expression of surprise. As we will see in other cases, questioning actions are regularly elaborated upon, and those elaborations may include the articulation of problems with previous talk.

Whether a response is produced as simple or expanded has to do with the actions that are combined in the question (see Ford, Fox & Hellermann 2004; Schegloff, 2007 among others). Questions do not uniformly introduce sequences which are expanded, but as I examined my meeting collection, it became clear that questioning was one way in which women moved into expanded participation in these meetings.

Questioning turns and sequences: expertise and challenge

In her 1994 book, *The Business of Talk*, Dierdre Boden introduces a distinction between questions leading to minimal expansion and "queries." Queries are questions that are "loaded" and call for further expansion into a longer sequence (1994:122 ff.). She notes that queries create a shift in a course of action:

> Queries [. . .] are frequently used in sequences, chained together by the same speaker to follow a particular line of reasoning or lead to a particular position. A query breaks frame as the first stage of a series of same-speaker turns that may address broader organizational issues or selectively narrow a topic along relevant lines.

(1994:124)

Boden notes the power of queries to create expanded sequences in which "the thrust of the talk is sustained across several (or many) intermediate moves as one participant reveals a specific agenda" (1994:126).

While Boden looks at question forms rather than questioning conceived of in more general interactional terms, her notion of a loaded question or "query" bears resemblance to the work of questioning in the current meeting data. Boden's observation that a "query breaks frame as the first stage of a series of same speaker turns" is nicely related to the patterns I find in which women's questions open expanded sequences. In this next section, we look at such expansions. We also examine how questioning turns and the sequences they open can display expertise and involve the elaboration of challenges.

As we have noted, turns doing questioning can lead to expansions, and questions and their expansions can also serve as vehicles for displaying knowledge and thus a form of power within a group. Example (4) offers an initial case in which a questioning action sets in motion a course of action in which the questioner receives another opportunity to speak. In this case, the questioning turn and its later expansion both include displays of expertise.

Ned, an internationally recognized expert on osteoporosis, has been speaking at length to a group of medical practitioners with whom he works. They are evaluating treatments for bone density loss. Jill is also an expert in a closely related area of medicine. In her questioning turn (example [4], line 10, first arrow), Jill renews the construction of Ned as the local expert, by asking him a factual question about his experience with the treatment under discussion: the drug alendronate (prescribed to inhibit bone density loss). Yet even as Jill constructs Ned as possessing knowledge that she does not, in the way she delivers her question and speaks again, after Ned's lengthy response, Jill also exhibits her own expertise (20–2); thus, an action that can be done in a questioning turn is to the knowledgeability of the speaker as well:

(4) [Medical] Questioning and expansion, with displays of expertise

1 Ned: And so if you've g̲o̲t somebody, who's >just< dev̲astated by osteoporosis,
2   and those people ex↑i̲s̲t̲,(.) I think >that< thi̲s̲ is s̲o̲mething to consider.
3   (0.8)
4 Ned: *((sniff))*
5   (2.3)
6 Ned: °okay° *((turns toward screen while touching laptop keyboard))*
7   *((N turns to face group as J moves hand out & up))*
8 Ned: Okay. *((N reverses head movement to look specifically at J))*
9   *((N gestures toward J, places hands in lap & leans back in chair))*

10⇒ **Jill: Ned, uhm what- what's the- percent of alendronate users, (0.4)**

11   **have you seen that ar- you would call sort of <u>fai</u>lures.**

12   (0.4)

13 Jill: **Bone marrow d<u>e</u>nsity failu°res.°**

   //[. . . Ned responds at length--partially deleted for space reasons . . .]//

15 Ned: (ya know) It's just no:t that- It's just no:t, i- In my: practice, I-

16   I see basically <u>none</u>. .hh uhm, *((clears throat))* (.) I think tha:t,(1.0) that,

17   eh- (2.1) the literature suggests that failure, (.) would be <u>r</u>eally

18   high, because of non-ad<u>he</u>rence.

19   *((Jill nods and points toward Ned))*

20⇒ **Jill: And that's what it sounds like. I mean if y- if you: .hh If you >can<**

21   **loo:k, I mean if you kn<u>o</u>w you have good ad<u>he</u>rence,(.) it sounds like the**

22   **likelihood of failure is very, (.) [very low .**

23   **[*((Ned nods repeatedly))***

24 Ned: (Correct) .

25 Jill: **°Okay:,°**

As part of her question on the success rate of the treatment (10–13), Jill refers to "alendronate users" and "bone marrow density failures." Thus, within her questioning turn, Jill already displays knowledge of terms and concerns relevant to the treatment at issue. Jill's question also initiates a sequence leading to an additional opportunity for her to speak (19–20 onward). While she later produces a sequence-closing turn ("°Okay:,°" line 25), she does this after first using her returned turn slot to produce more than a simple receipt. In lines 20–2, she acknowledges Ned's answer but also asserts that she had already inferred just what Ned states in his response. She even begins her turn at line 20 with the conjunction *and*, indicating that she is expanding upon what Ned has just said:

20⇒ Jill: And that's what it sounds like. I mean if y- if you: .hh If you >can<

21   loo:k, I mean if you kn<u>o</u>w you have good ad<u>he</u>rence, (.) it sounds like the

22   likelihood of failure is very, (.) [very low.

23   [*((Ned nods repeatedly))*

24 Ned: (Correct) .

25 Jill: °Okay:,°

Thus, within her questioning turn and the talk she adds in the slot after Ned's response, Jill constructs herself as a co-expert with Ned. Ned, it should be noted, seems to be reasserting his role as arbiter of accuracy in

his area of expertise when he evaluates Jill's assertions with "(Correct),"
line 24, though this is not clearly decipherable on the recording.

In (4), Jill does not expose a problem with what Ned has been saying
nor does she challenge him. This appears to be the case with Gwen's
turn in the next example as well. Example (5) is from the same meeting.
Here Gwen raises the issue of race as a possible factor in the study of
osteosarcoma as a side effect of a particular treatment. Gwen's first turn,
though not initially formed as an interrogative, addresses the domain in
which Ned is an expert and can be heard as doing questioning (lines
5–9). At the end of her turn, Gwen explicitly marks it as questioning
with the tag, "right?"

The context of Gwen's tag brings to mind the cases in Fishman's
data where tags were added when recipients were minimally responsive. Note that, at line 7, Ned produces a minimal response, and
though enough of Gwen's point is clear earlier in lines 8 and 9,
he does not initiate a response. In fact, even after Gwen has passed
one point of possible completion and has produced the tag, a silence
ensues (line 10). When Ned does speak at lines 11–12, he produces a
paraphrase of what Gwen has said, and this serves as a confirmation,
without elaboration:

(5) [Medical] Questioning, expanding, and possibly challenging

```
 1   Ned: [So I think, osteosarcoma is still on the plate. as a concern.
 2        [((G starts to raise hand and then retracts by end of N's "I think"))
 3   Ned: [That's the punch line, °of all of this.°
 4        [((G raises hand, begins speaking with hand up while looking at article))
 5⇒Gwen: [I mean this just caught my eye, and I don't know if this is relevant,
 6⇒      but, this case report is in a black woman, [a hundred percent of the (.)=
 7   Ned:                                           [umhm
 8⇒Gwen: =at least in the male study, were white, and there is some calci-
 9⇒      trophic axis (.) bone difference between blacks and whites, right?
10        (0.8)
11   Ned: Yeah, blacks tend to have (.) have lower bone turnover (.) than, than
12        whites,
13⇒Gwen: So, does that- do you think that's just a coincidence, or is there
14⇒      anything to make of that,
15        (0.8)
16   Ned: I'm:, I don't know, but you're right, I- all- I-I think essentially
17        every patient that's: received PTH in the clinical trials has been
18        caucasian,
```

19   Gwen: **And the <u>one</u> case report is in a black woman.**=
20   Ned: =<u>A</u>ctually, they they cite three other cases.
21   Gwen: um
22   Ned: So, there are now <u>four</u> cases of (0.3) concomitant osteosarcoma with
23   primary hyperparathyroidism, whether that's (.) <u>cau</u>sative or simply (.)
24   coi<u>n</u>cidence, I don't know, but if uh- the point that I'm making is if
25   somebody simply tells ya that (.) PTH is <u>sa</u>fe because it's never been
26   eported to cause- to coe<u>xist</u> with osteosarcoma, (.) and primary
27   hyperpara, you can say, well:, yeah, not exactly.

Gwen's questions in example (5) display her expertise. She uses a technical description, "calcitropic axis bone difference," (lines 8–9) for what Ned then paraphrases as "lower bone turn over" (line 11). Gwen's initial questioning action gains her access to further opportunities to speak beyond her initial turn. At lines 13–14, Gwen uses the opportunity to produce a further question, working to get some conclusive response from Ned with regard to the racial make-up of the case studies and the clinical trials. But again there is first a pause; and when Ned speaks, he confirms the accuracy of Gwen's observation, but he does not take up the issue of racial representation beyond that confirmation. While Gwen pushes further, adding, "and the one case report is in a black woman," Ned closes the issue by correcting her and then moving back to "the point" he is making, "I don't know, but if uh- the point that I'm making is" (line 24).

Example (5) illustrates how questioning can open a sequence and lead to further talk by the questioner, and it also demonstrates how questioning sequences can also serve as displays of knowledge. And although Ned may be resisting taking up the issue of racial bias in large clinical trials, Gwen's questions have clearly brought that problematic issue to the surface.

In other cases, questioning turns are not merely treated as potentially indicating problems with what has been said so far; questions are indeed responded to as challenges, with recipients producing accounts to defend their positions and/or proposals for solutions to a problem implicit in the question. In example (6), Jan has been outlining an aspect of the committee organization. The committee is divided into subgroups to follow up on particular plans or "initiatives," and Jan is asking that these subgroups choose leaders. In Beth's turn (line 4), she asks where the group she is in fits into the chart Jan has passed around. She draws attention to the fact that the evaluation and research group is missing from the table of subgroups, a lack that Jan interprets as a challenge. In the sequence that this question opens, Jan as well as others treat the question as having presented a problem they must respond to with an account or solution:

(6) [Diversity] Questioning as challenging and leading to accounts and solutions

1 Jan: [. . .] we'd like each of the groups to be coordinated by somebody in
2   the leadership team so that we can regularly get reports back on on how
3   these connections are going.
4⇒ Beth: Jan is the evaluation:, and research part under, just the committee
5   itself?
6   (.) *((J looks at sheet))*
7 Beth: down at the bottom,
8   (0.8)
9⇒ Jan: It's not really an initiative?
10⇒Beth: [Okay.
11⇒Jan: [we we-=that's why I kind of ended up taking it <u>out</u>. um (.) eh- and
12   maybe we just need a separate grouping or maybe it's overarching, I don't
13   know.
14   (.)
15 Beth: How about under, (.) <u>lack</u> of initiative. eh huh
16 Virg: uh huh [huh huh
17 Lenn: [eh hah
18⇒Jan: e(hh)'Cause it- it sort of pertains to everything in here, and the
19   evaluation team is going to have to have a connection with each of the
20   five leaders so that's why I left out, but then do you think it should be
21   on here.
22⇒Gwen: It sort of cuts across:
23   (.)
24⇒Gwen: We'll <u>think</u> about these.
25   (.)
26 Viv: ↑Maybe under the overarching, so that- questions like that,
27   [don't come up.
28 Jan: [Okay.
29 Jan: Okay.
30   (.)
31 Jan: *((writing))* @great.@

                                                    @ = creaky voice

Beth's question (lines 4–5) certainly displays that she is following what Jan is saying; she is onboard as she looks for where her group fits into Jan's request. However, it is not the knowledge Beth displays but the way her question becomes contextualized as a challenge that is of interest here. In line 9, Jan provides an initial account for why the research and evaluation group is missing; that group is not an "initiative," and the list includes initiatives. Jan produces this first account with rising intonation, appearing to be offering it as a candidate rationale. While Beth produces "okay," as an accepting action in her next turn (line 10), she is overlapped by Jan's continuing account for why the group is missing from the document (line 11). As Jan expands her turn in lines 12–13, she begins to explore a solution to what is now clearly treated as a problem rather than merely a question of information.

Jan suggests that they may need a "separate" or an "overarching" category for the missing group, and Beth responds with a joking turn, playing on the word "initiative." After a bit of laughter, Jan returns to her pursuit of a solution (lines 18–21), prefacing her return with a single breathy token of laughter—"e(hh)". At 22 and 24, Gwen joins in treating a solution as relevant, either right in the meeting or in the future: "It sort of cuts across:" and "We'll think about these." The deliberations end when Jan accepts Vivian's proposal that the group be included on the document as "overarching" (lines 26–31).

Example (6), then, presents another case of questioning leading to expansion, and it also provides a clear example of how a question can be interpreted as a challenge to an aspect of the talk so far. In the development of the sequence, over a number of turns and participants, we find specific actions: accounts and solutions. These responsive actions demonstrate that the questioning action here is interpreted as presenting a problem.

In another case, example (7), Pam's questioning is responded to as a challenge. John is the Dean of Applied Sciences and Charles is Associate Dean. Pam, a scientist and professor, is a member of another college. John has been reporting on an oversight plan he has personally instituted in his college. The plan is aimed at diversifying the pool of applicants for new faculty positions. Charles collaborates in describing John's new policy. In response to the report of the plan, Pam produces two questions, both of which address the timing of the plan, something Pam seems to think should be done differently. Pam's entry into participation is initiated by a *yes/no* question (line 9), and in the abstract, Pam's question might be presumed to be answerable by a simple *yes* or *no*. However, Pam's question is followed by delayed (so potentially dispreferred) responses from John and Charles. They treat

Pam's question as more than merely answerable with a *yes* or *no* (lines 12–15):

(7) [Diversity] Questioning as challenging and leading to expansion

```
1       John: ah to make sure that they've done a good job. of uh
2             selecting the poo:l.
3                (.)
4       John: And I'm going to (.) reject some on the fact that they
5                ↑haven't. done, that. if they can't convince me.
6       Jan: mm hm,
7       John: I'll °send it back.°
8       Jan: mm
9⇒      Pam: Is there anything you could do:, (.) a step sooner, than
10               tha:t,
11                  (1.3)
12      Charl: WEll our our [inten-
13      John:                 [Oh we're- they- our training is a step
14             sooner [is to show them how they get to the
15      Charl:        [Our our intention is to yeah=
16⇒     Pam: =That's maybe two steps sooner.
17                 (0.4)
18⇒     Pam: °Is° there something SOMewhere betwee:n (.) how they
19             ought to conduct the search, and the short list.
20      John: Oh [Oh yeah I'm sorry. Sure.
21        Charl: [Oh ye-
22⇒     Pam: There might be some- I'm tryin to think wher:e but
23             the- it's a very interesting idea,= ↑I thought of
24             doing that for the- high- high: b- high position, (.)
25             search committees,=I hadn't °thought of it in that.°
```

After a significant delay (line 11), itself a sign of potential trouble, Charles begins to provide an account of the intentions of the plan (line 12), and John joins in with a statement that counters the basis for Pam's question itself (lines 13–14). Whereas Pam has asked if the plan could involve "anything a step sooner," John insists, "our training is a step sooner." Pam responds to John with a further counter: her own insistence that his training plan is "two steps sooner" rather than one step sooner (line 16). The sequence thus far includes a question, a counter by the question recipient (John), and a further counter, a kind of other correction by Pam; the potential challenging force of Pam's question is reinforced by the successive counters.

In lines 18–19 Pam restates and clarifies her question, now succeeding in pointing to the missing "step" in the dean's plan as one
"Somewhere between." To this both the deans respond by acknowledging their revised understanding, lines 20–1 (e.g., the "change of
state token," *oh* [Heritage, 1984a]). Pam continues her expansion by
presenting her own previous and independent thinking about the
training of search committees (lines 23–5). In this segment of the
expansion, Pam harvests the fruit of a sequence she set in motion
through her questioning turns. One feature of Pam's original question
is that it is first presented in a minimal and unelaborated form. As we
will see again in excerpt (10) and the discussion that follows, it may
be a feature of challenging questions that they are not specific as to
the nature of the challenge. In the present case, as Pam presents the
background to her question (lines 23–5), she appears to be more interested in getting ideas from and with the deans than in calling into
question their plan. Nevertheless, her questioning has been treated as
a challenge, at least initially, and she has succeeded in initiating an
expanded sequence in which she has the opportunity to elaborate her
thoughts.

Questioning as challenging is further illustrated in example (8),
where another question from Pam leads to expansion, this time by
Jan and Beth. While Pam does later explicate her stand, the expansion
leading to the points she makes from lines 33–53 is initiated by her
questioning turn, an understanding check at lines 11–12. Jan is pro-
posing a plan to use a survey of workplace climate that the committee has just conducted, but to use it for a different group and for a
different purpose. She would like to see how the deans, a small and
elite group in the institution, would respond to the climate questions.
The plan is that, after the deans respond, Jan would compare their
responses to the responses of other staff members, using this as an
opportunity to raise awareness of differing experiences of workplace
climate:

(8) [Diversity] Questioning, challenging, expanding

6   Jan: . . . we'd like to go to one of the deans meetings and, do the same set
7   of questions with the <u>deans</u>, and then, Jim has a way of (.)
8   pro<u>jec</u>ting the, um, at the e- at the very end, after <u>all</u> the questions,
9   projecting both sets of data, the data we generate <u>that</u> day with the
10   <u>deans</u>, and then the data that we've °uh° [generated °(before)°
11⇒Pam: [**(Is it) using the ex<u>act</u> <u>same</u>**

12   **questions?**
13   Jan:°Ye(h)ah.° *((vertical head movement; gaze toward Pam))*
14   (.)
16   Jan: I mean, some things won't apply perfectly, bu[t
17   Beth: [>It'd be interesting,<
18   °(>ya know<)°? Well, >I mean< (another) even °the general observation
19   (that)° we don't have that (any) male responses of of how gender ih-
20   (.) issues (.) figure in your [work life, (then we can't getting that=
21   Jan: [um hm
22   Beth: =be very).
23   Jan: Yeah.
24   Beth: (Interes[ting)
25   Jan: [>Yeah<,(.)or, y'know the- I- one >of the things< that struck
26   me in both, um, sessions was the pessimism about the climate. And I
27   would bet most of the dea:ns just think that climate's gonna get better
28   in the future, and I think more than half of our respondents said that it
29   would (either) get worse, or stay the same. so, yeah, I'm sure there'll
30   be some interesting (.) °out[comes.°
31   Pam: [*((Pam raises hand))*
32   Jan: yeah,?=
33⇒**Pam**: =**Yeah, one thing that- (.) I think is:, (.) that I've come to**
34   **appreciate a great deal, >(just)< even recently, (.) is: (.) getting (.)**
35   **if not an equal number of responses from males, certainly a substantial**
36   **°number,°=**
37   Jan: =°um hm°
38   (0.8)
39⇒**Pam: And I don't think that they::, (.) that- getting responses from-**
40   **(.) deans, who are male, is going to be quite the same as getting**
41   **responses from people in the ranks, who are (.) male, and it would be**
42   **very good at some point to do this. (.) to do this °for men.°**
43   (0.3)
44   Jan: Yeah, one of the things that I think, [(.)tha- the purpose of the deans
45   Pam: [( )
46   Jan: is more >just< to share with them, what we've lear:ned,
47   and [I think
48   **Pam: [°(Yeah.)°**
49   Jan: that people are more interested in data than had th- (.) answer the
50   same questions [themselves, (so in that eventual)
51⇒**Pam: [(I agree), THA- THAT'S NEAT, I think it's a neat**
53   **thing to do:, but it's (.)ah- we do need something from men.**

In Pam's question (lines 11–12), she checks her understanding of Jan's reference (lines 6–7) to "the same set of questions." Pam asks if the survey questions will be exactly the same when they are presented to a very different group. Jan offers an affirmative response, after which there is a brief pause. Treating the pause as indicating a need for further accounting, Jan expands with a concession that displays her understanding of the potential challenge in Pam's question, "I mean, some things won't apply perfectly, bu[t." In other words, Jan's expansion demonstrates that she takes Pam's question not merely as a neutral inquiry but as pointing to a problem with using the same survey items with a group for whom they were not designed.

At line 17, Beth joins in on Jan's behalf, overlapping with Jan's prosodically trailing off "but" (line 17) (Local and Kelly, 1986; Local and Walker, 2005). In her response Beth attempts to support the idea of using the same survey items on men, noting that at the time they have no males in their sample and that including males could be "interesting." Jan goes on to explain why she is interested in giving the survey to the deans. The women faculty and staff members who have responded have been pessimistic about the likelihood of improvement in climate, whereas she expects the deans (at that time all men) would respond more optimistically.

Both Jan and Beth orient to Pam's question as a challenge to the validity of the plan. Both treat Pam as the recipient of their talk, and as Jan articulates her reasons for wanting to try the plan, she looks directly at Pam. When Jan nears a possible completion of her extended turn (in lines 29–30), Pam raises her hand and is recognized to speak again:

(9)

⇒Pam: =Yeah, one thing that- (.) I think is:, (.) that I've come to appreciate a
      great deal, >(just)< even recently, (.) is: (.) getting (.) if not an equal number
      of responses from males, certainly a substantial °number,°=

Jan: =°um hm°

       (0.8)

⇒Pam: And I don't think that they::, (.) that- getting responses from- (.) <u>deans</u>,
      who are male, is going to be quite the same as getting responses from people
      in the ranks, who are (.) male, and it would be very good at some point to do
      this. (.) to do this °for men.°

That Jan has continued to gaze toward Pam during her response and that Pam does indeed speak again both support the observation that questioning can serve as a way into further participation, as I have been suggesting. Furthermore, as Pam takes her turn and expands her contribution, she confirms what Jan and Beth have already understood: that she has a particular position on the issue at hand. However, Pam's problem is not with surveying men. The problem she elaborates is that the deans will not be the ideal group of men to sample. Beth and Jan were accurate, then, in interpreting Pam's initial question as a challenge, but they were not on the mark regarding exactly what Pam was challenging. It could be that initial questions in this sort of challenge sequence project expansion in a next turn but do not provide more than that projection; that is, they do not specify the nature of the challenge. Recipients, nevertheless, address possible grounds for a challenge.

With respect to the challenges inherent in some questioning actions, we can also find questioning turns accompanied by accounts themselves. These are cases in which the questioner produces an additional turn component, after the question, with the addition being support for the argument or stand implied by the question. Examples (9) and (10) are such cases.

Just before the segment in (9), a member of the committee has proposed that readings relevant to their shared work be put on a website as pdf files. As the turn begins, Flor and Gwen both produce positive assessments of the idea, but at line 4, Jan asks, "Is that legal?" While this question alone could be taken as a challenge, Jan moves rapidly into a second unit to her turn, a unit introduced with the connector, "cause"; this addition adds support to what can be now seen as the stand or argument implied by the first unit of her turn, i.e., that putting pdfs on the website may be illegal. As the sequence initiated by Jan's question is expanded, we find Mary and Wendy joining in to support the legality of putting library materials on the web, and Jan also speaks again. In line 13, Jan produces a turn that is a syntactic continuation of Mary's turn at 10–11. Jan begins with "Even though," extending her challenge, and she completes that turn with the rising intonation of a *yes/no* question:

(10) Questioning plus supporting for an argument in a single turn

```
1      Flor:    I like that idea, (.) >of<- (.) putting pee dee ef [=pdf] documents
2               on the website, so people can have access °to them.°
3      Gwen:  That's a great ide [a.
4⇒    Jan:                          [Is that legal?>Cause I just heard that when you
5               p:ut pdf- (.) documents of- published papers on your website, it's:
6               (.) copyright- infringement
7      Mary:   If the library owns it,
8               (.)
```

9   Mary: it's legal.
10   Mary: So as I understand it.>if the university library system owns a copy
11   of it, it's fine.
12   (.)
13⇒   Jan: Even though: (.) then anyone has access to it, because the website's
14   [public?=
15   Mary: [mm hm.=
16   Wendy: =Anyone can come in the library and check it out.=
17   Mary:=Yeah.
18   Wendy: That's- I was on the- university library committee last year and-
19   and that was my understanding.

In (10), then, the challenging force of a question is confirmed in the same turn as the question, as the questioner adds support to what must be understood as an argument rather than a simple *yes/no* question.

The fragments in example (11) also illustrate the dual functions and potential hybrid nature of questioning. This is part of a much longer discussion of a workshop format that two visitors to the Diversity Committee are offering to help the committee conduct. Maureen has been describing a pair activity that would be part of the planned event. I present only a bit of context and I have also deleted most of the responses. What is included are two turns by Marge, both of which combine functions of questioning and challenging:

(11)

1   *((Marge raises hand))*
2   **Gwen:** °Marge°?
3⇒   **Marge:** Could you tell us a bit more what- after they jus- had their
4   paired discussions, (.) what do ↑you- what do you end up with.
       // **[Maureen describes a process of writing down the group's ideas]** //
17⇒ **Marge:** But it se̲e̲ms to me, that we have a hundred an fifty, (0.8) (h)how
18   do you get everybody's ideas up there.

In lines 3–4, Marge begins with a request for elaboration, "Could you tell us a bit . . .," but she inserts an adverbial clause ("after . . ."). When she continues after that insertion, her request is in a different form, one that seems to challenge the process by questioning what it will lead to (line 4, "what do you end up with"). Maureen's response (not reproduced here) comes across as merely explaining rather than defending against the challenge, but at line 17, Marge takes a further turn in the sequence. Here she begins an observation, formulated declaratively, but she pauses before its completion. When she starts again, she produces another interrogative clause, and, like her question in line 4, this seems to imply incredulity: "<u>how</u> do you get everybody's ideas up there."

The formulation of turns in examples (10) and (11) further evidence that questioning can also serve as challenging. In these cases, however, it is not through the responses to the questions or through their expansion by the questioner that we first recognize their challenging function. In these cases, the questioning turns already reveal that they contain arguments or stands. Comparing Marge's questions with Jan's (in example [10]), we see that, although Marge does not add supporting clauses, as does Jan in lines 4–6 and 13–14 of (10), Marge reveals the challenging force of her turns in the ways she produces repairs. In lines 3–4, her repair changes what looks like a polite request into a question that implies a problem with what the pair work will "end up with." In lines 17–18, she moves from an assertion regarding the large size of the group to another question indexing a problem with managing "everybody's ideas"—all the ideas that are generated in the many pairs in the exercise. So we can see that it is not just in their expansions that questioners compose, reveal, and elaborate their challenges; there are also challenge-displaying features in the composition of the questioning turns themselves.

This section has provided cases of questioning turns that in themselves display knowledge and enact challenges. We have also examined how the responses that these questions receive and the expansions added by the questioner display an understanding of questioning as challenging. Thus, in addition to providing a way into participation for the women in these meetings, their questioning turns also enact the relatively powerful acts of showing expertise and of challenging one's co-participants. In the final section of the chapter, we see how questioning may lead not only to expanded participation by the questioner, but that it can also open participation opportunities for others.

Opening space for others to participate

As we have seen in the cases so far, the person who initiates a questioning sequence regularly uses a subsequent turn to either accept the answer or to expand upon the question and on any challenge it may imply. But participants other than the questioner may also join in the sequence. This is a further way in which questioning shifts participation. We can see this in cases from the previous section, such as (8), where Beth joins in defending Jan, and (10), where Mary and Wendy respond to Jan's questions. Some of the other question-initiated sequences above were expanded by further comments or questions by other participants. For example, the questioning sequence initiated by Jill's question in (4), is expanded when Beth, a pharmacologist, adds to Ned's response (see Chapter 4, example [12]), and then Xavier asks a further question. Thus, although there is a tendency for the original questioner to be the participant who elaborates on issues raised and who ultimately acknowledges the response, it is also common for other participants to expand on issues touched off by the question. In other words, the questioning action can open space for participation beyond the talk of the questioner.

This is true in the next example, where Virginia does a questioning action, and she also expands a bit, but others take leading roles in further expanding the sequence her question initiates. Example (12) demonstrates that questioning can shift the dynamics of participation such that participants other than the questioner can be provided with opportunities to speak, but, as we will see, it also underscores the relevance of a third action by the original questioning participant, a recognition of the three-part action sequence.

In example (12), the discussion of putting articles on the web is closing (see example [10]). Virginia takes the opportunity to introduce another issue; at arrow 1 she expresses confusion about the committee's charge. Gwen's response at arrow 2 is non-serious, as what she points to as the committee's accomplishment is minimal; but Virginia does not reciprocate Gwen's laughter. At arrow 3, Virginia further elaborates her question, and from that point on a multiparticipant sequence develops; during a span of one minute and 20 seconds Virginia does not speak again, though it is the sequence she initiated that is expanded. This is a case in which one participant's questioning action opens a space for other participants to contribute:

(12) One person's question opens a sequence which others expand

> Wendy: It's called a fair use doctrine.
>   (1.0)
> Jan: Yeah I'll get a copy of it cause it was actually a case so: we might
>   wanna just look at it. (   )
>   (2.2) ((*V raises hand*))

1⇒ Virg: **One other just question about how we're organizing**. .h There
        was that matrix of: who was gonna do what, and now there's this
        new group or whatever. (.) and eh- I've had some questions about

like- (.) What is the committee actually doing, and I keep telling
people that (we) only started a month ago, so huh but

2⇒ Gwen: We nominated Heddy Sade. eh heh

Virg: Right exactly.=

Gwen:=uh huh huh

3⇒ Virg: **But ih- I- I guess I- just wanna know kind of what's the**
procedure by which these different groups or tasks or whatever
will actually ge:t (.) charged to go: >do something.<
(1.2)

Pam: Make them write their own charges.
(0.7)

Gwen: We'll yeah uhm (.) *((looks toward Jan))* Well you >we're< getting
there, do you wanna say (   )

Jan: Well once: w:e have people who are gonna head them all, (I mean)
one possibility would be to have the group leaders meet, (.) and talk
about what kind of process >they'd each like to use<

// [. . . 1 minute 20 seconds of people other than Virginia talking. . .] //

Jan: Uh but then we can also bring it back to the leadership team, and
talk about it there, (.)and I agree with Pam, I think ultimately
we have to have some discussion of having each one write their
own charge.
(1.0)

Pam: That's what I'm trying to do on the Recreation Board, (.) Trying to
figure out what it's about.

Gwen: mm hm

Jan: mm hm.

Pam: They've never had a charge (   )

Gwen: eh heh

Jerry: huh
(4.7)

4⇒ Gwen: *((facing toward Virginia))* **So did you [get your question ans-**

5⇒ Virginia: [*((multiple head nods))*

6⇒ Gwen: **I think once there's a leader, once they [(.) know they**=

7⇒ Virginia: [**Yeah.**

Gwen: =**ya know (.)write they'll write it's charge,**

After a substantial expansion on the question of subgroup charges,
Gwen turns toward Virginia and asks whether Virginia's original question has been answered (arrow 4). At arrows 5 and 7, Virginia produces
minimal affirmative response tokens, first non-vocal and then vocal.
In addition to illustrating a shift in participation dynamics—the

opening up of space for other—, (12) also offers evidence for the continuing relevance of the three-part action sequence—question-response-
acknowledgement/elaboration.

In the next case, from the church staff meeting, we see an issue first
introduced by one member of the staff and later elaborated by a second
participant. The question is first treated as an understanding check, but
later, when it is reformulated by a different participant, its challenging
import is taken up.[5]

Paula, the administrator for St. Barnabas, handles the overall calendar
of events. At this moment she is reading aloud from the master calendar.
At line 1, she voices confusion about one entry, and the rector, Flo,
responds by reading it aloud, "Pack five forty? It sounds like boy scouts."
With the identification shared, Paula asks the potentially challenging
question, "Do we allow boy scouts?" The relevant background here is
that there has just been a legal judgment (at the federal level) allowing
the Boy Scouts of America to discriminate against gay Scout leaders.

(13) [Church] Paula initiates a questioning challenge; Karin reasserts the
challenge

```
1   Paula: An' now I see something that I don't understand here. .hhh
2   Flo:   ((looking at Pam's calendar)) Pack five forty? °It° sounds like
3          boy scouts.
4          (0.3)
5 Paula: Do we allow boy scouts? Eh(h) Heh heh heh heh
6          (1.0)
7          .hhh uh [heh .hhh
8   Flo:          [Resurec-*
9   Paula: Right.
10  Flo:   I think it's cub scouts.
11         (1.2)
12  Paula: Hmm.
13         (1.7)
14  Flo:   I bet (.) Mrs. Jim Daniels** has got herself a scout troop.=
15  Paula: =U:hm ° umm.° °okay.° mm[m
16  Flo:                          [What do you bet.
17  Paula: °eh heh° huh huh you didn't mention that one to me on the phone.
18         (0.5)
19  Flo:   .hh I: didn't hear. This's the first time I heard of it.
20         (1.8)
22⇒Karin: Girl scouts or boy scouts.
23  Flo:   Pack.=
```

24 Paula: =Packs are <u>boys</u>.
25   (0.8)
26⇒**Karin: Are you gonna let 'em <u>have</u> (.) are you**
27   g[onna <u>let</u> them <u>have</u> uhm (0.2) <u>boy</u> scouts=
28 Paula: [> °That's what I was gonna say.°<] *((turning towards Flo))*
29 Karin: =**in your <u>church</u>?**
30   (4.0)
31 Karin: You know tha[t's ha- it's happening,
32 Flo: [Oo:::::::::::::::::::::::hh
33 Kari: [that tha[t that people are saying people are=
34 Flo: [°My::::::::: °
        // [[**discussion of allowing boy scouts to use the church continues**] //]

        *Church of the Resurrection uses the facility of St. Barnabas.
        **Jim Daniels leads that congregation.

Though Paula stresses the word "allow" (line 5), she also follows her question with laughter tokens, potentially undermining the seriousness of the challenge. In responding (lines 8, 10, 14, 16, 19, and 23), Flo does not immediately register that having Boy Scouts meet at St. Barnabas may violate principles of openness and diversity that the church works to represent. Though the discrimination issue is very topical in the media at the time of this meeting, no one has yet explicitly connected the discrimination issue with the Boy Scouts. It is not until after Karin's turn at 26–7 and 29 (with no laughter tokens) that Flo registers the problem. As we have noted, in this case, it is only when the question is redone by another participant that the pastor finally gets the implication of the question.

The discussion of whether to allow the Scouts continues for a number of further turns, including talk by Paula, Karin, and Richard. While more could be said about Flo's other repair (line 10) and the way that action displaces the relevance of a response to Paula's question at line 5, what we can take away for the purposes of this section is that questioning, in this case two questions, can open space for others to come in. Here, and in other cases, the full expansion is done collaboratively with other participants building on and responding to the challenge implicit in the question.

Conclusion: questioning as opening participation, displaying expertise, and challenging

By questioning, women in these meetings could simply initiate two-part sequences, that is, adjacency pairs, the most basic structure of collaborative action in conversation. That is, viewed in terms of immediate turn-taking consequences, questioning actions hand the floor to another speaker, the recipient, for response. On the face of it, then, the questioner might appear to present herself as uninformed and needing to enlist the help of the recipient, putting the recipient in a "one up" position. However, analysis of the current meeting interactions has revealed other ways that questioning functions, including new perspectives on the work of such actions to position participants and to expand opportunities for participation.

Questioning, as a sequence-initiating action, opens opportunities for talk by the same participant and/or by others who have not been speaking in the most recent interactional context. While the additional opportunity for the questioner to speak is sometimes used only minimally, it is most common for at least a three-part sequence to emerge: a question, a response, and a minimal third turn of acceptance (vocal or non-vocal).

Looking closely at how questioning turns open participation opportunities for others has also led to observations regarding other significant actions that may be combined with questioning. Specifically, question actions may be vehicles for displaying expertise. Knowledge in itself is considered a source of power in these workplaces from the perspectives of the women I interviewed; but in the interaction, we can find evidence of a further kind of power enacted through questioning.

In addition to projecting further slots for speaking, and beyond the display of expertise, questions can challenge. Examining the talk of the recipients of questioning turns, we find evidence that they recognize the challenges implicit in questions. Recipients produce accounts, rationales, and other defensive actions. And, in questioning turns themselves, we find other moves such as accounts that index the taking a stand or presenting argument in the questioning action. With respect, then, to women's discursive agency, we find that the women in these meetings are treated as consequential, individuals whose expertise and whose challenges warrant and receive serious responses and expansions.

In the next chapter we look closely at the work of two women as they take issue with the ideas of other participants. The formulation of these two extended turns involves particular care and persistence, and a detailed examination of the interactional dynamics that these women manage offers further evidence of women's competence in doing disaffiliative actions, even in the face of potentially disruptive talk by high-ranking recipients.

6
Placing and Designing Disaffiliative Actions

While it is clear from excerpts in Chapter 5 that women are perfectly able to produce questions that challenge co-participants, we should note that taking issue with others' ideas is a delicate and disaffiliative action, as has been amply demonstrated in studies of ordinary conversations. Disaffiliative actions are regularly formulated with care: they are delayed, prefaced, and interwoven with displays of hesitancy. Once launched, such turns are formulated in ways that further delay and also mitigate the disaffiliative action itself. Disaffiliative actions are regularly accompanied by accounting, with such accounts or excuses indexing a speaker's recognition of deviation from the normative preference for agreement (Sacks, 1987; Pomerantz, 1984). That delicate and dispreferred actions are presented with care is one way in which interactants display the general orientation to avoid such actions. But, of course, disaffiliative actions cannot be avoided altogether, particularly in workplace meetings.

The meetings taped for this study were task-based encounters in which participants arrived at decisions and agreements on shared understandings of the shape of future action (Huisman, 2001:70). The outcomes of meetings directly affect the worklives of meeting members. Thus, when the plans in question were consequential for any individual, it was in that person's interest to raise questions, voice objections, and to offer revisions or counter proposals—all less than affiliative actions in that they entail treatment of what others have said as deficient and needing to be revised or corrected.

The current chapter examines in detail how two different women successfully initiate and expand turns that deliver disaffiliative actions.[1] We look specifically at how these women carefully design turns that point to shortcomings in the proposals of previous speakers, and we analyze how these women manage potentially disruptive recipient responses. This fine-grained analysis of one continuous span of talk supports understanding of the local and contingently adapted work of meeting participants as they formulate such actions. Attending to the position and composition of each turn offers a detailed picture of the interactional work involved in taking issue with other participants' ideas, ideas originally put forward and agreed upon by high-ranking members of the group. The close analysis presented here also provides evidence that in meeting interaction, as in ordinary talk, pauses, hesitations, repairs, overlaps, and other apparent hitches in turn delivery should not be understood as faulty articulation but as skillful means of formulating particular actions in particular unfolding interactional contexts. This final analytic chapter further evidences women's competence in contributing to workplace interactions; and more generally, this detailed analysis provides new insights into practices for raising problematic issues, producing extended turns, and managing competing talk.

Analyzing a single segment

Continuing to draw on basic conversation analytic methods, we now look more closely at turn and sequence organization in a single segment from a meeting of the Diversity Committee. In this span, Stephie and Mary voice ideas clearly bearing on the committee's charge: the advancement of underrepresented groups in the institution. The themes of Stephie's and Mary's contributions are particularly relevant to the topic at hand: plans for supporting searches for more diverse applicants for new positions at their university. At the same time, both women's actions are potentially face-threatening and disaffiliative in relation to previously agreed upon plans by high-ranking members of the committee.[2] Each woman addresses deficiencies with what has been discussed so far regarding the purpose and scope of a plan for supporting more diversified hiring practices.

Looking at these two contributions within one span of talk recommends itself on methodological grounds, as it imposes a degree of control on who the participants are in the meeting, and, in these instances, it is the same particular participants that each woman's disaffiliative action addresses. Both women are taking issue with aspects of a plan the committee chair and the deans of the College of Applied Sciences (CAS) have just outlined and agreed upon. Both women gaze more frequently toward the deans than toward other committee members, with both this non-vocal pattern and the topic of the turns placing the deans in positions to acknowledge or otherwise respond to the womens' actions.

The deans do indeed respond vocally and non-vocally to Stephie's and Mary's contributions at possible completion points in their turns.

In what senses are Stephie's and Mary's turns interpretable as disaffiliative with previous talk? The fact that Stephie and Mary raise concerns that have not yet been addressed by the participants in a lengthy discussion can, in itself, be taken as problematic, particularly given that the previous agenda item is being treated as coming to an end. The issues raised by Stephie and Mary, though clearly relevant, might not have been aired in this meeting were Stephie not to use the potential closing of the discussion as a point to intervene and initiate further elaboration.

Just prior to the focal contributions, there has been a seven-minute interchange, primarily between the chair, Jan, the CAS dean, John, and the CAS associate dean, Charles. This has resulted in an agreement between the three to collaborate in designing anti-bias workshops for committees charged with selecting candidates for new positions at the university (referred to as "search committees" for "new hires"). With no further comments from others in the meeting, Jan begins to close the discussion and to make moves toward opening another. Stephie initiates a turn just at that moment (line 4, example [1], below). Stephie's ultimate action is to urge the group—though she is specifically addressing the deans—to take a "broader" approach to diversifying hiring practices than what has been proposed so far (lines 38–40):

(1) Stephie's plea (intervening talk is here deleted, but discussed later)

1   Jan: .Summer (scheme), anyway. [(.) It'll be fun to work ou:t, I think.
2   Jan: [((*nods, gazes at & turns over notes*))
3   (0.6)
4⟹ Steph: [.hh Can I make a- (.) brief comment on tha:t,
            // [. . . .] //
34   .hh (.) I think what we wanna-(.) do:, the issue here is:
35   is: (.) locating a good poo:l. and .h (.) uh: (.) and insuring
36   that we've at least eh uh stimulated. (.) interest in the school,
37   >even if we haven't gotten a hire out of a pool,
38⟹   .h An' the- **so I- I guess I want- wanna eh make a plea: for a**
39⟹   **broader approach to searching, than once the committee is**
40⟹   **formed.**

Stephie's plea comes after she first develops background through a long set of preliminaries to her plea. Her reference to a "broader approach" contrasts with the approaches proposed by Jan and the deans, whose current plans is to limit anti-bias education to a point after specific search committees have been formed.

Mary's turn follows the deans' responses to Stephie. In her turn, Mary ties back to previous mentions by both deans of a "two year" period after new faculty are hired, but before they arrive at the university to begin their appointments. Notably, the deans have referred to the "two years" as a time for new hires to establish their research agendas and laboratories so that they will be competitively positioned for continuing productivity right when they arrive at the university. In Mary's turn, she specifically reminds the deans that diversity in hiring practices needs to involve attention not only to the research competitiveness of new faculty but also to the needs of their families, which may include another career as well as childcare challenges:

(2) Mary's reminder. John=Dean of CAS; Charles=Associate Dean of CAS

83 Mary: [. . .] **the two years**
84   **would (.) enable you >not only >>then<< to set up< a la:b,**
85   **but to find (.) possible dual- dual career po[sitions:.**
86 Vivian: [₀(I see)₀
87   ₀Dual careers are huge.₀
88 Mary: **Or [childcare,**
89 John: [Oh: y[es.
90 Charl: [Yep. Yep
91 Mary: **Uhm but that's probably [obvious (and)**
92 John: [and and
93 Mary: **Maybe not.** *((quick smile toward John))*
94 John: THAT by the way=
95 Mary: = > **AN' AND OF COURSE THAT<** (0.5) **bmuh increases rates to**
96   **tenure, [₀as well.₀**

The deans did not refer to the needs of dual career couples and persons with children, nor the effects of attention to such needs on the likelihood of success in the tenure process. As is true with most research universities in North America, this institution has not traditionally attended to family concerns in the hiring process, though policies are on the books in favor of such attention. Difficulty with partner hires and childcare are major obstacles to faculty hiring and retention.

Thus, the contributions of Stephie and Mary have in common that they introduce considerations that have been missing in the previous discussion. Also common to the turns of both women, though with differences in degree and length, is that at least one of the deans speaks during what each woman ultimately treats as the continuing course of her turn. By extending her talk beyond the deans' responses, each woman treats the deans' talk as occurring within rather than at the end of her contribution. Stephie and Mary use different practices to construct and extend their turns, but each deals artfully with the deans' interventions, and each succeeds in expanding her turn.

In the remainder of this chapter, I first give an overview of the meeting and the segment in which both turns are embedded, including a summary of the topic and actions so far. This sketch of the talk leading up to the focal segment offers a sense of the work Stephie and Mary may need to do to articulate their concerns in a manner adapted to the local dynamics of the prior, present, and unfolding context. I then consider each woman's contribution in some detail, drawing attention to how she places her action relative to the talk so far; how she shapes the early parts of her turn such that she is able to incorporate possible perspectives of her recipients and thereby show a degree of deference toward them; and how she manages to extend her talk beyond the responses from her recipients. I also consider the uptake each turn receives.

Close attention to a single segment serves to deepen our sense of the contingent and locally managed nature of turn organization in real-time interaction in meetings, and the cases analyzed further evidence the skillful work women in these data do as they contribute to meetings.

Previous talk: plans for anti-bias workshops

As background, let me review the talk leading up to the focal segment, highlighting points that are explicitly taken up and addressed by Stephie and Mary. The major contributors to the discussion have been Jan, the committee chair and professor of microbiology, John, the Dean of the College of Applied Sciences (CAS), and Charles, the Associate Dean of CAS. Stephie is a professor in a department within CAS and is thus answerable to these deans. Jan is a faculty member in another college in the sciences. Mary is an assistant professor in a social science department, placing her outside the physical and biological sciences. The fact that she is of a different academic background than the other participants is relevant to how she frames her contribution, and two members of this committee, also from social sciences, reported in my interviews that they perceived a bias in the way their ideas were treated relative to others from science departments.

The talk revolves around plans to increase the number of persons hired who are from underrepresented groups. The problem, well recognized by Jan and the deans, is that white men continue to be overrepresented among new faculty hires, particularly, though not exclusively, in the sciences. Working from an agenda sheet and notes on the table in front of her, Jan has been reporting what she learned at a recent symposium on the advancement of women in professional workplaces. For Jan, the highpoint of the symposium was Virginia Valian's presentation on "gender schemas" (Valian, 1998). Jan was impressed by the "neutral feel" of Valian's review of experiments on gender biases:

(3) Jan on the power of Virginia Valian's presentation

   Jan: The power of what she does (.) is that she she talks entirely from data. She
         talks from from really good experiments that look at the way people perceive
         men and women. (.) and it's- it has a very neutral feel, (.) a lot of that's
         because both men and women have the same prejudices, about men and
         women, and so it's not a finger pointing men are bad, or, men hate us, or
         anything like that, it's just (.) we've all grown up with these gender schemas,
         and, we expect certain things, we believe certain things, and very often, our
         stereotypes play out, there's a reason that stereotypes exist. But they also
         block the advancement of people, in certain situations,
                    //   [. . . . .]   //
         People rea:d, men's and women's C Vs. an' ... the sa:me, information, on a C
         V, that has a man's name at the to:p or a woman's name at the to:p, has a
         very different on- th- on (   ). (.) Something that can help men, (.) or raise
         the potential salary for men, can actually be a detriment, for women. (.) An'
         she had >like< data after data example after example. And, it gave me some
         (.) really, I-I think some, um, (.) somewhat new ideas about how we should
         be (.) approaching the issues and training people in the issues, an' I think by
         bringing more of the da:ta, into it, (.) we may be able to make some more gains.

Jan goes on to add what she frames as a "small digression," a plan that turns out to be of considerable interest to the group and which occupies the discussion for several minutes. This idea leads to a joint plan, and it becomes the target of the additional contributions of Stephie and Mary:

(4)

   Jan: so that led to the idea of maybe, an' this is just a s:mall digression,
         developing a plan, for training search committee chairs, which was

something that Maya Read, has been working on anyway, but bringing in some of the recognition, of these issues, to the chairs, so that i-if you become a little bit aware of these issues, maybe you can sort of fight against those prejudices, an' an' an' then accountability [. . .] So I'm gonna work with Maya on that this summer.

Jan also shares her idea of studying the effectiveness of the training program by creating control and variable groups. Half the search committee chairs would receive training and half would not. As she details her proposal, John produces non-vocal displays of heightened interest: he leans forward, placing his arms on the table; he smiles two times, and he looks toward Charles, his associate dean, at two points (see discussion of non-vocal cues to incipient speakership, Chapter [4]). Another administrator, Ingrid, is seated to John's left, and she takes note of John's movements. Ingrid works closely with deans and has special access to shared information from earlier interactions with John as she demonstrates at lines 10–11. She turns toward John and offers an interpretation of his non-vocal actions:

(5)

```
 1 Jan: I think it'd be a- an °interesting experiment,°
 2      (3.4)
 3 Viv: °Nice.°
 4      (1.4)
 5 Jan: °so°.
 6      (1.4)
 7 Jan: SO THAT was a: (.) °wht- kinda° just [ta
 8 Viv:                                       [°What
 9      comes (of it may be) other things, but°
10⇒Ingr: ((gazes toward John)) You need uh all of yours,
11      [in the non-cont(h)rol gr(h)oup, ri(h)ght?=
12 John: [Ye- Your idea to get this study
13 Ingr: =[eh heh heh eh heh heh
14⇒John: [I want mine in the non-control group.
15⇒John: Could I [have'em all in the-in the non-control group.
16 Jan:         [uh huh hah hah hah
17 Ingr: hah hah
18 Char: I don'-I don't think we're gonna- we're gonna wait to be the control
19      gro[up.
```

Ingrid's turn (lines 10–11) acts as a prompt for confirmation by John,[3] and indeed both John and Charles produce confirming actions (lines

14, 15, 18–19). John introduces an elaboration on the plans he and Charles have for search committees in their college:

(6)

20 Ingrid: Uh heh heh
21 John: **No [the the uh yeah**
22 Ingr: [uh heh heh uh .hh
23⇒John: **Let me comment on that. because [we're actually putting=**
24 Jan: [okay:.
25 John: **=together, (.) training for all the search committees.**
26   **[We're going to go through this kind of training for all:=**
27 Jan: [°oh.°
28 John: **=search committees, uh in the college of °next year°?**
29 Jan: mm hm,
30 John: **And then I am going to uh (.) have them meet with the equity and**
31   **diversity committee, and then after they come up with their short**
32   **list, I'm going to revie:w the short list,**
33 Jan: °mm hm.°
34 John: **ah to make sure that they've done a good job. of uh selecting the**
35   **poo:l. (.) And I'm going to (.) reject some on the fact that they**
36   **↑haven't. done, that. if they can't convince me.**
37 Jan: mm hm,
38 John: **I'll °send it back.°**

It is to the deans' and Jan's plans to give anti-bias workshops to hiring committees that Stephie ultimately responds with her plea for a broader approach.

A further element of John and Charles' plan for diversifying new faculty hires involves targeting job candidates whom they believe need more experience before taking faculty positions in CAS. As a way of insuring that the new hires get "seasoning" (John's term) before starting their new positions, John is devising a model through which the new hire is offered a position at the university but is encouraged to first take a two-year post-doctoral fellowship at another institution in order to be more productive and competitive in research before starting to work at John's college:

(7)

Char: maybe searching now constitutes something different, it's: uh finding uh new
        P-H-Ds who are willing to accept an offer, (.) but wanna do a two year post doc.
        (.) [You'd say fine. =We'll wait.<

Jan: [mm hm
              (1.0)
Char: So a little bit of this is not necessarily have the center of the
         activity is to (.) also get groups to think differently about
              [what it means to search.
Pam: [Tell the rest of us about it, please.
              (.)
John: Okay. hhh.hh yeah well, he's >commenting< about the post doc< I'm
         actually pushing uh I've seen some- several candidates that- look like
         potential to really be (.) be really good. But they look like they need a little
         bit more, (.) ↑seasoning, frankly. (.) So I- you would like to see them (get a
         po-) you know you'd like to make them an offer. (and set up thi-) Take a
         p<u>o</u>st do:c, (.) [get a
Char: [We- We'll wait two years,
John: Gu- ga- yeah go some- (an then I can) recommend places to go ↑w<u>o</u>rk, and
         then (.) by the time you show up h<u>e</u>re, we want you to have ordered all your
         equipment, your lab should be ready to go so you won't miss a- you don't
         miss a beat or anything like that in the w<u>o</u>rk.

John describes the post-doctoral position, the "two years," as a time for
the junior scholar to become more experienced in research and also a
time for the new hire to coordinate with the university in setting up a
lab. As articulated by John, the value of this two-year period is that it
allows new faculty members to arrive at this university and not "miss
a beat" in establishing their research agenda and academic productivity. No attention is drawn to potential needs of domestic partners of
new hires or their childrearing responsibilities. In Mary's later
contribution, she points to these non-traditional needs that should
also be addressed in the two-year period the deans have proposed.
  As John and Charles describe the plan for their college, Jan proposes
that she coordinate with them on a combined plan aimed not only at
committee chairs but at all members of search committees. After about
seven minutes of talk about educating search committees, Jan moves
to close the discussion. She does so with familiar summative actions:
she restates the importance and value of training search committees
and then refers back to the agreement to work with the deans to come
up with a coordinated plan. She continues to contextualize the topic
as nearing a close with her assessment of what they will jointly do,
"It'll be fun to work out," and she references a future return to the

plan, suggesting the coming summer as a good time for their collaborative work:

(8)

Jan: Summer (scheme), anyway. [(.) It'll be fun to work ou:t, I think.
Jan: [*((nods, gazes at & turns over notes))*
        (0.6)

It is at this potential closing juncture for the discussion that Stephie raises her hand and projects a "brief comment." She reopens the discussion of hiring strategies, which continues for three more minutes, during which time Mary also joins in.

The focal segment

We are now prepared to consider the focal segment in its entirety, including both Stephie's and Mary's turns and the responsive moves of their co-participants.

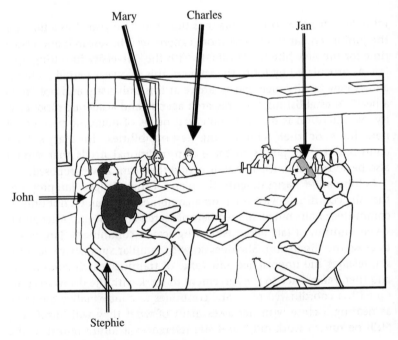

Figure 6.1 Seating of primary participants

John: **Dean, College of Applied Sciences (CAS)**
Mary: **Assistant Professor, Social Science**
Charles: **Associate Dean, CAS**
Jan: **Chair of meeting, Professor of Microbiology**
Stephie: **Professor in a department within the CAS**

Example (9) presents the entire focal segment. Stephie develops a lengthy turn from lines 4–50, and Mary's first action is to raise and hold up her hand (both open and closed) from lines 65–82. Mary begins her vocal turn at line 82 and extends that turn several times, through line 86:

(9)

```
 1 Jan: Summer (scheme), anyway. [(.) It'll be fun to work ou:t, I think.
 2 Jan:                          [((nods, gazes at & turns over notes))
 3         (0.6)
 4⇒ Steph: [.hh Can I make a- (.) brief comment on tha:t, I-[ eh- uhm:
 5         [((S raises & lowers hand))                      [((Jan gazes at S))
 6         (1.6) ((John turns toward S))
 7⇒ Steph: Being on- the other side of the
 8              co(h)lleg(h)[e.
 9 John:                   [huh eh heh
10              (0.6)
11 Steph: We've never had a search committee in our °department.°
12              (0.5)
13 Viv: >↑What,<
14 Steph: We've never had a search committee.
15 Charl: Sounds like you will now.
16 Steph: [So I'm not- Well I-
17 John: [You w- you will now. ((looks toward C))
18 Steph: I mean it's-
19 John: [huh huh huh
20 ???:  [((overlapping laughter, visible smiles & head movements))
21 Charl: [ huh huh [huh
22 Steph:          [There's a- there >see< there's a NUMber
23         of or- of of orders of thi- We have a recruitment
24         committee,
25 Charl: Mkay,
26 Steph: that oversees recruitment, for the department,
27         which is- to me has a functions in a very different way
28         than a search committe[e.
```

29 Charl: [uh huh
30   (0.6)
31 Steph: A:nd uhm I-eh whether we go to search committees, or go
32   with recruitments, or we've got (.) somebody who's (.)
33   seen uh- bright person at a at a research conference,
34   .hh (.) I think what we wanna-(.) do:, the issue here is:
35   is: (.) locating a good poo:l. and .h (.) uh: (.) and insuring
36   that we've at least eh uh stimulated. (.) interest in the school,
37   >even if we haven't gotten a hire out of a pool,<
38   .h An' the- so I- I guess I want- wanna eh make a plea: for a
39   broader approach to searching, than once the committee is
40   formed.
41   (0.6)
42 Steph: So:: what are faculty doing, at a (.) conference, when they're
43   seeing,=
44 Charl: =mm=
45 Steph: =someone who's in their second- year of their P-H-D, giving
46   their first poster. .h And how does that ha- >you know thi- is-
47   they're so it's not it isn't,< (.) okay now we have (.) permission
48   to hire, one person, in two years, and we'll search for this one, it's
49   it's mo:re integrating the- the idea of >of< searching for a broad pool
50   as a me- as a natural [>mechanism   of facu[lty °(hiring)°.<
51   [(((C lateral head movement))[
52 Charl: [>I think< ultimately
53   that may be the message particularly in applied sciences
54   because literally everybody is alway[s on the search committee.=
55 Steph: [Yeah.
56 Charl:=[and okay we [think-=
57 John: [Right.   [
58 Steph: [Yeah. [YEAH.
59 John: [Right
60 Charl: =we choose a subset when we're actually got a posi[tion=
61 John: [bu-
62 Charl:=to hire, but
63 John: Yeah, but it [- but it i:s (true),
64 Charl: [>but< We're e- We're always looking.
65   ((M raises hand, keeps it up until she speaks at line 82))
66 John: It is true that I I:'ve said recruiting, is is year round (.)=
67 Steph: Yeah.=
68 John: =activity, in college of applied sciences.
69   (.)

70 John: And also being a former recruiter, I found that, your chances of
71   hiring somebody, [(.)
72 Steph: [m hm.
73   (0.4)
74 John: are m:uch better, if you establish, (0.5) a interactional
75   relationshi[p.=
76 Steph: [Right,
77 John: =early o:n, and meet with 'em, year in, year out,
78 Charl: °mm hm°
79 John: couple of times a yea:r, *((John turns toward M, whose hand is up))*
80   (.)
81 John: °Sorry.° *((quick pointing gesture toward M))*
82 Mary: >Oh no no no (infac)< keh- (.) and this may be stating-
83   (.) stating the obvious, bu:t uh the two years
84   would (.)enable you >not only >>then<< to set up< a la:b,
85   but to find (.) possible dual- dual career po[sitions:.
86 Viv: [°(I see)°
87   oDual careers are huge.°
88 Mary: Or [childcare,
89 John: [Oh: y[es.
90 Charl: [Yep. Yep
91 Mary: Uhm but that's probably [obvious (and)
92 John: [and and
93 Mary: Maybe not. *((quick smile toward John))*
94 John: THAT by the way=
95 Mary: = > AN' AND OF COURSE THAT< (0.5) bmuh increases rates to
96   tenure [°as well.°=
97   [*((M rests head on right hand, gazes toward John))*
98 John: An I do think there's a- I think there's a much bigger issue with
99   the dual career. m-uh (.) situation. Than a lot of the faculty members
100   that have been here a long time recognize.
101   (0.9)
102 John: Cause they tend to bring in, the faculty candidate, (.) and ignor:e
103   (.)
104   the other person. Until the last minute.
105 Ingr: *((cough))*
106 John: And then they come runnin' to the dean to get help.
                  [Topic of dual career hires continues]

Within the newly extended discussion, there are several intercon-
nected courses of action, including the contributions of Stephie and

Mary. Stephie reopens the discussion by raising the problem of her department's approach to hiring, distinguishing a "search committee" from a "recruitment committee" (lines 11–40). By established practice in the university more generally, search committees are only put together for specific hires, and the proposal by the deans and Jan has been to begin the anti-bias education once search committees are formed. However, Stephie's department, as she informs the others in her turn, has the innovative practice of maintaining a standing "recruitment committee," which is always searching and building a pool of potential candidates to draw upon when official permission to search and hire is granted by the college. As the deans' respond to Stephie's plea for a broader approach to hiring, Mary takes an opportunity to bring up the importance of attending to dual careers and childcare (lines 82–96), tying back to the deans' earlier references to a two-year time period before new faculty would start up their positions (example [7]).

With this basic sketch of background and with an initial view of the full segment, we are prepared to consider the work Stephie and Mary do as they initiate and manage their potentially disaffiliative contributions.

Positioning and composing disaffiliative actions

The two women's turns have in common that they raise concerns previously overlooked but clearly relevant to the topic at hand and to the charge of the committee. Both women point to problems or deficiencies in the way hiring has been discussed so far. In terms of position in a wider sequence of action, both turns come after the chair, Jan, has moved toward closing the topic ([9] lines 1–2). Thus these contributions are placed late relative to the material to which they respond. Indeed, had Jan succeeded in closing the topic of diversifying the hiring process, it is likely that neither Stephie's nor Mary's ideas would have been raised at this time.

A general task that these women share is the formulation of disaffiliative actions. At an extreme of boldness, displaying strong aggravation, for example, they could articulate their actions as very directly and explicitly counter to what has been agreed upon by prior speakers. Alternatively, they can shape their turns with displayed caution, showing orientations toward the norm and preference for agreement. Pomerantz (1984), Sacks (1987) and Schegloff (2007) report on regularities in both placing and formulating potentially disagreeing actions. In the segment we examine here, Stephie and Mary draw on familiar practices for delivering disaffiliative actions.

In line with previous studies of the position and composition of disaffiliative or delicate actions, Stephie's and Mary's turns are characterized by delay, preface, mitigation, and accounts which expand the base actions. As noted earlier, relative to affiliative turns, disaffiliative turns are normatively delayed, with late placement serving as a practice for both avoiding disagreement and for displaying that one is doing disagreement. That is, in research on interaction among smaller groups with less formal agendas than these meeting events, delaying a response has been understood as projecting possible disagreement. In such cases the full articulation of disagreement may even be avoided if recipients pick up on the hesitancy and revise their actions with reference to possible disagreement. Of course, in a large group such as this one, the fact that any given member has not yet responded will not be necessarily interpreted as a lack of response or as a delay in responding, unless that individual is the clear recipient of the previous turn. It is hardly expected that all participants will respond to every turn, whereas specific addressees in dyads, for example, are more likely to be interpreted as delaying responses if they do not speak at relevant turn endings. As in ordinary conversation, however, late placement, prefaces, and hesitations may demonstrate that the disagreeing party is being careful in introducing her action. She is displaying sensitivity to the way her action may be interpreted and responded to by recipients. Thus, even when the disagreement is ultimately articulated, the presence of delays and hesitations displays that one has at least demonstrated hesitation before delivering the dispreferred action.

Consider the placement of Stephie's and Mary's contributions. Both contributions relate to information introduced well before these women initiate their turns. In the case of Stephie's plea, she is addressing the plans shared by Jan and the deans. Jan began the previous discussion with a proposal to train search committee chairs (example [4]), and John shared his plan for his college (and the college that Stephie's department is in), as part of his response to Jan's plan (examples [5] and [6]). In absolute time—that is, time measured by clock without reference to interactional boundaries—Stephie does not introduce her objection until seven minutes after Jan first introduces her plan, and about three minutes after John shares his idea of training all search committees in his college. Mary initiates her contribution, regarding dual career hires and childcare, about two minutes after the deans first outline their plan to have new hires take two-year post-doctoral positions to get more "seasoning." More interactionally relevant than time lapse is the fact that both Mary and Stephie allow the sequence and topic to come very near closure before introducing their concerns. In fact, it is doubtful that Mary would have added her comment had Stephie not first reopened that topic.[4, 5]

Thus, the placement of both turns is delayed relative to the actions they respond to, with these delays being local instantiations of the more general practices of avoiding and/or delaying disaffiliative actions. Either woman could have intervened earlier, but in placing a potentially disagreeing or face-threatening action either during or just after one of the earlier turns by Jan or the deans, each woman would have risked coming across as doing stronger disagreement. At the other extreme, waiting until Jan had actually opened a new agenda item would have meant more work on the part of Stephie or Mary. That is, either could also have waited until the group was in the midst of a new topic and sequence, in which case the action of introducing something relevant to the previous topic would have required halting a current course of action and requesting that the now closed topic be reopened. The position of each woman's turn relative to the talk each addresses stands as evidence of their interactional skill. Each achieves late placement of her contribution, and this placement helps her avoid a more aggravated articulation of disaffiliation that might well be enacted through earlier placement.

Both women vocally and non-vocally display that the deans are their primary recipients, and in the ways that they address the deans, they work to show degrees of care in designing their turns toward these men. Furthermore, their turns are characterized by pauses and restarts, which are also normative displays of treating actions as delicate and potentially face-threatening, with the hesitations associated with difficulty in articulation.[6]

In addition, and in line with general findings on the shape of disagreeing turns, both women preface their actions with framing and projection devices, further delaying the actual disaffiliative actions; here the delays are within the turns themselves. Stephie explicitly projects a "brief comment," while Mary uses the beginning of her turn to mitigate the newsworthiness of what she is about to say, "This may be stating the obvious but … ." Stephie uses "brief" to diminish the projected imposition of her comment. Mary initiates her turn by acknowledging that the others may be well aware of what she will share ("the obvious"), and in so doing, she shows deference while also orienting to a more general preference not to report what recipients already know. Stephie assures her recipients that she will not take much of their time, and Mary designs her preface to avoid treating the deans and others as not knowing what she is about to tell them, though she tells them nonetheless. As it turns out, Stephie's comment is far from "brief," and Mary's addition regarding the concerns of couples and parents have not been mentioned at all, and are far from "obvious" in the context of this institution.

To summarize, through multiple practices, Stephie and Mary display that their upcoming actions may be disaffiliative. Delay and forms of prefacing constitute ways of shaping turns toward agreement, delivering disagreement in a maximally "agreeable" way, avoiding more bold and aggravated presentations in terms of turn position and composition.

With these commonalities in mind, we now move to a closer examination of the work each woman does within the contingent and dynamic context of her turn.

Stephie's turn: managing participation

Stephie's turn is complex in a number of ways.[7] My concentration here is on Stephie's attested skill in designing her turn such that it is shaped toward agreement (Sacks, 1987), while at the same time positioning and composing a disaffiliative action. In reporting that her department does not follow the official practice of forming search committees, she publicly reveals the deans' lack of knowledge about innovations and differences in her department, one which the deans oversee. As she elaborates on her department's policy, she raises a consequential problem for the deans' authority and for the plans the deans and Jan have just agreed upon: to begin anti-bias workshops after committees have been formed. Indeed, John has presented it as policy for CAS that search committees will be closely monitored for compliance with his vision of diversity. How does Stephie manage to articulate her problem and her plea? How does she control the tone of her objection, extend her turn, and arrive at agreeing uptake from the persons for whom her contribution might be most problematic?

Initiation, projection, and prefacing

We have noted that Stephie enters the discussion just as the topic is moving toward closure; late placement of turn initiation being in line with normative practices for doing disaffiliation. Thus, Stephie displays skill in turn positioning. Further artfulness can be seen in Stephie's projection of an extended turn or multiunit turn. CA research (Sacks, 1974; Sacks *et al.*, 1974; Jefferson, 1978; Goodwin, 1984; Houtkoop and Mazeland, 1985; Schegloff, 1987; Selting, 2000; Ford, 2004) has documented the fact that such long holds on primary speakership require

negotiation and collaboration on the part of interactants, both to enter
into these extended turns and to end them. Though long turns are
common in the present meeting data, they regularly involve specific
work for projection and extension. This is particularly true when a
speaker self-selects, as opposed to being called upon by the chair to give
a report.

Not only does Stephie precisely place her turn initiation at the latest
possible position before a new agenda item is begun, but she projects an
extended turn through the specific composition of the initial clause in
her turn. As Jan looks down at her agenda sheet, Stephie produces an
audible in-breath (represented by a period followed by one or more
"h"s), a regular indication that a participant is preparing to speak,
preparing others to attend.

(10)

Jan: Summer (scheme), anyway. [(.) It'll be fun to work ou:t, I think.
Jan: [((*nods, gazes at & turns over notes*))
    (0.6)
⇒Steph: [.hh Can I make a- (.) brief comment on tha:t, I- [eh- uhm:
    [((*S raises & lowers hand*))   [((*Jan gazes at S*))

She raises her hand just as she finishes her audible in-breath, and she
goes on to produce a hybrid form of question. The clause is grammatically a polar or *yes/no* question, a form that, when delivered as a prompt
for recipient response, is normally produced with a final rise in pitch in
Stephie's variety of English. Stephie produces the clause with falling
intonation normally associated with declaratives. Furthermore, she does
not allow a pause for response from Jan. Rather, Stephie moves immediately into a new unit, "I- eh- uhm:" Had Stephie used rising intonation and had she paused after the first clause, she would have opened
an interactional slot for Jan, inviting Jan to respond with a go-ahead or
a blocking action (Schegloff, 2007). Through this hybrid grammatical
and intonational practice, Stephie combines the politeness and deference of an interrogative request with a strong claim of continuing
speakership. In her first clause, not only does she project a multiunit
turn, but before pausing, Stephie moves into another clause, thereby
continuing without explicit permission from the chair.

As noted in Chapter 4, Stephie also uses the initial portion of her turn
to project further talk in the form of a "brief comment," and she ties
back to the prior discourse with the broad reference "that." As has been
detailed in a number of studies of the construction of longer turns in

interaction (Sacks, 1974; Goodwin, 1996; Houtkoop and Mazeland, 1985; Selting, 2000 among others), turn-projecting prefaces such as Stephie's "Can I make a brief comment ..." allow a speaker to reach a point of possible turn completion (in terms of grammar and prosody) while projecting a more extended hold on the floor. Because extended turns contain multiple points of grammatical and prosodic completion, recipients must monitor for other clues as to when one is coming to completion. Note that Stephie provides such guidance in her initial clause and in the next clause, which she only partially produces before a 1.6 second pause.

Steph: **.hh Can I make a- (.) brief comment on tha:t, I- eh- uhm:**
    (1.6)

The type of action that Stephie's first turn is explicitly preliminary to is specified by her vernacular speech-act term *comment*, and its content is bounded, though quite flexibly, through its deictic link to the previous talk. The comment will be "on that," that is, interpretable as related to the topic of training search committees to arrive at more diversity in their ultimate hires.

As already noted, by projecting her comment will be "brief," Stephie adds to the deference of the interrogative grammar a diminution of the projected length of her turn. Her projection of a "brief" use of the floor is arguably, then, a further display of deferential politeness. Stephie's use of *that* (in, "Can I make a- (.) brief comment on tha:t") not only links back to the previous talk, it simultaneously provides a guide for recipients regarding what will follow. Stephie projects that her turn will comment on the previous talk, which the participants know has centered on the training of search committees. This means that the recipients, should they choose to collaborate in allowing this extended turn, will know Stephie is nearing possible completion of that multiunit turn when she articulates a "comment" on the plans from the previous discussion ("that").

While her utterance, "Can I make a- (.) brief comment on that" could relevantly be followed by a response by the meeting chair, we have noted a combination of features of her delivery of this utterance that preclude uptake. It is delivered without rising intonation, and Stephie allows no pause for uptake from Jan. This first turn unit, as we have observed, also projects further action: it projects a comment on the discussion of workshops for search committees. However, Stephie's production of the projected *comment* is still contingent on the recipients granting her some form of go-ahead to continue with the extended turn she has projected. In other words, even if Stephie pushes ahead with her talk, collaboration with her move to primary speakership is required of her recipients. If the chair or another participant does not correspondingly adjust their orientations to display recipiency of an extended turn, Stephie's continuation would face obstacles. For example, the committee chair, Jan, might interrupt and request that further discussion be put off until a subsequent meeting. However, in response to Stephie's turn beginning, the go-ahead response is manifested as participants, including the chair, make no moves to speak. Jan abandons her moves toward closing the topic, and other members of the group move their bodies and their facing directions toward Stephie in visible displays of recipiency.

As discussed in the previous sections, through late placement of this turn relative to what it addresses, Stephie may already be projecting what is interpretable as a disaffiliative action. In addition, and in line with previous descriptions of the construction of disaffiliative actions, once Stephie initiates her turn, she then delays delivery of the disagreeing part (Pomerantz, 1984; Sacks, 1987; Schegloff, 1980). She does not produce her explicit "plea for a broader approach" (counter to the plans so far expressed) until lines 38–40. Her initial clause is not the main action of her longer turn. Instead, as it projects a longer turn it also delays the comment it projects, and even as she begins her next turn unit, she stops short of completing it. On ending her *yes/no* interrogative clause (without rising intonation), Stephie proceeds immediately and without any pause into the beginning of another clause, "I- eh- uhm:," which she cuts off. Notably, Gail Jefferson (1973) has demonstrated that, when elements are begun in this way but then cut off and replaced by other terms, this can be a practice for bringing the full projected unit (the unit that is not completed) into consciousness, while not actually producing that full unit. In other words, by beginning with the pronoun *I*, Stephie may indicate that her projected "comment" will ultimately begin with that pronoun. However, she now produces a pause in place of continuing the clause she has begun.

Stephie's turn beginning is an example of a pre-expansion or pre-sequence (Schegloff, 2007). Through pre-expansion she has gained non-vocal compliance and collaboration from her interlocutors. As noted, the type of action that Stephie's first turn is explicitly preliminary to is specified by the vernacular speech-act term *comment*, and its content is bounded, though quite flexibly, through its deictic link to the previous talk: the comment will be *on that*, that is, interpretable as related to the topic of training hiring committees to arrive at more diversity in their ultimate hires. As motivation for this pre-expansion or preface, we note that Stephie is projecting a possible disaffiliative action. Stephie's next clause, initiated with *I*, could have delivered her plea right at that moment, with the preface serving to prepare the recipients for the delicate action she is formulating; prefaces have been observed to introduce delicate actions (Schegloff, 1980). Instead, Stephie only gives a clue as to how her comment may begin (i.e., it may begin with *I*) but then delays its delivery. When she does continue after her pause, she has abandoned the *I*-initiated clause, replacing it with "Being on-the other side of the college" (line 7).

The format of Stephie's turn bears similarity to a much shorter case of prefacing and then delaying a delicate action discussed by Schegloff in his 1980 article on preliminaries. While prefaces may be used to gain an extended turn in which to offer background or preliminary actions before the projected base action, Schegloff pays particular attention to prefaces that serve to introduce delicate actions. In the case of delicate actions, prefaces may do the simultaneous tasks of providing for an extended turn which includes background material before the ultimate (and initially projected) base action, and also creating a delay and warning associated with dispreferred actions. Thus, first prefacing, then beginning a next unit, but then delaying its completion, can serve as a complex format for composing a delicate, disaffiliative, or face-threatening action.

In (11), I reproduce the example Schegloff offers of a delicate question which is prefaced, initiated and then delayed. The formulation of the extended turn in this case bears fundamental similarities to the practices used by Stephie. Speaker A has just reported having rented out a property she owns, whose former occupant recently suffered the death of her husband. Speaker B projects and then further delays a question about the fate of the widow:

(11) From Schegloff (1980); [bold highlighting is mine]

1⇒ B: Say, tell me something, Bea, **what is** the uhm
2   I always feel sorry for someone when they lose
3   their husband or the husband loses the wife,
4   A: Uh huh,
5⇒ B: **What** uh **is** this wife, **what** is she going to do.
6   A: Oh well she has always worked.

B prefaces, initiates and then abandons and delays the delicate action of inquiring about a person whom A may have treated unkindly.

In comparing B's talk in (11) with Stephie's extended turn (fully shown in [9]), we find commonalities. Rather than directly delivering the base action, both B and Stephie use a first clause to project their actions. For B, "tell me something" does the projection. For Stephie it is "Can I make a- (.) brief comment on tha:t." Both speakers follow their prefaces with abandoned clause beginnings ("what is the uhm" and "I- uh- uhm:"). And both B and Stephie return to the abandoned turn beginnings when they ultimately deliver the delicate base action:

(11a) B's return to her abandoned *what is* clause

B: **What** uh is this wife, **what is** she going to do.

(10a) Stephie's return to her projected *I*-initiated comment (lines 38–40 of Stephie's turn in 10)

38   Steph: .h An' the- so **I- I** guess **I** want- wanna eh make
39   a plea: for a broader approach to searching, than
40   once the committee is formed.

B delays but returns to "What is," finally completing her question; Stephie returns to "I" and completes the projected comment.

While B, in Schegloff's example, provides only a brief preliminary (2 lines on the transcript) after she abandons her second clause, Stephie enters into much longer and interactionally complex preliminaries to her plea for a different conception of the hiring process. Interactionally, the practice of prefacing, beginning a grammatical unit, and then abandoning it, serves as a very handy mechanism. With "I- eh- uhm:," Stephie could be launching her just projected comment; that is, she could at that moment and in that unit say, "I want to make a plea for a broader approach to searching than once the committee is formed." With this clause beginning, Stephie suggests the possible form her comment will take, i.e., it will begin with the first person pronoun, *I*.

The significance of beginning with the pronoun *I* but failing to complete the clause becomes evident as Stephie returns several times to using *I* as the subject of clauses she again fails to complete. She reinforces the relevance of her projected "comment" by reusing the subject pronoun *I*. At lines 16, 31, and 34, Stephie begins units with *I* but she again cuts those units off before completion.

(12) Abandoned *I*-initiated utterances

16 Steph: [So **I**'m not- Well **I**-
     // [. . . . .] //

31 Steph: A:nd uhm **I-eh** whether we go to search committees, or go
32　　with recruitments,
　　　// [. . . . .] //
34　　.hh (.) **I think what we wanna-(.) do:,** the issue here is:
35　　is: (.) locating a good poo:l.

By reintroducing but then abandoning *I*-subject clauses in this way, Stephie renews the relevance of such units, and she simultaneously continues to delay her delicate action. She does not complete any *I*-subject clause until she delivers the upshot of her turn. At lines 38–40, she explicitly makes a plea for a broader approach to hiring, thereby also implicitly indexing her judgment that the plan for anti-bias training that was agreed upon in the prior discussion was not broad enough.

In carefully positioning and crafting her turn initiation, Stephie makes use of multiple methods to project an extended hold on the floor and postpone the main action of her turn, the "comment." A next task she addresses involves engaging the recipients with whom she is disaffiliating but with whom she appears to aim at a revised new plan, thus, ultimately, affiliation and agreement.

Structuring participation

We have noted Stephie's skill at speaking up, projecting an extended turn, at providing cues as to the grammatical form her projected comment will take, but delaying that comment, the ultimate action of her turn. We turn now to the skill she demonstrates in positioning herself relative to the deans of her college. This is interactionally important work because it is the deans' plan for training search committees in their college that is the target of the plea Stephie articulates in the upshot of her extended turn. As we will see, in building this turn Stephie walks a narrow path between deference and insubordination. Stephie specifically secures the demonstrated recipiency of John and Charles, and she also positions herself as an insider to the college they share but also as an outsider relative to the central concerns and top-down structure of the college. In managing her position relative to the deans as she develops her turn, she is faced with the need to regain control of the direction and tone of the shared course of action.

By the end of her sequence-initiating turn at line 4, *Can I make a- (.) brief comment on that*, Stephie has projected a multiunit turn and has begun to receive displayed orientations by others to that extended turn. However, she has not secured the displayed recipiency of two participants whose alignment is crucial for the rest of her talk, namely, John and Jan. Jan's recipiency matters because she is chairing the meeting, and also because she is the one who first proposed anti-bias education for search committees. John's recipiency is important because he is the dean of the college in which Stephie is a faculty member, and also because John has just reported on a policy he plans to implement with regard to training and evaluating hiring committees in that college. Jan, John, and Charles were the most prominent speakers in the discussion that Stephie's turn addresses through its placement and through her use of *that* in line 4. Given their status as special recipients of Stephie's talk, it is problematic that neither John nor Jan is looking at Stephie at the end of her first unit. At that point, Jan has begun putting down the agenda sheet in front of her and is moving her face in Stephie's direction:

```
4  Steph: [.hh Can I make a- (.) brief comment on tha:t, I-[ eh- uhm:
5         [((S raises & lowers hand))                    [((Jan gazes at S))
6              (1.6)
```

C. Goodwin (1979, 1980, 1981) has demonstrated that repair initiation (Schegloff *et al.*, 1977), including hitches or breaks in the projectable continuation of a turn, regularly elicits the gaze of non-gazing recipients. While the hitches in Stephie's speech stream and her delay in continuing should make gaze movement relevant, the hitches do not immediately secure John's gaze.

Stephie allows a fairly long silence to grow at this point.[8] Having secured the floor, as is evident by the silence and the recipient behavior of most members of the meeting, Stephie can use this silence to delay continuation until she gains the gaze of the crucial recipients, a delay that also follows the pattern associated with dispreferred, disaligning turns, as we have discussed (Sacks, 1987; Pomerantz, 1984). During this silence, John brings his gaze to Stephie, and it is only when John's gaze has been secured that Stephie begins once more and this time continues to the end of a clause, though it is a dependent clause that projects at least a main clause to follow:

```
6              (1.6) ((John turns toward S))
7⇒ Steph: Being on-the other side of the
8                co(h)lleg(h)[e.
9  John:              [huh eh heh
```

Through her participial clause at 7, "Being on- the other side of the co(h)lleg(h)e" Stephie positions herself in competing ways, while also introducing a note of humor. Using the definite article in referring to "the college," she establishes an insider relationship among herself, John, and Charles, the Dean and Associate Dean of her college. She also thereby proposes a shift in participation structure, highlighting the institutional connection between herself and these men. No other person at this particular meeting belongs to that college. Yet by describing herself as located "on the other side of the college," she positions herself as separate and different from the deans. Articulating the word *college* with laughter tokens (transcribed with parenthetical *h*s) displays a stance of humor toward her talk at this point, and it invites responsive laughter. Note that John produces laughter tokens in overlap with Stephie's production of the word *college*. Let's consider how Stephie works to formulate an exclusive circle of participants, and why reference to "the other side of the college" might be colored with humor.

While her definite reference to *the college* locates her within the shared sphere of the deans and excludes others, with her reference to herself as inhabiting the "other side of the college," she distances herself from the everyday knowledge of the deans. In this way, rather than constructing the deans as possibly "knowing recipients" of what she is about to say in a projected grammatical continuation (after the participial clause), she instead constructs them as possibly "unknowing recipients" (Goodwin, 1979). Through this formulation, she highlights the fact that she and the deans inhabit distinct worlds, both geographically (a different building on the campus) and intellectually (different subject matter). The distance she proposes through reference to herself as from *the other side* creates a prospective frame, a projection that what she is about to say will be news to them (as well as to everyone else in the room, none of whom is from either *side of the college* in reference). That is, through this participial clause, she projects another clause which will deliver news from "the other side."[9]

Recall that in example (6), from the discussion upon which Stephie is now launching a comment, John presented himself as both author and evaluator of a college policy on hiring and diversity in his college (see especially lines 30–8). With this in mind, we can understand that Stephie's positioning herself as from the "other side" may come off as resistant to the scope of John's power and knowledge. In forming up this potentially insubordinate move, it is significant that Stephie inserts laughter tokens in her production of the word *college*. In so doing, Stephie creates a humorous mitigation of her stance. This is a strategically important modulation in relation to her further disaffiliation, her plea for a broader approach to searching. Her laughter (and its reciprocation by John) may also serve to reference the distinct work, the otherness, of Stephie's department within the college. Hers is a highly interdisciplinary department in comparison with other more purely scientific departments in the college. Faculty in Stephie's department address problems and employ methods not traditionally part of the college (i.e., in some ways closer to social scientific inquiry). That John is the only participant who reciprocates Stephie's laughter is evidence for success of the exclusivity that this unit of Stephie's extended turn proposes.[10] While Jan has been a major player, and remains so as chair of the meeting, even she is sidelined as a recipient through Stephie's reference to "the college."

This section has detailed how Stephie uses her pause at line 6 and her participial clause, lines 7–8, doing intricate interactional work to gain the recipiency of John and to position herself and her developing action relative to both deans, whose job it is to oversee what her department does. That her department has instituted a faculty search process at odds with college policy is news to the deans, which she delivers with humor. She reminds them that she is both a member of the college and that she is also at a distance from the center of the college in campus geography and disciplinary methodology. Stephie's laughter is reciprocated, but the humor begins to be managed by the deans, independent of Stephie's purposes. Let's now examine the development of that joking interchange.

Managing the tone

Stephie's laughter tokens in "college" invite laughter as a further display of insiderness between herself and the deans, but the humor takes on a life of its own. Stephie follows her reference to being on the other side of the college with a now projectable news delivery: news that the deans have been set up to receive as outsiders. She informs the deans that, their plan for training search committees notwithstanding, her department has never had search committees:

(13)

```
7  Steph: Being on-the other side of the
8      co(h)lleg(h)[e
9  John:        [huh eh heh
10      (0.6)
11⇒ Steph: We've never had a search committee in our °department.°
12      (0.5)
13  Viv: >↑What,<
14⇒ Steph: We've never had a search committee.
```

15 Charl: Sounds like you will now.
16 Steph: [So I'm not- Well I-
17 John: [You w- you will now. *((John looks toward Charles))*
18 Steph: I mean it's-
19 John: [huh huh huh
20 ???: [*((overlapping laughter, visible smiles & head movements))*
21 Charl: [huh huh [huh

Vivian, another member of the committee but not one connected with CAS, the college headed by John, responds with a high pitched token of surprise, an open class repair initiator, "What" (Drew, 1997; Selting, 1996b; Curl, 2004, 2005). Given that Stephie's report directly undercuts the assumptions behind the plans for search committee training that the deans and Jan have just detailed, surprise would seem the predictable response to Stephie's news. However, even after being designated as Stephie's primary recipients, John and Charles remain silent, both during the pause at line 12, and through Stephie's response to Vivian's repair initiation. Given that John is the dean of CAS, it is problematic indeed that he might be the public recipient of this significant news about a department in his domain. It would certainly not be a display of authority for John to reveal here that he does not have full knowledge of the workings of (or non-existence of) search committees in his college. Thus, it is skillful of John not to display surprise, whereas for Vivian such a display does not carry the same social and organizational significance.[11] It is only after Stephie produces a partial repetition of her news (leaving off "in our department") that one of the deans responds.

Lucky for John, his associate dean, Charles, finds a way to respond that simultaneously acknowledges news of the problem with Stephie's department and reinforces the deans' authority over her department's practices. In line 15, Charles produces a simultaneous tease and display of power: he says, "Sounds like you will now". In his response, Charles displays recognition of how her news relates to the anti-bias education plans the deans have initiated in the college.

14 Steph: We've never had a search committee.
15⇒ Charl: Sounds like you will now.

Charles treats the news that there has never been a search committee in Stephie's department as a problem. However, his response, though produced in a sing-song and teasing manner, nevertheless proposes that the lack of search committees will be dealt with in a top-down manner: Stephie's department will now change to comply with college policy. Charles' turn both indexes and invokes the power of the deans, despite his playful prosodic delivery.

Although Stephie has both proposed a special connection with and simultaneously distanced herself from John and Charles with her earlier reference to being on the "other side of the college," Charles now invokes power over, rather than connection with, Stephie (and her department). It is through the deans' power that the deviance of Stephie's department will be corrected. With this turn Charles puts Stephie and her department in their place. Though Stephie makes an attempt to regain control of the floor at line 16 ("So I'm not- Well I-"), John speaks in full overlap with Stephie's attempts.

15 Charl: Sounds like you will now.
16 Steph: [So I'm not- Well I-
17 John: [You w- you will now. *((John looks toward Charles))*

John's action is an upgrade of what Charles has said: "You w- you will now." By formulating his version of Charles' admonition without the evidential frame of *sounds like* (see Charles' turn, line 15), John enacts his direct policy power over departments in his college.

At this moment, Stephie seems to be losing control of the course of action and the extended turn she has projected, or at the very least, she is losing control over the tone of the interaction. Others are now joining in with the laughter initiated by the deans, but Stephie, if she is to continue her comment, must reassert her role as primary speaker. What we witness next is Stephie's skill at managing to return to the seriousness of her extended turn while remaining on her careful path between deference and autonomy.

Stephie withholds reciprocating the humorous stance that the deans have now invited and to which others have responded with laughter. That is, in dealing with the deans' teasing but pointed responses, it is significant that Stephie does not laugh but instead produces her next vocal actions without a shade of humor (lines 16, 22–4, 26–8) (Drew, 1987).[12]

15 Charl: Sounds like you will now.
16 Steph: [So I'm not- Well I-
17 John: [You w- you will now. *((John looks toward Charles))*
18 Steph: I mean it's-
19 John: [huh huh huh
20 ???:   [*((overlapping laughter, visible smiles & head movements))*

```
21  Charl: [ huh huh [huh
22  Steph:           [There's a- there >see< there's a NUMber
23         of or- of of orders of thi- We have a recruitment
24         committee,
25⇒Charl: Mkay,
26  Steph: that oversees recruitment, for the department,
27         which is- to me has a functions in a very different way
28         than a search committee[e.
29⇒Charl:                       [uh huh
```

Stephie delivers two short *I*-subject units ("So I'm not- Well I-," line 16), but she then restarts at line 22 with a clause initiated with *there's*. She restarts two more times: "There's a- there >see< there's a NUMber of or- of of orders of." Rather than take these restarts purely as errors, a conversation analytically informed analysis relates this to well-documented practices associated with the resolution of overlapping talk (Schegloff, 2000). Disfluencies and hitches in sound delivery are capable of attracting the gaze and attention of recipients (Goodwin, 1980). Through multiple restarts at lines 22–4, along with louder volume ("NUMber," line 22), Stephie reasserts her position as primary speaker. She also succeeds in not only subduing the laughter, but also in shifting from a humorous to a serious tone and prompting a non-laughing recipiency token from Charles, "Mkay" (line 25) and "uh huh" (line 28). Charles aligns vocally with Stephie's serious stance, while the others, including John, align by producing no further laughter.

Completion and uptake

I have suggested that Stephie is successful in managing to project and expand her contribution. She is adept at speaking up, and at projecting an extended turn. She is adept at delaying the explicitly disaffiliative portion of her turn, while gaining the active recipiency of specific participants and positioning herself as both an insider and as one who is simultaneously outsider enough to have news to share. And, after having her control of the developing turn and its tone challenged by Charles and John, she demonstrates further skill in reclaiming the floor and eliminating the joking tone. The final task I will touch upon here is her arrival at the comment itself, the projected goal of her turn. Here what we see is that she cedes the floor over to Charles as he begins to show agreement.

As noted, Stephie has provided repeated clues that her ultimate action will be a comment initiated with the pronoun *I*. After beginning *I*-initiated units on several occasions, only to cut them off and replace them with other formulations, at lines 38–40, she finally completes an *I*-initiated turn, her plea:

```
38      .h An' the- so I- I guess I want- wanna eh make a plea: for a
39      broader approach to searching, than once the committee is
40      formed.
41                (0.6)
```

Here there are multiple markers that indicate that Stephie is about to produce the projected comment or upshot of her long turn. She introduces this next segment with an audible in-breath, *and*-prefacing, and a discourse marker associated with the upshot of a discourse unit, *so* (Schiffrin, 1987).

Stephie allows a pause for potential uptake, but at this moment there is no visible or audible response. To manage the lack of immediate uptake, Stephie adds lines 42–4, providing a more concrete picture of what "a broader approach" would entail. By line 44, Charles begins to provide both vocal and non-vocal indications of agreement and readiness to speak. At line 44, he not only delivers a recipiency token (*mm*), but he produces a series of nods (vertical head movements) as Stephie continues.

```
42  Steph: So:: what are faculty doing, at a (.) conference, when  they're
43      seeing,=
44  Charl: =mm= ((produces 7 vertical head movements, through line 47))
45  Steph: =someone who's in their second- year of their P-H-D, giving
46      their first poster. .h And how does that ha- >you know thi- is-
47      they're so it's not it isn't,< (.) okay now we have (.) permission
48      to hire, one person, in two years, and we'll search for this one, it's
49      it's mo:re integrating the- the idea of >of< searching for a broad pool
50      as a me- as a natural >[mechanism of facu[lty °(hiring)°.<
51                              [((C lateral head movement))[
52  Charl:                                                [>I think< ultimately
53          that may be the message particularly in Applied Sciences
54          because literally everybody is alway[s on the search committee.=
```

Interestingly, just before Charles begins to speak (line 52), he produces a head shake (lateral movement), which, in this context may be combining a display of strong agreement and disagreement. Such head movements can do both and more, depending on the context (Schegloff, 1987). As Charles begins his head movement at 51, Stephie speeds up the completion of her turn, while simultaneously trailing off in volume. The floor is transferred to Charles and he produces an agreeing turn, but not a simple agreement, lines 48–55 (Raymond, 2003). Charles agrees by stating his perception that what Stephie is describing is "the message in applied sciences because everybody is always on the search committee." In agreeing with Stephie in this manner, Charles also claims that what she has delivered as news is already the practice in CAS. At line 55, Stephie produces "yeah" along with multiple head nods, thus treating Charles' talk as agreement indeed.

In a partial recognition of Stephie's point, Charles concedes that "okay we ... choose a subset [of candidates] ... when we're actually got a position to hire" (56–62). However, he goes on to repeat the fact that what Stephie has said is the general practice in the college, "but We've al- We're always looking." John, overlaps with an agreement formulated with an upgrade of authority, "It is true that I I've said recruiting is a year-round activity in the college of applied sciences." Here John confirms what Charles has said, thereby asserting authority, and he uses "I" rather than "we" (Charles' pronoun choice) when stating the position of the college.

Stephie has succeeded in delivering her delicate and disaffiliative comment, and the deans have succeeded in receiving the idea as one they already practice. That is, in a sense, the way the deans produce their agreeing uptake is to claim prior ownership of the idea and practice that Stephie has presented as particular to her department. Thus, Stephie is skillful in getting her idea taken up and agreed with, but the problem she has raised is not acknowledged nor the already agreed upon plan for training search committees altered. If the deans and Jan were to incorporate Stephie's comment into the plan to give anti-bias training, then the training plan itself would need to be revised to include not just search committees but all faculty members.

Stephie is successful in her turn initiation, and in the manner she carefully articulates her continuation and arrives at agreement. She sets up the participation in such a way that she designates the deans as her primary recipients. She uses reference to being "on the other side of the college" to highlight both insider and outsider status and provide a context for delivering the news that her department has no search committees. And she reclaims control of the talk and of the tone, after the deans produce a set of heckling responses. When she completes her turn, Charles agrees and John seconds Charles' response, both deans treating Stephie's plea as in concert with general trends and policies in their college. It is unclear, however, whether the problem Stephie has introduced will be acted upon with respect to the anti-bias education plan.

At this point, Stephie does not pursue the revision of the plan, instead offering only tokens of recipiency compatible with agreement at lines 55, 58, 67, 72, 76. What is clear is that Stephie is skillful in delivering disagreement agreeably, and that her idea has interactional consequences in the meeting. This is not a clear case of a woman's idea being "ignored," as Stephie's contribution is responded to, but the case suggests how talk and ideas can be taken up even as no action is taken beyond the meeting. One factor that may derail further expansion of Stephie's plea is that Mary intervenes in the discussion just as John is responding to Stephie and Charles.[13] We now examine Mary's intervention.

Mary's turn: Deference and Persistence

As already noted, there are similarities between Mary and Stephie's turns in that both introduce issues that were missing from the previous treatment of the topic. Furthermore, the concerns they introduce are directly relevant to the diversifying faculty-hiring practices at the university, the specific goal of the anti-bias education plans that the deans and Jan have agreed to work on together. Mary brings up dual career hires (lines 83–5) and childcare (88). She bolsters the importance of this issue by noting that attention to family issues improves rates of retention of faculty beyond the probationary period ("rates to tenure,"

Figure 6.2   Mary holds hand up throughout John's extended turn

lines 95–6). On the other hand, in comparison with Stephie's turn, Mary's is relatively brief. Taking into account the increments of talk she adds after possible completion (lines 88, 93, 95–6), Mary ends her turn in 19 seconds; Stephie acts as primary speaker for a total of two minutes. In addition, whereas Stephie begins speaking simultaneously with her hand raise and continues without being given a go-ahead, Mary gains entry to speaking through her hand raise alone.

Mary holds her hand up throughout a long stretch of talk by John, and she does not begin her vocal action until she is given the floor, in this instance by John rather than Jan, the chair:

60 Charl: =we choose a subset when we're actually got a posi[tion=
61 John: [bu-
62 Charl:=to hire, but
63 John: Yeah, but it[- but it i̱ːs (true),
64 Charl: [>but< We're e- We're al̲ways looking.
65⟹ ((*Mary raises hand, keeps it up until she is called upon by John, line 81–2*))

   // [20 seconds of John speaking, see full presentation in (9), above] //

77 John: . . . and me̱et with 'em, ye̱ar in, ye̱ar out,
78 Charl: °mm hm°
79 John: co̱uple of times a ye̱aːr, ((*John gazes to his left, taking in M, whose hand is raised*))
80   (.)
81⟹ John: °Sorry.° ((*John produces quick pointing gesture toward M*))
82⟹ **Mary: >Oh no no no (infac)< keh- (.) and this may be sta̱ting-**
83   **(.) sta̱ting the o̱bvious, buːt uh the two ye̱ars**
84   **would (.) ena̱ble you >not only >>then<< to set up< a la̱ːb,**
85   **but to find (.) possible dual- dual career po[sitions:.**
86 Viv: [°(I see)°
87   ◦Dual careers are huge.°
88 **Mary: Or [childcare,**
89 John: [Oh: y[es.
90 Charl: [Yep. Yep
91 Mary: Uhm but that's probably [obvious (and)
92 John: [and and
93 **Mary: Maybe not.** ((*quick smile toward Jan*))
94 John: THAT by the way=
95 **Mary: = > AN' AND OF COURSE THAT< (0.5) bmuh increases rates to**
96   **tenure [°as well.°=**

```
97               [((M rests head on right hand, gazes toward John))
98 John: An I do think there's a- I think there's a much bigger issue with
99       the dual career. m-uh (.) situation. Than a lot of the faculty members
100      that have been here a long time recognize.
```

While the specifics of Mary's turn position and composition are distinct from those of Stephie's, through a combination of deference and persistence, Mary's succeeds in articulating an issue which matters to her. Let's consider how she does this.

Mary's hand raise

Charles has been responding to Stephie's plea that searching for diverse new faculty be an ongoing practice, when John speaks up directly, without negotiation and in overlap with Charles' continuing turn (line 61 and 64):

(Simplified)

```
Charl: >I think< ultimately that may be the message particularly in
       applied sciences because literally everybody is always on the search
       committee. and okay we think- we choose a subset when we've actually got a
       posi[tion to hire, but
⇒John: [bu-
⇒John: Yeah, but it[- but it i:s (true),
⇒Charl:            [>but< We're e- We're always looking.
```

Charles has produced a concession, "okay we think- we choose a subset when we've actually got a position to hire, but." (Ford, 1994, 2000a & b; Couper-Kuhlen and Thompson, 2000).[14] John, by initiating his talk in overlap and thereby speaking before the projectable completion of Charles' turn, has already set up his claim on the next turn at the earliest possible point.[15] Other participants may be waiting for Charles to arrive at projectable completion before they initiate turns, but John claims a turn before a transition relevance place arrives. In fact, it is just when Charles completes his turn—which is now in overlap with John's turn—that Mary raises her hand (after "We're always looking."):

```
63 John: Yeah, but it[- but it i:s (true),
64 Charl:           [ We've al- We're always looking.
```

65⇒ *((M raises hand, keeps it up until she speaks at line 82))*
66 John: It is true that I I:'ve said recruiting, is is year round (.)
67 Steph: Yeah.=
68 John: =activity,in college of applied sciences.

In Chapter 4, hand raises were included among practices for getting turns, but there was indication that these non-vocal bids could be trumped when another participant launches a vocal action without waiting to be officially recognized. In the present case, Mary raises her hand just at the end of Charles' turn, but after John has already begun but cut off a vocal action. John speaks again (line 66), at the same moment as Mary raises her hand.[16] While Mary's hand raise is precisely coordinated with Charles' turn completion, her bid to speak is not acknowledged at this point. Instead, John recycles his prior turn. In line 66, John repeats most of what he has said in line 63 (minus the agreement/confirmation).

Mary's use of a hand raise is a relatively deferential practice of turn seeking, in comparison with John's directly speaking up and doing so in overlap. But even in her non-vocal action, Mary is not fully deferential. Notably, rather than lowering her hand as John speaks at length, Mary keeps her hand up throughout the course of John's turn (lines 65–82). As we will see, when Mary finally launches her turn, she expands it incrementally past points of possible completion, even as John begins to speak again (lines 92 and 94). We'll look at that now.

Getting the floor

I examine Mary's turn in some detail now, focusing on its beginning and on work she does to present herself as in a less central and powerful position in the group. Recall that she is an assistant professor in a social science, and she is addressing a group primarily composed of scientists and engineers, specifically John, the dean of the College of Applied Sciences. These identities do not determine the way that she speaks, but they are parts of the institutional context to which she may be orienting in choosing how to deliver her turn. After highlighting ways that Mary performs deference, I document features of her turn that display strength and persistence.

As we have seen, to get the floor, Mary raises her hand (line 65) with no vocalization, and she waits as John talks (lines 65–81). At first, John does not display any recognition of Mary's continuous bid to speak, and he speaks beyond several points of possible completion in his extended turn (lines 68, 75, 77, and 79). At the end of line 79, as he turns his head in a direction that clearly takes in Mary (though he is probably looking toward Charles), John pauses and issues a quick apology as he gestures toward Mary (line 81):

79　John: <u>couple</u> of times a <u>yea</u>:r, *((John turns toward M, whose hand is up))*
80　　　　(.)
81　　John: °Sorry.° *((quick pointing gesture toward Mary))*
82⟹ Mary: >Oh no no no (infac)< keh- (.) and this may be st<u>a</u>ting-

Mary does not immediately move into the gist of her turn. She first reacts to John's *sorry* (line 81) by producing a refusal of the apology, "Oh no no no (infac)< keh" (line 82). As she produces the rapid succession of *no*s, she holds her right hand palm up and out toward John, gazing in his direction through a short pause before continuing:

82⟹Mary: >Oh no no no (infac)< keh- (.) and this may be st<u>a</u>ting-
83　　　　(.) st<u>a</u>ting the <u>o</u>bvious, bu:t uh the two y<u>e</u>ars
84　　　　would (.) en<u>a</u>ble you >not only >>then<< to set up< a l<u>a</u>:b,
85　　　　but to find (.) possible dual- dual career po[sitions:.
86　Viv:　　　　　　　　　　　　　　　　　　　　[°(I see)°
87　　　°Dual careers are huge.°
88　Mary: Or [childcare,
89　John:　　[Oh: y[es.
90　Charl:　　　　[Yep. Yep
91　Mary: Uhm but that's probably [obvious (and)
92　John:　　　　　　　　　　　　[and and
93　Mary: Maybe not. *((a quick smile toward John))*
94　John: THAT by the way=
95　Mary: = > AN' AND OF COURSE THAT< (0.5) bmuh increases rates to
96　　　　tenure [°as well.°=
97　　　　　　[*((M rests head on right hand, gazes toward John))*
98　John: An I do think there's a- I think there's a <u>much</u> bigger issue with
99　　　the dual car<u>e</u>er. m-uh (.) situation. Than a lot of the faculty members
100　　　that have been here a long time recognize.
101　　　(0.9)
102　John: Cause they tend to bring <u>in</u>, the f<u>a</u>culty c<u>a</u>ndidate, (.) and ignor:e
103　　　(.)
104　　　the other p<u>e</u>rson. Until the last minute.
105　Ingr: *((cough))*
106　John: And then they come runnin to the dean to get help.

Mary's (polite) rejection of John's apology, her held gesture toward him, and the ensuing pause, combine to delay the beginning of Mary's base action. Perhaps in only a perfunctory way, they also offer John a chance to add further to his turn. So far, then, we see that she is balancing persistence (holding her hand up throughout John's talk) with deference: rejecting his apology and holding an open palm toward him as she delays her continuation. After she has created this delay and display of concern with John's actually being finished, Mary launches into further talk, again with deference.

Deferential framing

Mary's turn is a comment on the deans' conception of a two-year postdoctoral "seasoning" period, discussed more than two minutes earlier, and which has not been referred to in the intervening interaction. Despite the long referential distance between Mary's turn and the last reference to the post-doctoral period, Mary uses the definite article in referring to "the two years."[17] In so doing, she reaches far back across the intervening time and courses of action to reference the deans' earlier reference to a two-year period in which new hires can improve their research. Mary adds concerns that the two years could be used to address but which the deans have not referenced, and her additions relate to non-traditional or more "diverse" new employees.

As with Stephie's comment, had Mary placed her contribution during or immediately after the deans' report of their plans, her action could have been heard as more of a challenge to the deans. In that position, it would more explicitly be responding to and perhaps exposing the deans' failure to include reference to significant issues for non-traditional hiring. Instead, Mary delays her turn, positioning it at a juncture where it is less likely to come across as taking issue with the deans and more likely to be interpreted as a reminder. Heritage (1984b) notes that

> there is a 'bias' intrinsic to many aspects of the organization of talk which is generally favourable to the maintenance of bonds of solidarity between actors and which promotes avoidance of conflict.
>
> (1984b:265)

Mary's delay in making her comment follows with general tendency for interactants to position and compose disaffiliative actions distinctly from affiliative ones. As Mary continues, we see other ways in which she is formulating her action as delicate and dispreferred.

As Mary continues, she is explicitly deferential in a manner which brings to mind common stereotypes about women's talk (for critical reviews, see Crawford, 1995, Eckert and McConnell-Ginet, 2003). In contrast with the initial framing of Stephie's turn, which is primarily occupied with projecting a longer hold on the floor, Mary's first clause is entirely occupied with hedging and epistemic downgrading, "and this may be stating- (.) stating the obvious." Rather than drawing on commonalities between herself and her recipients, as does Stephie with her reference to "the college" she shares with the deans, Mary positions herself as a less-knowing member of the group, an outsider. Recall that she is a social scientist while the deans, Jan, and Stephie are in biology and engineering. Mary uses the first clause of her turn, then, to position herself as one who does not know whether what she is about to report is something that is already familiar to those in the know.

Another (compatible) view of this preface is that it is one through which Mary manages to design her turn beginning in a manner which is *fitted to* and *renewing of* her relationship with her recipients. By framing and projecting that her upcoming talk (referenced cataphorically with her prospective indexical "this") is potentially "obvious" to the recipients, she further delays her projected turn action and simultaneously underscores her marginal membership in a relevant community of knowledge. Most specifically she manages stance framing of her unfolding turn with respect to John, at whom she gazes predominantly throughout her developing turn. John, of course, has just completed an extended turn in which he has pointed to his considerable experience with the recruitment and hiring process. For Mary, an assistant professor from another college, to be informing John about the hiring process is certainly a delicate action.

Through Mary's manner of bidding for the floor (a hand raise) and through her turn preface, she displays deference as she initiates her contribution. Mary is at pains to acknowledge that she knows she is not an insider, and that she may be violating the principle of not telling people what they already know (Sacks and Schegloff, 1979; Schegloff, 2007). Although Mary frames her contribution as possibly "stating the obvious," the issues of dual career hires and childcare have indeed not been mentioned earlier by the deans or any other member of the committee.

Hybridity and "strategic constructivism"

It is fair to characterize Mary's turn as marked by deferential and mitigating devices. As we have just noted, she positions herself as a less knowing participant relative to her recipients. Furthermore, she uses multiple practices to counterbalance the critical and disaffiliative nature of what she is saying. For example, epistemic modal expressions mitigate associated talk:

>   may (line 82)
>   probably (line 91)
>   maybe (line 93)

Her talk also has spurts produced at a rapid pace, which literally diminishes the time she takes in producing parts of her talk:

>   >Oh no no no if I-< (line 82)
>   >not only >>then<< to set up < (line 84)
>   >AN' OF COURSE THAT< (line 95)

When she produces a rather direct formulation of the important, but missing, considerations for the two years, she follows this with a mitigating extension (arrowed below):

>   the two years would (.) enable you >not only >>then<< to set up< a
>   la:b, but to find (.) possible dual- dual career po[sitions:. [ ] Or [childcare,
>   ⇒Uhm but that's probably obvious (line 91)

And even as she persists in adding on to her turn, she trails off in volume, producing the final phrase of her turn very quietly:

>   °as well.° (line 96)

These devices seem to diminish the overall force with which Mary formulates her action, and this could have consequences on the ultimate uptake she receives.

However, there is hybridity in Mary's turn formulation. In addition to the forms just listed, she uses strategies that upgrade and strengthen her action. In other words, across and between her mitigating practices, she deploys practices that serve to counter balance her deferential stance. As we have noted, Mary is doing a delicate action: she is adding heretofore missing, but highly relevant, considerations related to the deans' plans. She is thereby drawing attention to the deans' failure to refer to central concerns of non-traditional faculty, those whose presence in this diversity committee is charged with increasing. The deans refer to research seasoning and productivity—traditional concerns for advancement in the university. They do not refer to dual career and childcare needs.

Furthermore, Mary is doing the delicate action of correcting this deficiency in an interactional context which includes her institutional identity in relation to her recipients. Though Mary has choices of how to present herself from moment-to-moment, she is indeed an outsider relative to her main addressees. Among her identities, she is a social scientist addressing a group dominated by faculty and staff in biological and physical sciences. Mary is also an assistant professor addressing high-ranking administrators, John in particular.[18] Bearing in mind these identities, we can see her current choice to delay her intervention and to present it with notable deference toward John as both practical and politic. Positioning herself in this way is well fitted to the delicate action she is taking, and, given the place she occupies in the hierarchy of the institution and the committee, it may reflect a compromise with respect to the forcefulness of her action. That is, Mary is not simply emanating a style of talk that reflects her predetermined and essential lower status in the group, but, like Stephie, Mary is also strategically positioning herself and her action in relation to issues, actions, and recipients at a specific moment in this meeting and in her career. I would argue that Mary is using what Yerian (2002) refers to as "strategic constructivism."

Yerian analyzes interactional work, both vocal and non-vocal, in a full-force self-defense course for women. In addition to documenting how women use their bodies and their voices to aggressively defend themselves, Yerian documents the use of passive and conciliatory strategies as components of an effective defense, with the women in the course encouraged to gauge their defense practices to emergent and unpredictable contexts of particular role-play attacks. The women she studied move between stances of assertiveness and compliance, adapting to the situations that arise as they practice in new scenarios of sexual assault by a (fully padded) mock assailant.

Since the course participants alternate between stereotypically feminine and masculine responses, Yerian does not call their practices strategic essentialism but rather strategic constructivism. With this new concept she captures "the relatively deliberate use of a variety of interactional strategies in the construction of stance and identity" (2002:393). This concept allows us to appreciate the interplay between Mary's deference and assertiveness in the current case, as Mary's formulation of her delicate action is not uniformly deferential and conciliatory.

We have noted multiple signs that Mary works to diminish the disaf-filiative force of her action. These include her manner of securing the floor, aspects of the composition of her turn, and her non-vocal behavior. At the same time, she uses a number of practices to counter these mitigating and deferential moves. To begin with, Mary counterbalances the deferential practice of raising her hand with persistence. She keeps her hand up even as a very high-ranking member of the group speaks at length. Then, in the unfolding design of her turn, Mary juxtaposes downgrading with upgrading practices, deference with power. She draws on contrasting stances in a contrapuntal manner, employing strongly assertive practices to reclaim the floor and add increments to her turn.

Beyond her initial preface, using the prospective indexical "this" to project further talk, Mary expands her turn past points of possible com-pletion through incremental extensions. These are in the form of coordinate noun phrases and clauses (lines 88, 91, and 95) and an adverbial (line 93, "maybe not"):

```
82  Mary: >Oh no no no if I-< keh- (.) and this may be stating-
83        (.) stating the obvious, bu:t uh the two years
84        would (.) enable you >not only >>then<< to set up< a la:b,
85        but to find (.) possible dual- dual career po[sitions:.
86  Viv:                                             [°(I see)°
87        ∘Dual careers are huge.∘
88⇒Mary: Or [childcare,
89  John:    [Oh: y[es.
90  Charl:         [Yep. Yep
91⇒Mary: Uhm but that's probably [obvious (and)
92  John:                         [and and
93⇒Mary: Maybe not. (( quick smile toward Jan))
94  John: THAT by the way=
95  Mary: => AN' AND OF COURSE THAT< (0.5) bmuh increases rates to
96        tenure [°as well.°=
97               [((M rests head on right hand, gazes toward John))
```

Although she comes to possible turn completion at the end of line 85, she adds a further concern at line 88, "or childcare." As she produces this extension, both deans overlap with her, producing forms of agreement. However, the way that John and Charles formulate their agreement treats Mary's contribution as already familiar; I discuss this in the next section. Just after her addition (88) and the overlapping agreements (89–90) by the deans, Mary again produces an extension through which she again reasserts the possibility that what she is saying is "obvious" (91). Were that the end of Mary's talk, she would have begun and finished by downplaying the newsworthiness of her contribution, but she goes on.

Before Mary has completed her addition at line 91, clearly not at a point of possible completion in her turn, John begins to overlap with "and and" (92). Despite this overlap by a high-ranking participant, Mary does not cede the floor but instead counters the downplaying action with "maybe not" (line 93). In so doing, she not only overrides John's attempt to speak, but she also suggests that, her prior downgrading notwithstanding, the importance of dual career hires and childcare may not, in fact, be obvious to the deans. Further hybridity and contrapuntal displays of deference and power can be found as Mary immediately follows "Maybe not" with a quick smile toward John. What she is doing with this smile, produced as separate from her vocal turn rather than simultaneous with its production, is not clear. However, in following her suggestion that the needs of families may not be obvious to the deans, her smile is interpretable as softening and moving back toward deference.

91 Mary: Uhm but that's probably [obvious (and)
92 John: [and and
93 Mary: Maybe not. *((M flashes a quick smile toward John))*
94 John: THAT by the way=

Mary's talk could end at 93, and we can see that John again attempts a turn beginning, "THAT by the way." Note that he produces "THAT" with louder volume than his previous talk. John may be deploying what Schegloff (2000) has analyzed as a "pre-onset perturbation" (17); a noticeable increase in volume can serve to prevent the entry of another speaker. But John is not successful in continuing here, as Mary further extends her turn. In so doing she also assumes a "competitive mode" through louder volume and repetition, "AN' AND OF COURSE THAT" (Schegloff, 2000:18):

94 John: THAT by the way=
95 Mary: => AN' AND OF COURSE THAT< (0.5) bmuh increases rates to
96   tenure [°as well.°=
97   [*((M rests head on right hand, gazes toward John))*

It is evident that John has not completed his turn at line 94, as the grammar, prosody, and action he has produced projects more to come.

Thus, Mary counterbalances her deference by cutting off John's turn beginning. In her final addition to her turn (95–6), she supports her action of calling attention to family issues by citing the fact that attention to such concerns results in greater faculty retention. By the end of this final extension of her turn, Mary again softens her stance. She trails off in volume on "as well," as she physically positions herself as an attentive listener to whatever John will say. On completion of her turn, she is resting her head on her right hand and gazing toward John.

Overall, then, in Mary's extended turn, she creates a hybrid formulation of stance, combining deferential actions with competitive and assertive ones. She draws upon multiple practices of upgrading and downgrading to produce a locally adapted presentation of an institutionally important, but potentially delicate, move in this interactional context.

Uptake of an artfully designed turn

Mary succeeds in getting her contribution recognized and the topic is continued at length in the interaction that follows. From the beginning of her turn, she receives agreement from Vivian, another social scientist in the group, and from both John and Charles. After she ends her turn, discussion continues on how to insure that new hires are offered information about the university policy on partner employment. Yet, as with the responses of Charles and John to Stephie's contribution, they again display agreement with Mary in ways that treat her concerns as already familiar to them:

```
89 John:    [Oh: y[es.
90 Charl:        [Yep. Yep
```

The display of prior access to knowledge is particularly clear in John's "Oh: yes." This response is comparable to those analyzed by Heritage (2002), cases Heritage describes as treating the prior turn as self-evident. When an assessment is followed by an *Oh*-prefaced response, Heritage demonstrates that the *Oh* token is "used to convey the epistemic independence of a second judgment or evaluation from the first" (219). In the present data, John, with his *Oh*-prefaced agreement at line 89, may also be enacting "epistemic priority" (219), similar to what Heritage has documented for assessment sequences. In this meeting, Mary explicitly references important concerns related to diversity in hiring, concerns that Charles or John have not yet voiced. But John's "Oh: yes," while doing agreement, also proposes that John is well aware of the issue Mary has raised.

Viewed in the light of Mary's careful turn design, we can see that Mary's displayed concern with "stating the obvious" may be appropriate as she addresses the deans. Without the deferential work and the down-grading of her authority, Mary might have come across as publicly treating John and Charles as not fully in tune with the concerns of dual career couples. It is not in fact clear that Mary does believe the deans are adequately aware of these concerns; they have not, after all, mentioned the concerns, while they have mentioned the seasoning of new faculty and the preparation of their laboratories so that they will not "miss a beat" in productivity (see example (7), above). Had Mary not spoken up at this late juncture relative to the original talk of a two-year seasoning period, all indications are that the topic would have been closed without mention of the crucial challenges of dual careers and childcare. There is thus good motivation for Mary to explicitly add these issues to the discussion, and she formulates this delicate action with a well-adapted hybrid turn design, combining deference with persistence, strength, and competitive turn practices. Like Stephie, though Mary is successful in airing her concern and getting agreement, the kind of agreement she gets may leave her wondering about what concrete action John will take with respect to her concerns.

Summary and conclusion

This chapter has documented skills two women use within a single continuous span of meeting interaction. Looking closely at two contributions to a single continuous segment (Schegloff, 1987) has supported a fine-grained examination of a constellation of practices through which each woman, in different ways, introduces and extends potentially face-threatening and disaffiliative additions to the discussion. While Stephie and Mary use different resources to initiate and expand their turns, each demonstrates local adaptation to interactional and institutional context and each extends her contribution by managing potentially disruptive talk by others.

Stephie extends a topic that the meeting chair was in the process of closing. She projects a multiunit turn and moves immediately into preliminaries that will situate her ultimate action with respect to specific recipients. Her preliminaries include work to create solidarity with the deans, while also projecting that she may have news that they are not privy to in their geographic and intellectually separate realm in CAS. She is able to cut short the power display and humorous tone that the deans introduce in response to a part of her turn. Mary also produces an extended turn, though in her case the added units come in the form of extensions rather than parts of an initially projected longer hold on the floor. Mary also manages overlapping talk by cutting short John's turn beginning. Thus, each woman successfully deals with competing moves by her recipients, and each works to make her turn come across as affiliative, using turn-design features that move between solidarity and deference. Viewed in the interactional context and with attention to the care displayed in her turn design, both Stephie and Mary succeed in addressing deficiencies in the talk of previous speakers, and they do so with skillful combinations of caution and forcefulness.

One cannot help but notice, however, that in a certain sense, neither Stephie nor Mary is successful in getting the deans or the committee chair to commit to changing the plans they had previously agreed upon. These women are skilled in raising issues, in managing intervening talk, and in extending their holds on turns, but that does not mean that their ideas, though not ignored in the local interactional context, result in change. This is particularly striking, from a feminist perspective, given the consequentiality of these women's contributions in relation to women's advancement: Stephie takes issue with a traditional approach to hiring, insisting instead that a "broader" approach is necessary in relation to the women and minority candidates the university claims to have interest in recruiting. Mary draws attention to the importance of thinking beyond the traditional plan to recruit based on a model of a single, research-focused head of household. She reminds the deans of dual career hires and childcare and how attention to these needs correlates with tenure. The deans, as we observed, receive both women's interventions with agreement, but their agreement is formulated in such a way as to treat the ideas as already known and familiar to them.

That institutions move slowly and that there is resistance to the large-scale changes that a more inclusive workplace will require, is not news. What we can conclude from these data is that these women are indeed capable of articulating innovative alternatives through their contributions to workplace interactions. In the concluding chapter, I return to the issue of local interactional power versus effects beyond moments in meeting talk.

7
Speaking Up in Meetings: Summary and Conclusions

As I began this research, I was struck by the gap between the practical concerns of my female colleagues and the theoretical sophistication of current scholarship on gender and language.[1] On the one side were ideas about women and language informed by popular representations, which, if they cited research at all, selected only those findings reinforcing a vision of stark gender differences (Cameron, 1995). On the other side were critiques of hegemonic, homogeneous, and dichotomous conceptions of gender. Viewed in light of the latter critiques, popular narratives of gender difference and gender bias—like those shared with me by my colleagues in traditionally male professions—might be considered naïve and essentialist. Contemporary views of the complications of gender and other social categories resonate with CA's early observations on the myriad possible identifications one might draw upon in any moment of interaction (Sacks & Schegloff, 1979), with momentary choices both reflecting and positing social identities and participant relations *in situ*. In the conclusion to her 2003 book *Gender and Politeness*, Sara Mills addresses the tensions between earlier homogeneous and categorical approaches to gender and contemporary critiques of those simple, dual oppositional categories, but she also acknowledges that we must remain aware of the degree to which women are disadvantaged in relation to men in material terms: in terms of the salaries they earn; their positions in hierarchies; their representation in Parliament; the amount of housework and child-care they are expected to do; the degree that they are at risk of sexual assault and violence; and so on.
Mills adds that

> [w]hilst within Third-Wave feminism, it is not now possible to say that all women are oppressed in similar ways and to the same degree,

it does seem to be possible to argue that women are still systematically discriminated against and that this discrimination occurs at both a structural level (institutions and the state) and at a local level (relationships and the family).

(2003:240–1)

The path I have taken in this book is to address the local enactment of interactional positions in workplace meetings, with an emphasis on women's contributions. Thus, whereas contemporary approaches to gendered discourse and feminist discourse analysis, along with recent feminist expressions of CA, focus on the interactional construction of gender categories and the intersection of multiple social identities, I have used CA to document women's agency in practice. I have treated the existence of institutionalized biases against women's advancement as a backdrop rather than as an object of investigation itself. Based on analysis of interaction in videotaped meetings, this book provides a CA documentation of turn-taking and turn-building in workplace meetings, and it also provides evidence for women's observable competence at speaking up in such contexts.

In the introductory chapter, I situated this research with reference to several areas of inquiry: I provided a view of related studies of language and gender, and I sketched the connections between this project, applied linguistics, and conversation analysis. In subsequent framing chapters, I reported my data sources and described my analytic practices. I also presented selections from interviews with women who participated in the meetings to offer a sense of their concerns and perspectives regarding their multiple identities and the multiple challenges they face in workplace interaction.

With this background in place, three core chapters articulated findings from my analytic engagement with the meeting data. Chapters 4 through 6 presented new findings along with elaborated perspectives on meeting interaction and task-based, multiparty interaction more generally. These include findings on

- collaborative shifts to official meeting order,
- local management of speakership,
- structuring of turn beginnings,
- enactment of alliances and connections,
- multiple functions of questioning actions, and
- formulation of extended and disaffiliative turns.

I touch upon the major findings very briefly here, and I then turn to questions of power and application.

Represented in women's talk in these meetings were multiple methods for getting turns. Participants were called upon unilaterally by meeting leaders, and they also regularly used separate actions, both vocal and non-vocal, to bid for speakership; this involved the construction of small sequences: bids plus acknowledgment/go-aheads. Much as has been found in ordinary, non-institutional interaction, it was also common in these meetings for speakers to self-select without any formal bid to speak. In such cases, turn beginnings may be coordinated additions to prior talk or collaborative completions of ongoing turns. When speakers either gained the floor through separate bidding actions or simply started up, they could also initiate wholly new actions as well as new sequences, shifting participation and often opening slots for further turns by the same speaker. Turns that did questioning stood out in serving as vehicles for challenging previous talk, for displaying expertise, and for projecting possible expansion, affording further participation by the questioner or others.

In interviews, women, who also took part in the videotaped meetings, advised others of the value in building and maintaining workplace alliances. They see such connections as crucial to success in speaking up and receiving support in the meetings themselves. Connections and alliances were indeed evident in the meeting data itself. In framing turn beginnings, participants explicitly named prior speakers and articulated connections between current turns and prior ones. In various ways, colleagues also indexed and renewed their work relationships through the collaborative construction of turns and longer reports; they built upon and revised each others' turns.

With respect to extending contributions into multiunit turns, like other meetings, those in my collection regularly included long single-party talk. But the fact that this was possible and even normal did not eliminate the need for using initial units of turns to project multiunit turns. Thus, it is not only in casual conversation that special work is required in order to project longer holds on the floor, to provide guidance as to the organization of such extended turns, and to prepare recipients for actions yet to come. Among extended turns introduced through initial projecting work were turns doing disaffiliation, actions that are normatively designed with identifiable care.

While launching, a turn is essential to contributing to a meeting, designing more extended holds on the floor and doing disaffiliation both require interactional skill and the ability to adapt to the contingencies of ongoing recipient interventions. Relying on stereotypes, we might expect women to avoid disagreement and disaffiliation, especially in these more public interactions. However, CA research has demonstrated that avoiding disagreement is a tendency in interaction more generally, with examples drawn from both women and men. Though women may be more negatively evaluated when they do disaffiliative actions and when they take up interactional space in meetings through multiunit turns, in my data, there is no shortage of instances where women do disagreement and other forms of disaffiliation, and there are plenty of instances when they speak at length. My analysis of the extended and disaffiliative actions of two women in a single segment of meeting talk not only evidences their ability to do such action, but it also documents specific practices for managing potentially disruptive actions by institutionally powerful co-participants.

I looked closely at the coordination of vocal and non-vocal actions as women gained turns. As documented elsewhere for casual conversations, audible in-breaths worked along with non-vocal actions to draw attention to incipient speakers. In addition, in these data, body movements and shifts in gaze not only drew attention to possible bids to speak, but when such non-vocal behaviors were initiated during the course of an ongoing turn, they could be precisely timed to mark points in the current talk which the incipient speaker will respond to.

While hand raising was a common and functional non-vocal means for making a formal bid to speak, the alternative of simply speaking up, without any separate vocal or non-vocal bid, appeared to trump simultaneous non-verbal bids. While this is not surprising, it does underscore complications for workgroups attempting to combine informality and inclusivity. This may bias participation in favor of those willing to compete for speakership by starting up just as a current speaker comes to possible completion. However, Mary's persistence in her hand raise, detailed in Chapter 6, is interesting in this regard. Although John speaks up without a bid and initially gains the floor, Mary keeps her hand up during John's long turn, and she ultimately gains the floor. As she works to continue her contribution, she also uses generic methods to override John's self-selection to speak. Thus, getting a turn in these informally structured meetings does not require the willingness and ability to speak up without a separate formal bid, nor does hand raising imply lack of power both to get a turn and to expand upon it.

While women in the data showed deference through hedged pre-framing of turns (as did men in the data), they also spoke up in strong displays of unmitigated disagreement. They used increased loudness and pace to manage overlapping talk before they were ready to cede the floor. They also used pauses at points where more was projected before possible turn completion in order to hold the floor and to consolidate attention of specific recipients.

The current findings on turn-launching, turn-building, turn extension, action formulation, and sequence expansion contribute to a general CA-based understanding of turn-taking in meetings. However, my goal has also been to provide a feminist and applied CA response to women's concerns to be full participants in workplace interactions. By concentrating on women's turns and the sequences they initiate, I have documented ways that women enact local power in workplaces where, in the aggregate, women continue to be undercompensated and also underrepresented in the higher ranks. Taken together, the analyses in the three analytic chapters demonstrate that women, as represented in these data, command diverse, skillful, and adaptable repertoires for contributing to and affecting the flow of actions and ideas in meetings. My application of CA to understanding women's participation in a selection of workplace meetings celebrates the order and complexity with which women are *already contributing* to workplace talk, even in domains and events in which they are relatively new. Speaking up in meetings may be a skill that women find challenging, but bidding for a turn, projecting multiunit turns, opening sequences through questioning, and completing actions even in the face of disruption are practices available to participants of any social category. What women are doing when they speak up in workplaces in these data involves generic interactional practices, not specifically women's practice. But the fact that women speak up in these particular work settings needs also be recognized, at this point in history, as new and in that sense exceptional.

Talk and power

It has not been my goal here to theorize power, but I have done so implicitly by treating speaking up and affecting a group's local course of interaction as forms of power. These conceptions of power are similar to ones used by Nancy Ainsworth-Vaughn in her book *Claiming Power in Doctor-Patient Talk* (1998). As talk is a prime site for the co-construction of identity and power, we can witness and document the enactment of power in the moment-to-moment "actions that control the emerging discourse: participants' successful claims to speaker rights" (Ainsworth-Vaughn, 1998:43).

Viewing power as manifested through getting into participation and expanding one's participation, as I have in this study, is what Joanna

Thornborrow (2002) categorizes as "[p]ower as territory: gaining access to discursive space" (27–8). Thornborrow also demonstrates that power "can be construed as one participant's ability to affect or influence what the next participant does in the next turn." (136).[2] My analyses, in line with those of Thornborrow, document how varying contexts in emergent courses of action in institutional interactions afford shifting opportunities for participation.

Institutions are structured by positions and ranks, and just as current critical research is aimed at laying bare the restricted and restricting subject positions afforded by discourses conceived of abstractly, so CA can be used to support understandings of locally emergent interactional positions. These are specific moments in which participants may renew, resist, or improvise new spins on generic expectations. But how do moments of speaking up relate to the major changes in systems of oppression and bias in workplaces, changes that many women, including those who asked me to do this study, are committed to seeing?

Accessible CA and countering myths of women's (in)competence

This project contributes to CA-based findings on meeting interaction, and it adds to accumulating empirical evidence of women's competence in communicating. But while this is of value in itself, I am also interested in taking these perspectives beyond the realms of sociolinguistics, CA, and gender and language studies. Ideally, accessible CA supports appreciation of the underrecognized order in ordinary talk, and feminist perspectives on meeting interaction should help counter negative stereotypes of women. I have begun sharing this project as well as the basics of CA more widely, using these findings and the general perspectives they represent as a basis for public presentations. During the course of this study, I also shared my emerging observations with the women who prompted the project to begin with, colleagues for whom institutional change is a definite priority. These presentations have been opportunities to share a CA perspective on language, on agency, and on normative practices for interaction. I use the present section to outline ways I present CA in relation to gender and language to these nonspecialists, and in the last section of the chapter and the book, I consider feedback from these presentations along with some final thoughts.

Because I find people generally assume women speak differently than men, I begin my presentations by asking audience members to tell me what comes to their minds when thinking about gender and language.

As a way to motivate interest in feminist CA, after compiling a list of common conceptions about women's style of speaking, I invite consideration of the following facts:

(1) Women are evidently highly motivated to change. Literally and figuratively we "buy" popular fix-the-woman products of all sorts. We are socialized into the perpetual task of fixing ourselves in order to succeed both in relationships and at work.
(2) Workshops and self-help books offer contradictory advice from assertiveness training and the more recent development of training to soften our styles (our assertiveness work has not apparently served us).
(3) Empirical research on gender differences in language use is full of contradictions and far from conclusive. It does not support a view that women are deficient and in need of fixing.
(4) Experimental research points to more positive evaluations of men and more negative evaluations of women, even when competence and speech practices are controlled.
(5) Women are succeeding in traditionally male-dominated fields, despite the operation of social-evaluative biases against their advancement.
(6) My own work on turn-taking in meetings indicates that women are skilled participants.

In discussing these facts and how they relate to one another and to societally reinforced ideologies of gender and language, I cite the work of Kitzinger and Frith (1999) regarding the dangers of the dictum, "Just say 'No'." As Kitzinger and Frith note, on the basis of what we know about the typical delivery of refusals, women are being asked to break norms, while men are excused when they report failing to understand common practices for polite refusal. This underscores the need to question what we are told about how women talk—generalizations so often based on limited, decontextualized, or simply contrived examples. Kitzinger and Frith's piece not only introduces CA observations about the design of affiliative and disaffiliative actions, but it also serves as a powerful basis for debunking the advice that women are asked to follow in refusing sex.

I then use examples from my data to demonstrate that men as well as women use deferential strategies such as pre-framing hedges (Chapter 4):

(1) Richard: For what it's worth...
(2) Mary: This may be stating the obvious...

I also show that both men and women's turns include pauses, repairs, restarts, hesitations, and the notorious, but arguably useful phrases, *you know* and *I mean*. For example:

(3) Xavier, a physician participating in a workplace meeting, composes a turn containing features stereotypically associated with women's talk (bold type).

Xavier: This uh program for P-T-H, though uh it's it's very detail:ed, **>I mean**
          it's never< gonna- **you know:-**   **that- what you- the-** the treatment, and
          the monitoring,= it's never gonna **>kinda<** wo:rk, **yaknow**, in primary
          car:e, <u>or</u> uh: then the what uh-We [shd sh- We should send them to you:=

Ned: [eh ehm *((clears throat))*

Xavier: **Is that**, (0.5) Would that be : [**uh**

Ned: [I think for no:w, that's what I'd suggest.

Xavier, who speaks haltingly in example (3), is a successful physician, and Richard, who produces a hedged turn beginning in example (1), is a successful musician and director. These and other examples can complicate simple associations of speech production features with insecurity and with gender.

Attention to detail, as is evident in the transcribed examples I offer, introduces non-experts to the functionality of pauses, hesitations, hedges, and even laughter-infused production of words, all potentially effective practices for doing specific sorts of social actions in meetings and in interaction more generally. This can be illustrated through use of simplified versions of Stephie's and Mary's careful positioning, initiation, and progressive design of disaffiliative turns (Chapter 6).

I read or play the initial parts of both Stephie's and Mary's turns, with accompanying transcripts:[3]

(4)

1 Steph: .hh Can I make a- (.) brief c<u>o</u>mment on th<u>a:</u>t, I- eh- uhm:
2   (1.6)
3 Steph: Being on- the other side of the <u>co(h)</u>lleg(h) [e.W<u>e'</u>ve n<u>e</u>ver had a=
4 John: [huh eh heh
5 Steph: =s<u>ea</u>rch committee in our department.

(5)

Mary: >Oh no no no (infac)< keh- (.) and this may be st<u>a</u>ting - (.) st<u>a</u>ting the
      <u>o</u>bvious, bu:t uh the two y<u>ea</u>rs would (.) en<u>a</u>ble you >not only >>then<< to
      set up< a l<u>a:</u>b, but to find (.) possible dual- dual career po[sitions:.

Audience members usually have the same initial sense of Stephie's and Mary's turns as did I when I first transcribed them: we hear Mary as hesitant and unsure, while Stephie seems confident and commanding.

I ask the following questions as a way of guiding a simplified analysis of the turns in their contexts:

Where did the speaker place her turn in the flow of interaction?
Who is she addressing?
What kind of action is she doing relative to her recipients' prior actions (i.e., agreeing or disagreeing)?

As I guide a group through the cases and their interactional contexts, I note that Stephie's audible in-breath (line 1, example [4]), is a common and effective way to invite the attention of other participants. I point to her use of a question form (line 1) to show deference though she does not allow a slot for response after the question. Stephie's use of a long pause at line 2 exemplifies how an apparent disfluency serves to invite group members to align themselves, both physically and cognitively, as active recipients of her projected multiunit turn. By showing that a pause can be artfully deployed, and by introducing the notion of projection, I offer a new way to look at interaction.

I go on to consider Mary's turn and invite a rethinking of the work she is doing through it, whom she is addressing, and the immediate interactional context. I concentrate on how Mary succeeds in raising important themes for the committee, issues that were significantly absent from the deans' previous talk about diversity in hiring. I note her persistence in holding her hand up during the talk of a much higher-ranking dean. I also highlight the interactional practices Mary uses to expand and support her contribution, even as John begins a response. Though Mary is a relative outsider to this science-oriented group and also a lower-ranking member in the institution than John, she succeeds in adding to her turn by talking over John's turn beginning; she uses increased volume to resolve the overlap in her favor. In sum, I show how both Stephie and Mary expand and complete contributions in which they object to aspects of previous speakers ideas. Each uses different practices, ones that are specifically and effectively adapted to the challenges she faces in the local dynamics of interaction.

To end, I return to the original list of gender and language assumptions we compiled at the beginning of the presentation. I review them and point to what we have seen in the examples, i.e., how mitigation, hesitation, and other features and forms stereotypically associated with weakness are used by both men and women and clearly have their place in a repertoire of effective practices for meeting interaction. CA findings evidence the orderliness and functionality of such resources for turn composition. The examples of men using forms stereotypically associated with women ([1] and [3], above), and the simplified analysis of Stephie's and Mary's disaffiliative turns, together serve to counter a number of popular, but usually unexamined, beliefs. In my experience, audiences respond to this perspective and these materials with serious engagement as well as with animated questions and comments. They seem truly fascinated to find that features of spontaneous talk normally considered sloppy might actually be well-adapted to important functions in interaction. Women, in particular, are impressed with the possibility that women's speech may be perfectly alright as it is, and that obstacles must lie elsewhere.

No "silver bullet": feedback and closing thoughts

While CA and versions of my findings from this study are well received by the groups I have addressed, subsequent feedback from my female colleagues has also highlighted my use of what I think of as accessible CA. While my presentations are intended to educate about interactional practices and to counter myths of women's incompetence with them, and though I do not recommend adoption of any specific strategies, it is regularly the case that being exposed to evident orderly intricacies of normal talk creates more awareness of their operation in ones daily life. Several women have reported to me on their experiences and experiments with practices that I have touched upon in presentations.

Leslie, a research scientist, described using more movement of her torso and shifts in her gaze when she wanted to signal an interest in speaking. She found this effective for attracting attention of other participants and in getting her bid to speak recognized. However, Florence, a university administrator, tried using audible in-breaths to draw attention and was disappointed by the results. She explained that her new awareness of audible in-breaths meant she was able to observe how they functioned for her and for others. While Florence's audible in-breaths occasionally attracted attention, she reported that people in higher positions in the institutional hierarchy continued to get easier access to turns. She noticed that one higher-ranking woman, who was often at the same meetings as Florence, seemed to be more effective in using in-breaths than was Florence. It was as though this other woman's in-breaths were worth more in the institutional hierarchy as enacted in a particular meeting.

Florence reported her observations in this way (crediting me for "teaching" the use of audible in-breaths, which was not my intention):

> *You're teaching me. You talk about the breath intake that signals you want to talk. I'm very conscious of that now, and I can see other people doing it, and I find myself doing it. Many times that I do that signal, I still don't get to talk. And I've watched that happen to me at meetings, and I debate with myself, "Okay, I made the signal, I was ignored." You know, I'm not among the higher status persons in the room. There's kind of an editing of rank. It's the same for in-breaths. It's not a silver bullet.*

As other women in my interviews reported (Chapter 3), gender is only one of a number of intersecting social identities that affect their experiences in institutional interactions.

Another concern that women have reflected on is how much any instance of speaking up has effects beyond the moment of speaking. Ainsworth-Vaughn (1998) distinguishes power or control "claimed over emerging discourse" and power that is found in "future action" (1998:42). It is useful to consider whether an idea had a life beyond its interactional uptake in one meeting, and in the course of this research, I have also had occasion to observe the outcomes of meeting interactions, and I have had outcomes reported to me.

For example, in Chapter 6, I credited Stephie and Mary with effectively delivering disaffiliative actions, turns in which they took issue with the ideas of higher-ranking members of their committee, and turns which they successfully worked to expand. My last taping of the same committee was two years after Stephie and Mary raised issues regarding a broader approach to hiring and more attention to the partners and families of new hires. In the meeting two years later, the chair reported on and evaluated the group's efforts to educate against bias in hiring. At that time, only the more limited plan to educating hiring committees had been acted upon by the committee, and the committee discussed the idea that all faculty might need anti-bias workshops. By that point, I had been steeped in my analysis of the "plea" Stephie had made in a meeting of the same committee two years earlier, but though Stephie's suggestion was very fresh in my mind, no mention was made of it in the evaluative discussion, nor was there any change in the plan.[4]

And what of the outcomes of Mary's intervention? In Chapter 6, I noted the power Mary exercised in her talk as she raised the important issues of childcare and dual career hires to the committee's attention? These initiatives, though on record in her university's hiring and staff support policies, continue to be underfunded. They remain major reasons for faculty to seek jobs elsewhere, in hopes of achieving a healthier work-life balance, including childcare, jobs for their partners, and domestic partner healthcare benefits.

With regard to findings on the power of questions (Chapter 5), I can also see in the data that while a participant's questioning action can lead to further talk, this does not mean it will be responded to in affirming and supportive ways. Gwen, a physician, professor, and leader in women's health initiatives, is admired by other women as an activist in her workplace. She continually asks challenging questions about the exclusion of minorities and women at her institution and the neglect of minorities and women in clinical trials. In the meeting data I collected, there are instances of her asking such questions and raising challenging issues. She effectively gets them on the floor, but there is also evidence that her questions receive less than positive uptake.[5]

In our interview, Gwen reported on an experience she found particularly painful. Gwen was at a large meeting and the theme was how to recruit the best physicians:

> *I mentioned the thing about gender, and how if all the things that I was hearing were really true, people saying we want to get the best and brightest in medicine, we want to do this, we want to do that—I said we're going to have to address the gender issue, because women are leaving academic medicine at rates greater than men and we have to address these issues . . . No uptake, no comment, nothing.*
>
> *Then in the bathroom, the women came to me. Several women came to me and said, "Thank you so much for saying that." They said, "We wanted to clap but we felt squelched by the men around us who were rolling their eyes."*

Since rolling of eyes does constitute uptake, Gwen did get some public response, though non-vocal, off-record, and decidedly negative.

I see Gwen's story as containing seeds of change. In addition to the negative response in the large meeting hall, Gwen's call for attention to gender bias in hiring also received some positive uptake, even if only later and in the women's bathroom. I would argue that the women who later approached Gwen had witnessed her speaking up in the interest of meaningful change, change that they too supported, though less publicly in that moment. In my view, the public silence of these women is not the end of the story. They were moved by Gwen's courage in speaking up; they were moved to approach her and offer explanations for their public silence, accounts for their inaction in the larger group. Thus, they *did*, in fact, speak up in the safer space of the women's room. I am confident that they will speak up again in other settings.

Maureen Mahoney (2006) argues that, in a changing social world, a woman's choice to speak up should be understood as just one choice at one moment in time. Silence is "an active choice and an ingredient in resistance, either now or in the future" (2006:69). Mahoney adds that

> The capacity to speak out is nurtured in these episodes of nonspeaking . . . Far from being (only) moments of defeat, they also contain the possibility of strength and action.
>
> (2006:78)[6]

In the end, or at least at the end of this book, I agree with Florence that there is no "silver bullet" for success in meeting interaction. At times we will choose silence. At other times we will speak up. There is little doubt that we will often feel "squelched" by the silence of others, by "rolling eyes," or by other stronger negative responses. It is clear, however, that being exposed to positive perspectives and exercising our capacity to speak up constitute steps of the long and iterative process required to change institutions. Like many actions we take in the interest of change, once is not enough.

It was a group of educated, middle class North American women who originally invited me to investigate the challenges they face as they speak up in male-dominated workplaces. While socially and economically privileged, these women experience significant inequities in their worklives. By focusing on women's agency and skill rather than what holds them back, I have offered a serious empirical response to the self-reflection that these women, and others like them, exercise as they interact in their workplaces and as they absorb the contradictory representation of women and language in the popular media. The women who participated in this study, may not speak differently than do men, but nevertheless, by being women in the positions they hold (regardless of the methods through which they construct themselves and are constructed by others *as* women), they are exceptions to the norm. By their very presence, they are improvising new modes of being in their worlds.

Throughout my work on this project I have grappled with theoretical and practical challenges of studying women's talk in light of the complexity of current academic approaches to gender and language. One source of inspiration has been a chapter of the volume, *Identity and Agency in Cultural Worlds*, "The woman who climbed up the house" (Holland *et al.*, 1998). The authors reflect upon the actions of a Nepali woman, Gyanumaya. Gyanumaya needed to get to the second story balcony of a higher-caste home in order to meet with a western anthropologist. The problem was that getting to the second story of the structure would normally involve passing through the kitchen of a higher-caste family, a severe violation of culturally shared rules. Rather than being paralyzed by the problem, Gyanumaya quickly and effectively improvised a solution. She scaled the wall of the house to make her way onto the balcony. Reflecting on Gyanumaya's action, Holland *et al.* observe that

> Human agency may be frail, especially among those with little power, but it happens daily and mundanely, and it deserves our attention. Humans' capacity for self-objectification—and, through objectification, for self-direction—plays into both their domination by social relations of power and their possibilities for (partial) liberation from those forces.
>
> (1998:5)

What about the women in the meetings I studied, women moving into traditionally male positions and working for equity in those roles? What does liberation entail for these women and others like them? Among many other transformations, liberation includes liberation from stereotypical expectations. It requires that individuals of any gender begin to question and challenge common perceptions and interpretations of difference and the common, but biased, evaluations that accompany such perceptions. My experience with how applied, feminist CA is received by those outside and inside scholarly communities convinces me that attention to women's skills and practices for participating in workplace meetings can stimulate valuable reflection and support critical responses to cultural schemas that hold us all back.

I offer the findings from this study in hopes that they will serve, in some measure, to counter generalizations about women's lack of power to speak up articulately. I also offer them in celebration of the good work women are already doing.

Notes

1 Introduction: A Feminist Project

1. An ultimate goal, beyond this book, is to make versions of these methods and findings available to women and our allies to support reflection on women's competence and to counter myths of women's lack thereof. The success of such application remains to be seen.
2. But see Crawford (1988). Using more diverse evaluators than the usual college psychology students, and using "exploratory" factor analysis, Crawford found indications that

   assertiveness was evaluated differently depending on the sex of the assertive model and the sex and age of the research participant. Assertive women models received the lowest likeability ratings of all from older male participants and the highest from older female participants. However, the sex of the assertive model made no difference when competence was being judged.
   (1988, cited in Crawford, 1995:65)

3. It is an empirical question whether these practices are used asymmetrically based on social categories of speakers, though not one which I explore here.
4. For reviews of the history of gender and language studies see Holmes & Meyerhoff (2003), Eckert & McConnell-Ginet (2003) and Cameron (2005).
5. Cameron (2005:483) notes that though social constructionism may be the terminology used for the postmodernism of the 1990s, social constructionism in feminist research dates back to 1949, the year of the first (French) publication of Simone de Beauvoir's *The Second Sex*.
6. See Schegloff (1992 and elsewhere) on the "procedural consequentiality" of social identities. Schegloff argues on numerous occasions for analysts to attend not only to possible identities but to the ways that participants show that such categories are relevant to their conduct in the data at hand.
7. As we now better understand the interaction between language and gender, we might expect that further research would also reveal heterogeneity of male and female speech practices within the Malagasy speech community.
8. Keenan and Ochs are the same author.
9. These practices bring to mind the claims originally made by Lakoff in the 1970s that women commanded a form of language that both reflected and renewed their subjugation. The practices can also be understood as manifestations of women's taken-for-granted discourse labor as reported in earlier CA studies (Fishman, 1977; West & Garcia, 1988).
10. But see David Mulcahey's piece in *In These Times*, October 1, 2001 (http://www.inthesetimes.com/site/main/article/1624/):

    In a depressing field report on the inner void of the upper bourgeoisie, the *New York Times* describes a new kind of therapy for overly assertive female executives. Bully Broads, a program run by Jean Hollands of the Growth and Leadership Center in Mountainview, California, takes brassy, outspoken strivers (usually sent by their bosses, who find them a little too much to handle) and teaches them to hem and haw, blubber and just shut up. The results can be impressive. "Some of the, um, modifications Jean suggested have helped me," an ex-corporate shrew told the *Times*. "I just said 'um.' I never used to say 'um.' "

11. The pattern of men being evaluated more positively than women, even when other factors are equal, has been supported in a number of controlled experimental social psychological studies. These are reviewed in Valian (1998) and Ridgeway and Correll (2004). Of course, the construction of an individual as woman or man is a symbolic and discursive achievement itself, a process that my research subjects and I participated in for the current study. Much past and current conversation analytic, ethnomethodological, and poststructuralist research takes the social construction of gender as an object of study. That is not the goal of the current study.

12. At the time I entered a graduate program in AL, I had just completed a study of language-related prejudice (Ford, 1984), and I was exploring a discourse-based understanding of language structures (Ford & Thompson, 1987; Ford, 1993). The AL I refer to was manifested in the curriculum and faculty of the interdisciplinary Applied Linguistics Program in which I studied in the 1980s at UCLA. In that program I was able to form an interdepartmental dissertation committee co-chaired by a linguist and a sociologist.

13. See also the editorial introduction and collection of articles in a special 2005 issue of Applied Linguistics, "Applied Linguistics and Real-World Issues" (Cook & Kasper, 2005).

14. At the 2004 meeting of the American Association of Applied Linguistics, I worked with Junko Mori to coordinate an interdisciplinary panel entitled, "CA as Applied Linguistics: Crossing Boundaries of Discipline and Practice."

15. See also contributions to Sarangi and Roberts (1999).

16. For further examples of studies combining CA and other methods, see Goodwin 1990; Mangione-Smith *et al*, 2006; Kleinman *et al*, 1997; Pomerantz, 2005; Heritage & Stivers, 1999; Kitzinger & Frith, 1999 among others.

17. Of course, there is a great deal of research exploring such potential differences, in general terms and in specific communities of practice, some exemplars of which can be found in works cited earlier in this chapter.

2 Data and Analytic Practices

1. One instance involved the fine-tuned coordination of one recipient's postural movements with precise moments in the ongoing talk of another speaker.

2. My individual engagement with segments of talk became the basis for collaborative analyses in a number of forms including email sharing of short clips and messages back and forth; extended conversations with individuals at conferences; and intensive group analyses, CA data sessions, with students and colleagues in our interdisciplinary conversation analysis group at the

University of Wisconsin-Madison. Such second and third opinions and the insights generated from collaboration have been invaluable to my work with the data, but I, of course, articulated what I present in the following chapters, and my generous colleagues can only be held responsible for encouraging my quest.

3. Ned's stress may also serve to project upcoming possible turn completion. I thank Barbara Fox for bringing this to my attention.

4. See Sacks, Schegloff, and Jefferson (1974) for the first CA documentation of turn-taking and turn-constructional units.

5. The context and significance of Stephie's talk in this example will be examined in chapters 4 and 6.

6. Jefferson (2004) suggests ways of exploring a possible pattern whereby women respond more frequently to men's laughter than men respond to laughter initiated by women.

7. On the audience as "co-author," see Duranti and Brenneis (1986). Related illustrations are to be found in Schegloff (1987) and Goodwin & Goodwin (1987), Hayashi, Mori, & Takagi (2002), among other CA studies.

8. The principles elaborated in the 1974 article have been the subject of considerable criticism and refinement, but they have not received serious, databased challenges. For recent reviews and elaborations of the turn-taking and the notion of a TCU, see Ford and Thompson (1996), Schegloff (1996, 2000), Ford, Fox, & Thompson (1996), Selting (1996a, 2000), and Ford 2004), and chapters in Couper-Kuhlen and Ford (2004), among others.

9. For related reflections on research practice also see Cameron, Frazer, Harvey, Rampton & Richardson (1992) and Wilkinson & Kitzinger (1995).

10. I originally planned to videotape the same woman in two different meetings, but this was only possible with Wendy, Gwen, and Stephie. Here is a list of the formal interviewees; others, both female and male, were consulted with informally, without any recording:

Name	Meetings
Tilly	Zool 1
Carol	Zool 2
Lonnie	Plant
Gloria	Planning
Moira	Church
Lynn	Board
Pam	Diversity
Mary	Diversity
Wendy	Diversity
Florence	Diversity
Leslie	Diversity
Jan	Microbio, Diversity
Gwen	Medical, Diversity
Stephie	InfoGroup, Diversity

4 Meeting Organization: Openings, Turn Transitions, and Participant Alliances

1. Boden (1994:94) distinguishes directives from initiations through other actions with the terms "marked" or "unmarked"; to my understanding, she treats explicit directives and announcements of meeting beginnings as marked, and she considers other group-oriented actions (e.g., checking for a quorum) unmarked.
2. Deontic modality serves to make this a directive.
3. See Heritage (1984b) on conversational actions as "context-shaped and context renewing." (242).
4. See Beach (1993) and (1995).
5. I have not systematically investigated the ordering of choices to gesture, speak, use a name, or do all three simultaneously. Such choices may well be performing functions such as displaying special interest or downgrading interest, and they may also be adaptations related to other matters being managed.
6. I return to this case in Chapter 6 as I discuss ways of persisting in claiming a turn and in extending that turn.
7. I will return to Mary's turn and this sequence in my discussion of managing and expanding turns in Chapter 6.
8. Some of the women in my interviews report discomfort with this kind of competition, while others report that they may be "guilty" of not paying attention to others who may want to speak (see Chapter 3).
9. It is not the use of *no* that makes Stephie's actions disagreeing. The formulation of the turn is only part of the way meaning is made—its composition. We need also to attend to position in understanding agreement and disagreement. That is, we must see the *no* (or *yes*, or other vocal or non-vocal action) in its sequential context. The interpretation of Stephie's *no* tokens as strong disagreement, as in (20), is dependent on the context of activity. For example, in (10) line 14, which we have viewed above, Mary begins with "No no no," but her negative tokens, while formally doing disagreement, are used to politely reject the need for John to apologize for having talked while Mary's hand was raised.
10. Gareth does not provide a verbal response to Lonnie's request that he confirm remembering. He keeps his gaze toward her while leaning back in his chair and allowing her to continue with her answer to Jerry.

5 Questions: Opening Participation, Displaying Expertise, and Challenging

1. In a critique of Tannen's explanation of gendered patterns in asking directions, Mary Crawford (1995) reminds us that the interpretations we put on patterns of language use by women and men reflect our cultural expectations, what Wareing (1996, cited in Cameron, 1998) refers to as the "hall of mirrors." Crawford asks us to imagine how the same cultural assumptions might have been drawn upon if people reported that women rather than men were reluctant to ask for directions. Crawford suggests that if men had

reported a greater willingness to ask for directions, with women reporting avoidance of such interactions, one could draw upon another shared assumption: women experience more vulnerability in public than do men. Given women's position of relatively greater physical danger than men in most societies, one could reasonably interpret women's avoidance of asking for directions as stemming from not wanting to reveal vulnerability. In her discussion of this imagined reversal of gendered patterns in reported questioning behavior, Crawford highlights the need to be reflective regarding the cultural assumptions which drive our analyses.

2. This kind of "rush through" a point of possible completion is a familiar strategy for keeping the floor (Schegloff, 1996 and elsewhere).

3. I will return to this case in the next chapter, where I detail the position and composition of Stephie's turn and another turn that follows in the same meeting segment.

4. Schegloff (2007:151–5) discusses other-initiated repair and disagreement.

5. The fact that it takes two different articulations, by two different participants, before the question is heard as a challenge by the Rector is interesting with respect to the phenomenon of having one's ideas taken up or ignored. While both the first and second articulators of the question are women, the second one is of arguably higher rank: she is the education director at the church and Paula is the church administrator, sometimes taken to be the personal secretary to the Rector. Thus, as my interviewees suggest, gender is far from the only factor in getting uptake. And of course there is also the mere fact of an idea being articulated twice making it better understood because of persistence and repetition.

6   Placing and Designing Disaffiliative Actions

1. See Barske (2006) for analyses of disaffiliative and delicate actions in German business meetings.

2. See Heritage (1984b:265–9) for a discussion of connections between conceptions of "face" (Goffman, 1955, Brown & Levinson, 1978) and the CA notions of dispreferred or disaffiliative actions and/or turn design.

3. Ingrid's is a B-event statement, stating knowledge that is in John's domain. This contributes to the turn's prompting a response from John, but Ingrid also turns her torso and her gaze toward John.

4. Stephie also reintroduces reference to "two years" at line 48, although Stephie's is likely referring to the administration's practice of allowing two years in which to conduct a search.

5. Stephie's turn opens an interactional space that Mary uses to add her comment on the preceding discussion. However, unlike the cases discussed in the section on "alliances" in Chapter 4, Mary's intervention in the interaction takes the topic in a new direction, moving its development away from issues of "broadening" the notion of a hiring search. I thank Barbara Fox and Emanuel Schegloff for drawing my attention to relationships between Mary's turn and the issue that Stephie has raised. A full analysis of this must wait for another forum.

6. I don't mean to be overly wordy and obtuse in my description of the potential meaning of the pauses and hesitations, but it is obviously impossible to measure whether these women are truly having unavoidable problems in speaking or whether they are artfully "doing being" cautious and hesitant. In either case, both women construct their turns as such.

7. What I share here is dealt with in more linguistic and conversation analytic detail elsewhere (Ford & Fox, 2005). Thus, my analysis of Stephie's contribution depends crucially on the collaborative work I have done with Barbara Fox. We are exploring Stephie's use of clauses with *I* as subject pronouns and also features of affect management in her turn.

8. During the pause, there is a loud click sound on the video. This is likely not as loud for the participants, as it results from the researcher's handling of the camera as she finishes changing a digital cassette and checks the sound through headphones.

9. It was in close collaboration with Barbara Fox that the interactional significance of this participial phrase came to light.

10. John's joining in Stephie's laughter is particularly interesting given Jefferson's findings (2004) with regard to males resisting females' laughter.

11. I thank William Hanks for noting this possible motivation for John to withhold a surprised response after Stephie's news delivery.

12. This pattern goes against the trend for women to reciprocate men's laughter initiations more than the other way around, as suggested by Jefferson's (2004) data.

13. As mentioned in note 5, Emanuel Schegloff has suggested that Mary might be seen as hijacking Stephie's intervention by using the re-opened discussion of hiring practices to register her concern about couples and childcare. These issues are of clear relevance to the general discussion, but they do not build upon or support the theme that Stephie has just worked to raise.

14. A concession can project that a turn continues into a restatement of the contrasting claim (see Ford, 1994, 2000). Indeed just after Charles completes his concessive clause, he produces the contrastive connector "but" ("we choose a subset [...] but"). John's overlapping turn beginning is rhetorically coordinated with Charles' projected contrast, which means that the overlap is interpretable as collaborative (Lerner, 1991). By using the agreement token, "Yeah," John may also be enacting his power as Dean of CAS to confirm what his Associate Dean is saying. In spite John's turn beginning, Charles continues his own talk beyond the "but"; he persists to the completion of his projected contrast, now in overlap with John (arrows 2–3, p. 152).

15. See Lerner (1996) on the "'semi-permeable' character" of units in conversation.

16. Although John's talk at 63 is in overlap, we can note (and the other participants may hear) that he is projecting further talk. The "it" in "it <u>is</u> true," works as a cataphoric reference or prospective indexical.

17. See Fox (1987) for a related discussion of using long-distance anaphora to treat a sequence as still open.

18. Recall that during her turn and its extensions, Mary predominantly gazes toward John.

7 Speaking Up in Meetings: Summary and Conclusions

1. Cameron articulated this disjunct in a plenary at the 2004 AAAL conference, a piece later published in *Applied Linguistics* (2005).
2. Also see Hutchby (1996).
3. Although my digitized video is compressed to a degree that faces are not easily recognizable, in the interest of supporting confidentiality, I am cautious about using them in certain settings. At times I use audio only, and at times I read the examples rather than playing audio or video.
4. The workshops for hiring committees had gone forward, however, and I consider these innovative and important outcomes of the committee. My point here is to consider the consequences of speaking up in a meeting, as I happen to have access to an outcome in this instance.
5. One such case is presented in Ford (In press).
6. Also see Susan Gal (1991) for a cross-cultural and cross-linguistic critique of the interpretation of silence, which Mahoney and Thornborrow also draw upon.

References

Ainsworth-Vaughn, N. (1998) *Claiming Power in Doctor-Patient Talk*. New York: Oxford University Press.

Alcoff, L. (1991) The problem of speaking for others. *Cultural Critique, 20* (Winter 1991–2), 5–32.

Atkinson, J. M. & Drew, P. (1979) *Order in Court: The Organization of Verbal Interaction in Judicial Settings*. London: Macmillan.

Austin, J. (1962) *How to Do Things With Words*. Cambridge: Cambridge University Press.

Barrett, R. (1999) Indexing polyphonous identity in speech of African American drag queens. In M. Bucholtz, A. Liang, & L. Sutton (Eds), *Reinventing Identities: The Gendered Self in Discourse* (pp. 313–31) New York: Oxford University Press.

Barske, T. G. (2006) Co-constructing Social Roles in German Business Meetings: A Conversation Analytic Study. Unpublished Dissertation. Germanic Language and Literatures. University of Illinois at Urbana-Champaign.

Baxter, J. (2002) Competing discourses in the classroom: A post-structuralist discourse analysis of girls' and boys' talk in the secondary classroom. *Gender and Education, 14* (1), 5–19.

Baxter, J. (2003) *Positioning Gender in Discourse: A Feminist Methodology*. Basingstoke: Palgrave Macmillan.

Baxter, J. (2006a) Putting gender in its place: Constructing speaker identities in management meetings. In M. Barrett & M. Davidson (Eds), *Gender and Communication at Work* (pp. 154–65) Aldershot: Ashgate Publishing Ltd.

Baxter, J. (Ed.) (2006b) *Speaking Out: The Female Voice in Public Contexts*. Basingstoke: Palgrave Macmillan.

Beach, W. A. (1993) Transitional regularities for 'casual' "Okay" usages. *Journal of Pragmatics, 19*, 325–52.

Bergvall, V. L. (1996) Constructing gender through discourse: Negotiating multiple roles as female engineering students. In V. L. Bergvall, J. M. Bing, and A. F. Freed (Eds), *Rethinking Language and Gender Research: Theory and Practice*. (pp. 173–202) London: Longman.

Bilmes, J. (1995) Negotiation and compromise: A microanalysis of a discussion in the United States Federal Trade Commission. In A. Firth (Ed.) *The Discourse of Negotiation: Studies of language in the Workplace*. (61–81) Oxford: Pergamon.

Boden, D. (1994) *The Business of Talk*. Cambridge: Polity.

Brown, P & Levinson, S. C. (1978) Universals in language usage: politeness phenomena. In E. Goody (Ed.). *Questions and Politeness: Strategies in Social Interaction* (pp.56–310) Cambridge: Cambridge University Press.

Brumfit, C. (1995) Teacher professionalism and research. In G. Cook & B. Seidlhofer (Eds), *Principle and Practice in Applied Linguistics* (pp. 27–41) Oxford: Oxford University Press.

Bucholtz, M. (1999) Why be normal?: Language and identity practices in community of nerd girls. *Language in Society, 28* (2), 203–23.

Bucholtz, M. (2002) Geek feminism. In S. Benor, M. Rose, D. Sharma, J. Sweetland, & Q. Zhang (Eds), *Gendered Practices in Language* (pp. 277–307) Stanford, CA: CSLI.

Butler, J. (1990) *Gender Trouble Feminism and the Subversion of Identity.* London: Routledge.

Cameron, D. (1995) *Verbal Hygiene.* London: Routledge.

Cameron, D. (1997) Performing gender identity: young men's talk and the construction of heterosexual masculinity. In S. Johnson and U. Meinhoff (Eds), *Language and Masculinity* (pp. 86–107) Oxford: Blackwell.

Cameron, D. (1998) Gender, language and discourse: A review essay. *Signs: Journal of Women in Culture and Society, 23,* 945–73.

Cameron, D. (2005) Language, gender, and sexuality: Current issues and new directions. *Applied Linguistics, 26* (4), 482–502.

Cameron, D. (2007) *The Myth of Mars and Venus.* Oxford: Oxford University Press.

Cameron, D., Frazer, E., Harvey, P., Rampton, B. & Richardson, K. (1992) *Researching Language: Issues of Power and Method.* London: Routledge.

Cameron, D., McAlinden, F. & O'Leary, K. (1988) Lakoff in context: The social and linguistic function of tag questions. In J. Coates & D. Cameron (Eds), *Women in their Speech Communities.* New York: Longman.

Cook, G. & Kasper, G. (2005) Special Issue: Applied Linguistics and Real-World Issues. *Applied Linguistics, 26* (4), 479–581.

Couper-Kuhlen, E. & Ford, C. E. (2004) *Sound Patterns in Interaction: Cross-Linguistic Studies from Conversation.* Amsterdam: Benjamins.

Couper-Kuhlen, E. & Thompson, S. A. (2000) Concessive patterns in conversation. In E. Couper-Kuhlen & B. Kortmann (Eds), *Cause, Condition, Concession, and Contrast: Cognitive and Discourse Perspectives* (pp. 381–410) Berlin: Mouton de Gruyter.

Crawford, M. (1988) Gender, age, and the social evaluation of assertion. *Behavior Modification, 12,* 549–64.

Crawford, M. (1995) *Talking Difference: On Gender and Language.* London: Sage.

Cuff, E. & Sharrock, W. (1987) Meetings. In T. A. van Dijk (Ed.), *Handbook of Discourse Analysis* (pp. 149–60) London: Academic Press.

Curl, T. S. (2004) 'Repetition' repairs: The relationship of phonetic structure and sequence organization. In E. Couper-Kuhlen & C. E. Ford (Eds), *Sound Patterns in Interaction* (pp. 273–98) Amsterdam: Benjamins.

Curl, T. S. (2005) Practices in other-initiated repair resolution: The phonetic differentiation of 'repetitions.' *Discourse Processes, 39* (1), 1–44.

Davies, B. & Harré, R. (1990) Positioning: The Discursive Production of Selves. *Journal for the Theory of Social Behavior, 20,* 43–63.

Dietz, M. G. (2003) Current controversies in feminist theory. *Annual Review of Political Science, 6,* 339–431.

Drew, P. (1987) Po-faced receipts of teases. *Linguistics, 25,* 219–53.

Drew, P. (1997) "Open" class repair initiators in response to sequential sources of troubles in conversation. *Journal of Pragmatics, 28,* 69–102.

Drew, P. & Heritage, J. (Eds) (1992) *Talk at Work: Interaction in Institutional Settings.* Cambridge: Cambridge University Press.

Duranti, A. (1997) *Linguistic Anthropology.* Cambridge: Cambridge University Press.

Duranti, A. & Brenneis, D. (1986) The audience as coauthor. *Special Issue of Text,* 6 (3), 239–47.

Eckert, P. & McConnell-Ginet, S. (1992) Think practically and look locally: Language and gender as community-based practice. *Annual Review of Anthroplogy, 21,* 461–90.

Eckert, P. & McConnell-Ginet, S. (2003) *Language and Gender.* Cambridge: Cambridge University Press.

Edelsky, C. (1981) Who's got the floor? *Language in Society* 10, 383–421.

Egbert, M. (1997) Schisming: The collaborative transformation from a single conversation to multiple conversations. *Research on Language and Social Interaction, 30* (1–51).

Ehrlich, S. (2006) Trial discourse and judicial decision-making: Constraining the boundaries of gendered identities. In J. Baxter (Ed.) *Speaking Out: The Female Voice in Public Contexts.* (139–58) Basingstoke: Palgrave Macmillan.

Ervin-Tripp, S. (1976) Is Sybil there? The structure of American English directives. *Language in Society, 5,* 25–66.

Femø Nielsen, M. (In press) Falles fodslag. Mellenlederens arbejde med at skabe retnig og mening i mondtlig medarbejderkommonikation [Common ground: Middle managers working to create direction and meaning in verbal employee communication]. Copenhagen: Sanfundslitteratur, Spring 2008.

Femø Nielsen, M. (In prep a) *Doing being middle manager.* Manuscript, Department of Scandinavian Studies and Linguistics, University of Copenhagen, Denmark.

Femø Nielsen, M. (In prep b) *Interpretation management.* Manuscript, Department of Scandinavian Studies and Linguistics, University of Copenhagen, Denmark.

Femø Nielsen, M. (In prep c) *Observations on department meetings.* Manuscript, Department of Scandinavian Studies and Linguistics, University of Copenhagen, Denmark.

Femø Nielsen, M. (In prep d) *Opening up closings and closing down openings at department meetings.* Manuscript, Department of Scandinavian Studies and Linguistics, University of Copenhagen, Denmark.

Fenstermaker, S. & West, C. (2002) *Doing Gender, Doing Difference: Inequality, Power, and Institutional Change.* New York: Routledge.

Fishman, P. (1977) Interactional shitwork. *Heresies, 1,* 99–101.

Fishman, P. (1978) The work women do. *Social Problems, 25,* 397–406.

Fishman, P. (1980) Conversational insecurity. In H. Giles, WP. Robinson &. P. M. Smith (Eds), *Language: Social Psychological Perspectives* (pp. 127–32) Oxford: Pergamon Press.

Fletcher, J. K. (1999) *Disappearing Acts: Gender, Power, and Relational Practice at Work.* Massachusetts Institute of Technology: MIT Press.

Ford, C. E. (1984) The influence of speech variety on teachers' evaluation of students with comparable academic ability. *TESOL Quarterly* 18 (1), 25–40.

Ford, C. E. (1993) *Grammar in Interaction: Adverbial Clauses in American English Conversations.* Cambridge: Cambridge University Press.

Ford, C. E. (1994) Dialogic aspects of talk and writing: *because* on the interactional-edited continuum. *TEXT 14* (4), 531–54.

Ford, C. E. (2000a) At the intersection of turn and sequence: Negation and what comes next. In Couper-Kuhlen & M. Selting (Eds), *Studies in Interactional Linguistics* (pp. 51–79) Amersterdam: Benjamins.

Ford, C. E. (2000b) The treatment of contrasts in interaction. In *Cause, Condition, Concession and Contrast: Cognitive and Discourse Perspectives*, Bernd Kortmann and Elizabeth Couper-Kuhlen (Eds), in the series *Topics in English Linguistics*. Berlin: Mouton de Gruyter. 283–311.

Ford, C. E. (2001) Denial and the construction of conversational turns. In J. Bybee & M. Noonan (Eds), *Complex Sentences in Grammar and Discourse* (pp. 61–78) Amsterdam: Benjamins.

Ford, C. E. (2004) Contingency and units in interaction. *Discourse Studies, 6* (1), 27–52.

Ford, C. E. (In Press) Questioning in meetings: Participation and positioning. In S. Ehrlich & A Freed. (Eds), *Why Do You Ask?: The Function of Questions in Institutional Discourse*. Oxford: Oxford University Press.

Ford, C. E. & Fox, B. A. (2005) "Reference and Repair as Grammatical Practices in an Extended Turn." Plenary for the Annual Meeting of the Society for Text and Discourse. Amsterdam, July 6.

Ford, C. E., Fox, B. A. & Hellermann, J. (2004) Getting past 'No': Sequence, action and turn production in the projection of no-initiated turns. In B. Couper-Kuhlen & C. E. Ford (Eds), *Sound Patterns in Interaction* (pp. 233–72) Amsterdam: Benjamins.

Ford, C. E. & Thompson, S. A. (1987) Conditionals in discourse: A text-based study from English. In E. C. Traugott, A. ter Meulen, J. Snitzer Reilly, & C. A. Ferguson (Eds) *On Conditionals*. (pp. 33–72) Cambridge: Cambridge University Press.

Ford, C., Fox, B. A. & Thompson, S. A. (1996) Practices in the construction of turns: The "TCU" revisited. *Pragmatics, 6*, 427–54.

Ford, C. E. & Thompson, S. (1996) Interactional units in conversation: Syntactic, intonational, and pragmatic resources for the management of turns. In E. Ochs, E. Schegloff, & S. A. Thompson (Eds), *Interaction and Grammar* (pp. 134–84) Cambridge: Cambridge University Press.

Fox, B. A. (Ed.) (1987) *Anaphora and the Structure of Discourse*. Cambridge: Cambridge University Press.

Freed, A. F. (1992) We understand perfectly: A critique of Tannen's view of cross-sex communication. In K. Hall, M. Bucholtz & B. Moonwoman (Eds), *Locating Power: Proceedings of the Second Berkeley Women and Language Conference* (pp. 144–52) Berkeley: Berkeley Women and Language Group.

Freed, A. F. (1994) The form and function of questions in informal dyadic conversation. *Journal of Pragmatics, 21*, 621–44.

Gal, S. (1991) Between speech and silence: The problematics of research on language and gender. In M. D. Leonardo (Ed.), *Gender at the Crossroads of Knowledge: Feminist Anthropology in the Postmodern Era* (pp. 175–203) Berkeley: University of California Press.

Goffman, E. (1955) On face-work: An analysis of ritual elements in social interaction. *Psychiatry, 18*, 213–31.

Goodwin, C. (1979) The interactive construction of a sentence in natural conversation. In G. Psathas (Ed.), *Everyday Language: Studies in Ethnomethodology* (pp. 97–121) New York: Irvington.

Goodwin, C. (1980) Restarts, pauses, and the achievement of mutual gaze at turn-beginning. *Sociological Inquiry* 50 (3–4), 272–302.

Goodwin, C. (1981) *Conversational Organization: Interaction between Speakers and Hearers*. New York: Academic Press.

Goodwin, C. (1984) Notes on story structure and the organization of participation. In J. M. Atkinson & J. Heritage (Eds), *Structures of Social Action* (pp. 225–46) Cambridge: Cambridge University Press.

Goodwin, C. (1994) Professional vision. *American Anthropologist 96* (3), 606–33.

Goodwin, C. (1996) Transparent vision. In E. Ochs, E. Schegloff & S. Thompson (Eds), *Interaction and Grammar* (pp. 370–404) Cambridge: Cambridge University Press.

Goodwin, C. & Goodwin, M. H. (1987) Concurrent Operations on Talk: Notes on the Interactive Organization of Assessments. *IPrA Papers in Pragmatics* 1 (1), 1–55.

Goodwin, M. H. (1980) Directive-response speech sequences in girls' and boys' task activities. In S. McConnell-Ginet, R. Borker & N. Furman (Eds), *Women and Language in Literature and Society* (pp. 157–73) New York: Praeger.

Goodwin, M. H. (1990) *He-Said-She-Said: Talk as Social Organization among Black Children*. Bloomington: Indiana University Press.

Greenwood, A. & Freed, A. (1992) Women talking to women: The function of questions in conversation. In K. Hall, M. Bucholtz & B. Moonwomon (Eds) *Locating Power: Proceedings of the Second Berkeley Women and Language Conference*. (197–206) Berkeley Women and Language Group, Berkeley, California.

Gumperz, J. (1982) *Discourse Strategies*. Cambridge: Cambridge University Press.

Hall, K. (1995) Lip service on the fantasy lines. In K. Hall & M. Bucholtz (Eds), *Gender Articulated: Language and the Socially Constructed Self*. (pp. 183–216) New York: Routledge.

Hall, K. (2003) Exceptional speakers: Contested and problematized gender identities. J. Holmes & M. Meyerhoff (Eds) *The Handbook of Language and Gender*, (pp. 353–80) Oxford: Blackwell.

Have, P. ten (1999) *Doing Conversation Analysis: A Practical Guide*. London: Sage.

Hayashi, M., Mori, J. & Takagi, T. (2002) Contingent achievement of co-tellership in a Japanese conversation: An analysis of talk, gaze, and gesture. In C. E. Ford, B. A. Fox & S. A. Thompson (Eds) *The Language of Turn and Sequence*. (pp. 81–122) Oxford: Oxford University Press.

Heritage, J. (1984a) A change-of-state token and aspects of its sequential placement. In J. M. Atkinson & J. Heritage (Eds), *Structures of Social Action: Studies in Conversation Analysis* (pp. 299–376) Cambridge: Cambridge University Press.

Heritage, J. (1984b) *Garfinkel and Ethnomethodology*. Cambridge: Polity.

Heritage, J. (2002) Oh-prefaced responses to assessments: A method of modifying agreement/disagreement. In C. E. Ford, B. A. Fox & S. A. Thompson (Eds) *The Language of Turn and Sequence*. (pp. 196–224) Oxford: Oxford University Press.

Heritage, J. & Atkinson, J. M. (1984) Introduction. In J. M. Atkinson & J. Heritage (Eds), *Structures of Social Action* (pp. 1–15) Cambridge: Cambridge University Press.

Heritage, J. & Roth, A. (1995) Grammar and institution: Questions and questioning in the broadcast news interview. *Research on Language and Social Interaction, 28*, 160.

Heritage, J. & Stivers, T. (1999) Online commentary in acute medical visits: A method of shaping patient expectations. *Social Science and Medicine. 49* (11), 1501–17.

Holland, D., Lachicotte Jr., W., Skinner, D. and Cain, C. (1998) *Identity and Agency in Cultural Worlds*. Cambridge, MA: Harvard University Press.

Hollands, J. (2002) *Same Game, Different Rules: How to Get Ahead Without Being a Bully Broad, Ice Queen, or "Ms. Understood"*. New York: McGraw-Hill.

Holmes, J. (1984) "Women's language": A functional approach. *General Linguistics 24* (3), 149–78.

Holmes, J. & Marra, M. (2004) Relational practice in the workplace: Women's talk or gendered discourse? *Language in Society, 33*, 337–98.

Holmes, J. & Meyerhoff, M. (Eds) (2003) *The Handbook of Language and Gender*. Oxford: Blackwell.

Houtkoop, H. & Mazeland, H. (1985) Turns and discourse units in everyday conversation. *Journal of Pragmatics, 9*, 595–619.

Hutchby, I. (1996) Power in discourse: the case of arguments on a British talk radio show. *Discourse and Society, 7* (4), 481–97.

Hudson, R. A. (1975) The meaning of questions. *Language, 45*, 1–31.

Huisman, M. (2001) Decision-making in meetings as talk-in-interaction. *International Studies of Management & Organization, 31* (3), 69–90.

James, D. & Drakich, J. (1993) Understanding gender differences in amount of talk: A critical review. In D. Tannen (Ed.), *Gender and Conversational Interaction* (pp. 231–80) Oxford: Oxford University Press.

Jasperson, R. (2002) Some linguistic aspects of closure cut-off. In C. Ford, B. Fox & S. Thompson (Eds), *The Language of Turn and Sequence* (pp. 257–86) Oxford: Oxford University Press.

Jefferson, G. (1973) A case of precision timing in ordinary conversation: Overlapped tag-positioned address terms in closing sequences. *Semiotica, 9*, 47–96.

Jefferson, G. (1978) Sequential aspects of story telling in conversation. In J. N. Schenkein (Ed.), *Studies in the Organization of Conversational Interaction* (pp. 213–48) New York: Academic Press.

Jefferson, G. (2004) A note on laughter in 'male-female' interaction. *Discourse Studies, 6* (1), 117–33.

Jefferson, G. & Schenkein, J. (1978) Some sequential Negotiations in Conversation: Unexpanded and Expanded Versions of Projected Action Sequences. In J. Schenkein (Ed.), *Studies in the organization of conversational interaction* (pp. 155–72) New York: Academic Press.

Kangasharju, H. (1996) Aligning as a team in multiparty conversation. *Journal of Pragmatics, 26*, 291–319.

Keenan, E. (1974) Norm-makers, norm-breakers: Uses of speech by men and women in a Malagasy community. In R. Bauman & J. Sherzer (Eds), *Explorations in the Ethnography of Speaking* (pp. 125–43) Cambridge: Cambridge University Press.

Keisanen, T. (2006) *Patterns of Stance Taking: Negative Yes/no Interrogatives and Tag Questions in American English Conversation*. Acta Universitatis Ouluensis B71. Oulu: Oulu University Press. Available in electronic form at http:// herkules.oulu. fi/isbn9514280393/

Kiesling, S. F. (1997) Power and the language of men. In S. Johnson & U. H. Meinhof (Eds), *Language and Masculinity* (pp. 65–85) Oxford: Blackwell.

Kitzinger, C. (2000) Doing feminist conversation analysis. *Feminism & Psychology, 10* (2), 163–93.

Kitzinger, C. (2005) Heteronormativity in action: Reproducing the heterosexual nuclear family in 'after hours' medical calls. *Social Problems, 52* (4), 477–98.

Kitzinger, C. (2007) Is 'woman' always relevantly gendered? *Gender and Language, 1* (1), 39–49.

Kitzinger, C. (2007) Editor's introduction: The promise of conversation analysis for feminist research: Introduction to special feature on conversation analysis, gender and sexuality. *Feminism & Psychology, 16* (3), 133–148.

Kitzinger, C. & Frith, H. (1999) Just say no? Using conversation analysis to understand how young women talk about refusing sex. *Discourse and Society, 10* (3), 293–316.

Kitzinger, C. & Wilkinson, S. (1997) Validating women's experience? Dilemmas in feminist research. *Feminism & Psychology, 7* (4), 566–74.

Kleinman, L., Boyd, E. & Heritage, J. (1997, 13th Aug. 1997) Adherence to prescribed explicit criteria during utilization review: An analysis of communications between attending and reviewing physicians. *Journal of the American Medical Association, 278* (6), 497–501.

Koole, T & ten Thije, J. D. (1994) *The Construction of Intercultural Discourse: Team Discussions of Educational Advisers.* Amsterdam: Rodopi.

Labov, W. & Fanshel, D. (1977) *Therapeutic discourse.* New York: Academic Press.

Lakoff, R. (1975) *Language and woman's place.* New York: Harper & Row.

Lakoff, R. (2004) Language and woman's place. In M. Bucholtz (Ed.), *Language and Woman's Place: Text and Commentaries* (Revised and Expanded Edition). New York: Oxford University Press.

Land, V. & Kitzinger, C. (2005) Speaking as a lesbian: Correcting the heterosexist presumption. *Research on Language and Social Interaction, 38* (4), 371–416.

Lerner, G. H. (1991) On the syntax of sentences in progress. *Language in Society, 20*, 441–58.

Lerner, G. H. (1993) Collectivities in action: Establishing the relevance of conjoined participation in conversation. *Text, 13* (2), 213–45.

Lerner, G. H. (1996) On the 'semi-permeable' character of grammatical units in conversation: Conditional entry into the turn space of another speaker. In E. Ochs, E. Schegloff & S. Thompson (Eds), *Interaction and Grammar* (pp. 238–71) Cambridge: Cambridge University Press.

Lerner, G. H. (2002) Turn-sharing: The choral co-production of talk-in-interaction. In C. Ford, B. Fox & S. Thompson (Eds), *The Language of Turn and Sequence* (pp. 225–56) Oxford: Oxford University Press.

Lever, J. (1976) Sex differences in the games children play. *Social Problems, 23*, 478–83.

Linton, L. D. & Lerner, G. (Ms. Department of Sociology) (2004) Before the beginning: Breath taking in conversation. Santa Barbara: University of California.

Local, J. & Kelly, J. (1986) Projection and 'silences': Notes on phonetic and conversational structure. *Human Studies, 9*, 185–204.

Local, J. & Walker, G. (2005) Methodological imperatives for investigating the phonetic organization and phonological structures of spontaneous speech. *Phonetica, 62*, 120–30.

Mahoney, M. A. (2006) The problem of silence in feminist psychology. In S. J. Freeman, S. B. Bourque & C. M. Shelton (Eds), *Women on power: Leadership redefined* (pp. 61–83) Boston: Northeastern University Press.

Maltz, D. & Borker, R. (1982) A cultural approach to male—female misunderstanding. In J. Gumperz (Ed.) *Language and Social Identity* (pp. 196–216) Cambridge: Cambridge University Press.

Mandelbaum, J. (1987) Couples sharing stories. *Communication Quarterly, 35,* 144–70.

Mangione-Smith, R., Elliot, M., Stivers, T., McDonald, L. & Heritage, J. (2006) Ruling out the need for antibiotics: Are we sending the right message? *Archives of Pediatric and Adolescent Medicine, 160,* 945–52.

Maynard, D. W. (2003) *Bad News, Good News: Conversational Order in Everyday Talk and Settings.* Chicago: University of Chicago Press.

Mazeland, H. & Berenst, J. (in press) Sorting pupils in a report-card meeting: Categorization in a situated activity system. *Text and Talk, 28* (1).

McConnell-Ginet, S. (2000) Panel Discussion: How can language and gender research be best used in the work place? In J. Holmes (Ed.), *Gendered Speech in Social Context: Perspectives From Gown and Town* (pp. 124–27) Wellington, New Zealand: Victoria University Press.

McElhinny, B. S. (1995) Challenging hegemonic masculinities: Female and male police officers handling domestic violence. In K. Hall & M. Bucholtz (Eds, *Gender Articulated: Language and the Socially Constructed Self* (pp. 217–43) New York: Routledge.

McIlvenny, Paul (Ed) (2002) *Talking Gender and Sexuality.* Amsterdam: Benjamins.

Mendoza-Denton, N. (2004) The anguish of normative gender: Sociolinguistic studies among U.S. Latinas. In M. Bucholtz (Ed.), *Language and Woman's Place: Text and Commentaries* (Revised and Expanded Edition) (pp. 260–8) New York: Oxford University Press.

Mills, S. (2003) *Gender and Politeness.* Cambridge: Cambridge University Press.

Morgan, M. (2004) "I'm every woman": Black women's (dis)placement in women's language study. In M. Bucholtz (Ed.), *Language and Woman's Place: Text and Commentaries* (Revised and Expanded Edition) (pp. 252–9) New York: Oxford University Press.

O'Barr, W. & Atkins, B. (1980) "Women's language" or "powerless language". In S. McConnell-Ginet, R. Borker & N. Furman (Eds) Women and Language in Literature and Society (pp. 93–110) New York: Praeger.

Ochs, E. (1979) Transcription as theory. In E. Ochs & B. Schieffelin (Eds), *Developmental Pragmatics* (pp. 43–72) New York: Academic Press.

Ochs, E. (1992) Indexing gender. In A. Duranti & C. Goodwin (Eds) *Rethinking Context: Language as an Interactive Phenomenon* (pp. 335–58). Cambridge: Cambridge University Press.

Pomerantz, A. (1984) Agreeing and disagreeing with assessments: some features of preferred/dispreferred turn shapes. In Atkinson, J. M., J. Heritage (Eds) *Structures of Social Action: Studies in Conversation Analysis* (pp. 57–101). Cambridge: Cambridge University Press.

Pomerantz, A. (2005) Using participants' video stimulated comments to complement analyses of interactional practices. In H. Molder & J. Potter (Eds), *Talk and Cognition: Discourse, Mind and Social Interaction* (pp. 93–113) Cambridge: Cambridge University Press.

Pomerantz, A. & Fehr, B. (1997) Conversation analysis: An approach to the study of social action as sense making practices. In T.A van Dijk (Ed.), *Discourse as*

Social Interaction: Discourse Studies 2- A Multidisciplinary Introduction (pp. 64–91) London: Sage.

Raymond, G. (2003) Grammar and social organization: Yes/no interrogatives and the structure of responding. *American Sociological Review, 68*, 939–67.

Richards, K. & Seedhouse, P. (2004) *Applying Conversation Analysis*. New York: Palgrave Macmillan.

Ridgeway, C. L. & Correll, S. (2004) Unpacking the gender system: A theoretical perspective on cultural beliefs in social relations. *Gender and Society, 18*, 510–31.

Sacks, H. (1972) An initial investigation of the usability of conversational data for doing sociology. In D. Sudnow (Ed.) *Studies in Social Interaction* (pp. 31–74) New York: Free Press.

Sacks, H. (1974) An analysis of the course of a joke's telling in conversation. In R Bauman & J. Sherzer (Eds) *Explorations in the Ethnography of Speaking* (337–53) Cambridge: Cambridge University Press.

Sacks, H. (1984) Notes on methodology. In J. M. Atkinson & John Heritage (Eds), *Structures of Social Action* (pp. 21–7) Cambridge: Cambridge University Press.

Sacks, H. (1987) On the preferences for agreement and contiguity in sequences in conversation. In Button, G. & J. R. E. Lee (Eds), *Talk and Social Organisation*. Clevedon: Multilingual Matters: 54–69.

Sacks, H. & Schegloff, E. (1979) Two preferences in the organization of reference to persons and their interaction. In G. Psathas (Ed.), *Everyday Language: Studies in Ethnomethodology* (pp. 15–21) New York: Irvington Publishers.

Sacks, H., Schegloff, E. & Jefferson, G. (1974) A simplest systematics for the organization of turn taking for conversation. *Language, 50* (4), 696–735.

Sarangi, S. & Roberts, C. (1999) *Talk, Work and Institutional Order: Discourse in Medical, Mediation and Management Settings*. Berlin: Mouton de Gruyter.

Schegloff, E. A. (1968) Sequencing in conversational openings. *American Anthropologist, 70*, 1075–95.

Schegloff, E. A. (1980) Preliminaries to preliminaries: "Can I ask you a question?" *Sociological Inquiry*, 104–52.

Schegloff, E. A. (1987) Analyzing single episodes of interaction: An exercise in conversation analysis. *Social Psychology Quarterly, 50*, 101–14.

Schegloff, E. A. (1990) A contribution to the article: Defining our field: Unity in diversity (Special feature roundtable). *Issues in Applied Linguistics, 1* (2), 149–66.

Schegloff, E. A. (1991) Reflections on talk and social structure. In *Talk and Social Structure* (pp. 44–70) Cambridge: Polity.

Schegloff, E. A. (1992) In another context. In A. Duranti & C. Goodwin (Eds), *Rethinking Context: Language as an Interactive Phenomenon* (pp. 1991–227) Cambridge: Cambridge University Press.

Schegloff, E. (1993) Reflections on quantification in the study of conversation. *Research on Language and Social Interaction, 8* (2), 101–34.

Schegloff, E. A. (1996) Turn organization: One direction for inquiry into grammar and interaction. In E. Ochs, E. Schegloff & S. Thompson (Eds), *Interaction and Grammar* (pp. 52–133).

Schegloff, E. A. (1997) Whose text? Whose context? *Discourse and Society, 8* (2), 165–87.

Schegloff, E. A. (2000) Overlapping talk and organization of turn-taking for conversation. *Language in Society, 29* (1), 1–63.

Schegloff, E. A. (2007) *Sequence Organization in Interaction: A Primer in Conversation Analysis*. Cambridge: Cambridge University Press.

Schegloff, E. A., Jefferson, G. & Sacks, H. (1977) The preference for self-correction in the organization of repair in conversation. *Language*, 53 (2), 361–82.

Schiffrin, D. (1987) *Discourse Markers*. Cambridge: Cambridge University Press.

Schumann, J. (1990) A contribution to the article: Defining our field: Unity in diversity (Special feature roundtable). *Issues in Applied Linguistics*, 1 (2), 149–66.

Selting, M. (1996a) On the interplay of syntax and prosody in the constitution of turn-constructional units and turn in conversation. *Pragmatics*, 6 (3), 371–88.

Selting, M. (1996b) Prosody as an activity-type distinctive signalling cue in conversation: The so-called 'astonished questions' in repair initiation. In E. Couper-Cuhlen & M. Selting (Eds), *Prosody in Conversation: Interactional Studies* (pp. 231–70) Cambridge: Cambridge University Press.

Selting, M. (2000) The construction of units in conversational talk. *Language in Society*, 29, 477–517.

Sinclair, J. M. & Coulthard, R. M. (1975) *Toward an Analysis of Discourse*. New York: Oxford University Press.

Speer, S. A. (2005) *Gender Talk: Feminism, Discourse and Conversation Analysis*. London: Routledge.

Stockwell, R. P. (1990) A contribution to the article: Defining our field: Unity in diversity (Special feature roundtable). *Issues in Applied Linguistics*, 1 (2), 149–66.

Streeck, J. & Hartge, U. (1992) Previews: Gestures at the transition place. In P. Auer & A. di Luzio (Eds), *The Contextualization of Language* (pp. 135–58) Amsterdam: Benjamins.

Sunderland, J. (2004) *Gendered Discourses*. Basingstoke: Palgrave Macmillan.

Tannen, D. (1990) *You Just Don't Understand: Women and Men in Conversation*. New York: William Morrow.

Thornborrow, J. (2002) *Power Talk: Language and Interaction in Institutional Discourse*. Harlow, England: Longman Pearson.

Trechter, S. (2004) Contradictions of the indigenous Americas: Feminist challenges to and from the field. In R. T. Lakoff & M. Bucholtz (Eds), *Language and Woman's Place: Text and Commentaries*.

Troemel-Ploetz, S. (1991) Selling the apolitical. *Discourse and Society, 2* (4), 489–502.

Uchida, A. (1992) When 'difference' is 'dominance': A critique of the 'anti-power' cultural approach to sex differences. *Language in Society, 21*, 547–68.

Valian, V. (1998) *Why so slow? The Advancement of Women*. Cambridge, MA: M.I.T Press.

Wareing, S. (1996) "What do we know about language and gender?" Presented at the 11th Sociolinguistic symposium (5–7/September). Cardiff.

Wasson, C. (2000) Caution and consensus in American business meetings. *Pragmatics, 10* (4), 457–81.

West, C. & Garcia, A. (1988) Conversational shift work: A study of topical transitions between women and men. *Social Problems, 35*, 551–75.

Wilkinson, S. & Kitzinger, C. (Eds) (1995) *Representing the Other*. London: Sage.

Wilkinson, S. & Kitzinger, C. (2003) Constructing identities: A feminist conversation analytic approach to positioning in action. In R. Harré & F. M. Moghaddam (Eds), *The Self and Others: Positioning Individuals and Groups in Personal, Political and Cultural Context* (pp. 157–80) New York: Prager/Greenwood.

Yerian, K. (2002) Strategic constructivism: The discursive body as a site for identity display in women's self-defense course. In M. R. S. Benor, & D. Sharma (Eds), *Gendered Practices in Language* (pp. 389–405) Stanford: CSLI Publications.

Zimmerman, D. & West, C. (1975) Sex roles, interruptions and silences in conversation. In B. Thorne & N. Henley (Eds), *Language and Sex: Difference and Dominance* (pp. 105–29) Rowley, MA: Newbury House.

Index